W9-AZV-337

Boundary Issues in Counseling

multiple roles and responsibilities

SECOND EDITION

Barbara Herlihy
University of New Orleans

Gerald Corey
California State University, Fullerton

AMERICAN COUNSELING ASSOCIATION
5999 Stevenson Avenue
Alexandria, VA 22304
www.counseling.org

Boundary Issues in Counseling

multiple roles and responsibilities

SECOND EDITION

Copyright © 2006 by the American Counseling Association. All rights reserved. Printed in the United States of America. Except as permitted under the United States Copyright Act of 1976, no part of this publication may be reproduced or distributed in any form or by any means, or stored in a database or retrieval system, without prior written permission of the publisher.

10 9 8 7 6 5 4 3 2

American Counseling Association
  5999 Stevenson Avenue
  Alexandria, VA 22304

Director of Publications
  Carolyn C. Baker

Production Manager
  Bonny E. Gaston

Production Assistant
  Natasha Yetman

Copy Editor
  Kay Mikel

Cover and text design by Bonny E. Gaston. Cover photo by Garry R. Walz.

Library of Congress Cataloging-in-Publication Data
Herlihy, Barbara.
  Boundary issues in counseling: multiple roles and responsibilities/
Barbara Herlihy, Gerald Corey.—2nd ed.
      p.   cm.
  Includes bibliographical references.
  ISBN 1-55620-245-8 (alk. paper)
  ISBN 978-1-55620-245-2 (alk. paper)
  1. Counseling.   2. Counseling—Moral and ethical aspects.   I. Corey,
Gerald.   II. Title.

BF637.C6H423 2006
174´.91583—dc22   2006002169

 # Dedication

To our colleagues who struggle with the issues explored in this book.

# Table of Contents

About the Authors   vii
Guest Contributors   ix
Preface   xi

Chapter 1
Boundary Issues in Perspective   1

Chapter 2
Sexual Dual Relationships   21

Chapter 3
The Client's Perspective   41

Chapter 4
Issues in Counselor Education   53

Chapter 5
Issues in Supervision and Consultation   73

Chapter 6
Education and Training of Group Counselors   95

Chapter 7
The Counselor in the Community   115

Chapter 8
Focus on Specialty Areas   137
    Private Practice   137
    Group Counseling   145
    Couples and Family Counseling   150

Chapter 9

Focus on Specialty Areas   159
    Substance Abuse Counseling   159
    Counseling Clients Living With HIV   163
    Rehabilitation Counseling   166
    Forensic Psychology and Counseling   170

Chapter 10

Focus on Specialty Areas   175
    School Counseling   175
    Higher Education   182

Chapter 11

Key Themes, Questions, and Decision Making   191

References   199
Index   213

About the Authors

Barbara Herlihy, PhD, NCC, LPC, is a professor of counselor education at the University of New Orleans. She has served on the American Counseling Association (ACA) Ethics Committee as chair (1987–89) and as a member (1986–87, 1993–94), and as a member of the Ethics Code Revision Taskforce (2002–05).

Dr. Herlihy is the coauthor of several other books on ethical issues in counseling: *Ethical, Legal, and Professional Issues in Counseling* (2005), with Ted Remley; *Boundary Issues in Counseling* (1997, 2006); the *ACA Ethical Standards Casebook*, 5th and 6th editions (1996, 2006); and *Dual Relationships in Counseling* (1992), all with Gerald Corey; and the *ACA Ethical Standards Casebook*, 4th edition (1990), with Larry Golden. She is also the author or coauthor of more than 65 journal articles and book chapters on ethics, multicultural counseling, feminist therapy, supervision, and other topics. She is a frequent presenter of seminars and workshops on ethics across the United States and internationally.

Gerald Corey, EdD, ABPP, NCC, is a professor emeritus of human services at California State University, Fullerton, and an adjunct professor of counseling and family sciences at Loma Linda University. He is a diplomate in counseling psychology, American Board of Professional Psychology; a licensed counseling psychologist; and a fellow of the American Counseling Association, the American Psychological Association, and the Association for Specialists in Group Work (ASGW). He is the recipient of the California State University Fullerton Outstanding Professor of the Year Award in 1991 and, with Marianne Schneider Corey, the recipient of ASGW's Eminent Career Award in 2001.

Dr. Corey has authored or coauthored 15 textbooks in counseling, which are currently in print, and numerous articles and book chapters. Among his coauthored books is *Issues and Ethics in the Helping Professions* (2003, 2007), with Marianne Schneider Corey and Patrick Callanan. In the past 25 years the Coreys have conducted workshops for mental health professionals and students at many universities in the United States as well as in Mexico, Canada, Ireland, Germany, Belgium, Scotland, China, and Korea.

# Guest Contributors

Our guest contributors have enriched this book immensely. They have provided a diversity of perspectives, including those of student, counselor educator and supervisor, practitioner, and specialist. They have shared their thoughts and opinions and have raised issues that are well worth considering. These contributors (and the chapters in which their contributions appear) are as follows:

Jamie Bludworth, MA, is a doctoral student at the University of Arizona (Chapter 5).

L. DiAnne Borders, PhD, is Burlington Industries excellence professor and chair, Department of Counseling and Educational Development, University of North Carolina at Greensboro (Chapter 5).

Hal Cain, PhD, CRC, is a rehabilitation counselor and educator who lives and works in Canada. He is an adjunct faculty member in the School of Rehabilitation Therapy at Queen's University, Kingston, Ontario, Canada (Chapter 9).

Leon D. Caldwell, PhD, is associate professor of educational psychology at the University of Nebraska–Lincoln. He is currently a visiting research associate professor in the Psychology Department at the University of Memphis (Chapter 7).

A. Michael Dougherty, PhD, is associate dean of the College of Education and Allied Professions, Western Carolina University, Cullowhee, North Carolina (Chapters 5 and 10).

Holly Forester-Miller, PhD, is president of Wellness Consultants International, PLLC, and was cochair of the ACA Ethics Committee 1995–1997 (Chapters 6 and 7).

Harriet L. Glosoff, PhD, is an associate professor and director of the Counselor Education Program at the University of Virginia and was cochair of the ACA Ethics Committee 2003–2006 (Chapter 8).

Robert Haynes, PhD, is a licensed psychologist and was psychology internship director at Atascadero State Hospital for 25 years. He is currently associated with Borderline Productions (Chapter 9).

Mary A. Hermann, JD, PhD, is an assistant professor in the Department of Counselor Education at Mississippi State University and was a member of the ACA Ethics Committee 2004–2006 (Chapter 2).

Craig D. Kain, PhD, is a licensed psychologist in private practice, Long Beach, California (Chapter 9).

Arnold A. Lazarus, PhD, ABPP, is distinguished professor emeritus of psychology at Rutgers University (Chapter 1).

Amy Manfrini, PhD, is an adjunct faculty member in the Human Services Department at California State University, Fullerton, and a licensed marriage and family therapist in private practice (Chapter 8).

Michelle C. Muratori, PhD, is a senior counselor/researcher for the Center for Talented Youth at Johns Hopkins University (Chapter 4).

Thomas A. Parham, PhD, is an assistant vice chancellor for Counseling and Health Services and director of the counseling center at the University of California, Irvine (Chapter 7).

Sue Spooner, PhD, is a professor emeritus of college student personnel administration, University of Northern Colorado, Greeley (Chapter 10).

Holly A. Stadler, PhD, is professor and head, Department of Counseling and Counseling Psychology, Auburn University (Chapter 4).

Derald Wing Sue, PhD, is a professor of psychology and education at Teachers College, Columbia University; he also holds a joint appointment with the Columbia University School of Social Work (Chapter 7).

Laura J. Veach, PhD, LPC, LCAS, CCS, NCC, is an assistant professor of counseling and community counseling coordinator at Wake Forest University, and is also the current president of the International Association of Addictions and Offender Counselors (Chapter 9).

Susan L. Walden, PhD, is a counselor at Waltrip High School in Houston, Texas, and an adjunct professor of counseling at Sam Houston State University in Huntsville, Texas (Chapter 3).

# Preface

Dual or multiple relationships may be among the most controversial of all issues in the counseling profession. They have been the subject of extensive debate that has produced many questions and few answers. We expect that this book will be useful to others who share our interest in boundaries and dual or multiple relationships and who struggle, as we do, to find a clear personal stance on the issues involved.

We intend this book to be a resource that reflects the current thinking of our profession on the topic. We also want it to represent a diversity of opinion and perspectives. To that end, we have invited 19 guest contributors (6 of whom are new to this edition) to share their thoughts.

This revised edition represents a thorough updating of the literature and issues pertaining to multiple relationships. All of the chapters have been revised, and most chapters contain expanded discussions on the topics.

The previous edition addressed multiple relationships almost exclusively from the framework of the American Counseling Association's (ACA) *Code of Ethics and Standards of Practice* (ACA, 1995). This new edition has been updated to include not only the perspective of the revised *ACA Code of Ethics* (ACA, 2005) but also specific standards in the ethics codes of the American Association for Marriage and Family Therapy (2001), American Psychiatric Association (2001), American Psychological Association (2002), American School Counselor Association (2004), Association for Counselor Education and Supervision (1993), Association for Specialists in Group Work (1998, 1999, 2000), Canadian Counselling Association (1999), Commission on Rehabilitation Counselor Certification (2001), International Association of Marriage and Family Counselors (2005), and National Association of Social Workers (1999).

We have organized the book to begin with a general introduction and overview of dual or multiple relationships and a range of boundary issues in counseling practice. In the first three chapters, we define the issues and areas of concern (Chapter 1), then focus on sexual dual relationships (Chapter 2), and present the client's perspective (Chapter 3). In Chapters 4, 5, and 6, we examine issues in the preparation and supervision of counselor trainees. Chapters 7 through 10 focus on how dual and multiple relationships affect practitioners in various settings and aspects of their work. In Chapter 7 we discuss issues that confront counselors in the community as they work with a diverse client population. In Chapters 8, 9, and 10, we focus on unique boundary issues that arise in specialty areas of practice, including private practice, group counseling, couples and family counseling, substance abuse counseling, working with clients who are living with HIV, rehabilitation counseling, forensic work, school counseling, and higher education. Finally, in Chapter 11, we identify key themes, ask questions to encourage integration and reflection, and offer a decision-making model.

We make no claim to having discovered the answers to many complex and difficult questions. Rather, it is our aim to raise issues, present a range of viewpoints, and discuss our own position. Our hope is that you will use this material as a springboard for further reflection and discussion. We invite you to think about the issues that are raised, apply them to your own work, and discuss them with colleagues.

This work focuses on a specialized topic in counselor education and counseling practice. Because dual and multiple relationships are pervasive in the helping professions, this book can be used as a supplement to any of the textbooks that are used for courses in ethics and professional issues. It can also be used in practicum, fieldwork, and internship seminars. We hope that counselor educators, clinical supervisors, and students will find this book useful for getting a current view of the potential problems and solutions that are associated with dual or multiple relationships. Finally, we hope the book will aid practitioners who struggle with boundary issues in their work.

Boundary Issues in Perspective

Dual or multiple relationships occur when a professional assumes two or more roles simultaneously or sequentially with a person seeking his or her help. This may involve taking on more than one professional role (such as counselor and teacher) or combining professional and nonprofessional roles (such as counselor and friend or counselor and lover). Another way of stating this is that a helping professional enters into a dual or multiple relationship whenever the professional has another, significantly different relationship with a client, a student, or a supervisee.

Multiple relationship issues exist throughout our profession and affect virtually all counselors, regardless of their work setting or the client populations they serve. Relationship boundary issues affect the work of helping professionals in diverse roles, including counselor educator, supervisor, agency counselor, private practitioner, school counselor, college or university student personnel specialist, rehabilitation counselor, and practitioners in other specialty areas. These issues affect the dyadic relationship between counselor and client, and they can also emerge in complex ways in tripartite relationships (such as client/supervisee/supervisor or client/consultee/consultant) and in family therapy and group work. No professional remains untouched by the potential difficulties inherent in dual or multiple relationships.

This book is a revision of both of our earlier books, *Dual Relationships in Counseling* (1992) and *Boundary Issues in Counseling: Multiple Roles and Relationships* (1997), but with an expanded focus. Since we last wrote together about this topic, helping professionals have continued to debate issues of multiple relationships, roles, and responsibilities; power; and boundaries in counseling.

A *dual relationship*, as it pertains to the therapeutic relationship, has been defined by Jensen (2005) as "a separate and distinct relationship that occurs between the therapist and a patient, or a patient's spouse, partner, or family member, either simultaneously with the therapeutic relationship, or during a reasonable period of time following the termination of the thera-peutic relationship" (p. 17). Today this term seems somewhat simplistic as it does not adequately describe the complexity of issues that mental health practitioners, counselor educators, and supervisors face in trying to determine the appropriate boundaries of their relationships with those they counsel, teach, and train.

Professionals sometimes need to manage rather than avoid multiple roles, and there is an inherent duality even in some roles that are supposedly singu-lar. Because of these complexities, the term *multiple relationship* is often more descriptive than *dual relationship*. In the most recent revision of the *ACA Code of Ethics* (2005), both of these terms have been replaced with the term *nonpro-fessional interactions* to indicate those additional relationships other than sexual or romantic ones. In this book, we continue to use the terms *dual* or *multiple relationships* to describe these nonprofessional relationships.

This revised edition is based on the assumption that counseling profes-sionals must learn how to *manage* multiple roles and responsibilities (or non-professional interactions or relationships) effectively. This entails managing the power differential that is inherent in counseling or training relationships, balancing boundary issues, addressing nonprofessional relationships, and striving to avoid using power in ways that might cause harm to clients, stu-dents, or supervisees. This book rests on the premise that we can develop ethical decision-making skills that will enable us to weigh the pros and cons of multiple roles and nonprofessional interactions or relationships.

Over the past two decades, the counseling profession has become increasingly concerned with the ethical issues inherent in entering mul-tiple relationships and establishing appropriate boundaries. Much has been written about the harm that results when counseling professionals enter into sexual relationships with their clients. Throughout the 1980s, sexual misconduct received a great deal of attention in the professional literature, and the dangers of sexual relationships between counselor and client, pro-fessor and student, and supervisor and supervisee have been well document-ed. Today, there is clear agreement that sexual relationships with clients, students, and supervisees are unethical, and prohibitions against them have been translated into ethics codes and law. Even those who have argued most forcefully against dual relationship prohibitions (e.g., Lazarus & Zur, 2002) have agreed that sexual dual relationships are never acceptable. We examine the issue of sexual dual relationships in detail in Chapter 2.

Since the 1990s, nonsexual dual and multiple relationships have been receiving increased attention in professional journals and counseling text-books. The codes of ethics of the American Counseling Association (ACA, 2005), the American School Counselor Association (ASCA, 2004), the American Psychological Association (APA, 2002), the National Associa-tion of Social Workers (NASW, 1999), and the American Association for Marriage and Family Therapy (AAMFT, 2001) have all dealt specifically and extensively with topics such as appropriate boundaries, recognizing potential conflicts of interest, and ethical means for dealing with dual or multiple relationships.

These nonprofessional relationships are often complex, which means that there are few simple and absolute answers that can neatly resolve ethical dilemmas that arise. It is not always possible for counselors to play a singular role in their work, nor is this always desirable. From time to time we all will wrestle with how to balance multiple roles in our professional and nonprofessional relationships. Examples of problematic concerns associated with dual relationships include whether to barter with a client for goods or services, whether it is ever acceptable to counsel a friend or social acquaintance, whether to interact with clients outside the office, how a counselor educator might manage dual roles as educator and therapeutic agent with students, how to ethically conduct experiential groups as part of a group counseling course, whether it is acceptable to date a former client, and how to manage the budget for a caseload of clients in rehabilitation counseling.

In this chapter, we focus on nonsexual dual relationships that can arise in all settings. One of our guest contributors, Arnold A. Lazarus, makes a case for the potential benefits of transcending boundaries. He takes the position that benefits can accrue when therapists are willing to think and venture outside the proverbial box. The following questions will guide our discussion:

- What guidance do our codes of ethics offer about dual or multiple nonprofessional relationships?
- What makes dual or multiple relationships problematic?
- What factors create the potential for harm?
- What are the risks (and benefits) inherent in dual relationships, for all parties involved?
- What important but subtle distinctions should be considered?
- What safeguards can be built in to minimize risks?

Ethical Standards

The codes of ethics of all the major professional associations of mental health professionals address the issue of multiple relationships. To begin our discussion, consider these excerpts from the codes of ethics for counselors, marriage and family therapists, social workers, and psychologists.

The *ACA Code of Ethics* (2005) provides these guidelines regarding nonprofessional interactions:

> Counselor–client nonprofessional relationships with clients, former clients, their romantic partners, or their family members should be avoided, except when the interaction is potentially beneficial to the client. (A.5.c.)

> When a counselor–client nonprofessional interaction with a client or former client may be potentially beneficial to the client or former client, the counselor must document in case records, prior to the interaction (when feasible), the rationale for such an interaction, the potential benefit, and anticipated consequences for the client or former client and

other individuals significantly involved with the client or former client. Such interactions should be initiated with appropriate client consent. Where unintentional harm occurs to the client or former client, or to an individual significantly involved with the client or former client, due to the nonprofessional interaction, the counselor must show evidence of an attempt to remedy such harm. Examples of potentially beneficial interactions include, but are not limited to, attending a formal ceremony (e.g., a wedding/commitment ceremony or graduation); purchasing a service or product provided by a client or former client (excepting unrestricted bartering); hospital visits to an ill family member; mutual membership in a professional association, organization, or community. (A.5.d.)

The standard of the *AAMFT Code of Ethics* (2001) dealing with dual relationships cautions therapists to avoid exploitation:

Marriage and family therapists are aware of their influential positions with respect to clients, and they avoid exploiting the trust and dependency of such persons. Therapists, therefore, make every effort to avoid conditions and multiple relationships with clients that could impair professional judgment or increase the risk of exploitation. . . . When the risk of impairment or exploitation exists due to conditions or multiple roles, therapists take appropriate precautions. (1.3.)

The NASW (1999) *Code of Ethics* focuses on the risk of exploitation or potential harm to clients:

Social workers should not engage in dual or multiple relationships with clients or former clients in which there is a risk of exploitation or potential harm to the client. In instances when dual or multiple relationships are unavoidable, social workers should take steps to protect clients and are responsible for setting clear, appropriate, and culturally sensitive boundaries. (1.06.c.)

The *Ethical Standards for School Counselors* (ASCA, 2004) states:

The professional school counselor:
a. Avoids dual relationships that might impair his/her objectivity and increase the risk of harm to the student (e.g., counseling one's family members, close friends or associates). If a dual relationship is unavoidable, the counselor is responsible for taking action to eliminate or reduce the potential for harm. Such safeguards might include informed consent, consultation, supervision and documentation. (A.4.a.)

The APA (2002) code addresses multiple relationships quite extensively:

(a) A multiple relationship occurs when a psychologist is in a professional role with a person and (1) at the same time is in another role with the same person, (2) at the same time is in a relationship with a person closely associated with or related to the person with whom the psychologist has the professional relationship, or (3) promises to enter into another relationship in the future with the person or a person closely associated with or related to the person.

A psychologist refrains from entering into a multiple relationship if the multiple relationship could reasonably be expected to impair the psychologist's objectivity, competence, or effectiveness in performing his or her functions as a psychologist, or otherwise risks exploitation or harm to the person with whom the professional relationship exists.

Multiple relationships that would not reasonably be expected to cause impairment or risk exploitation or harm are not unethical.

(b) If a psychologist finds that, due to unforeseen factors, a potentially harmful multiple relationship has arisen, the psychologist takes reasonable steps to resolve it with due regard for the best interests of the affected person and maximal compliance with the Ethics Code.

(c) When psychologists are required by law, institutional policy, or extraordinary circumstances to serve in more than one role in judicial or administrative proceedings, at the outset they clarify role expectations and the extent of confidentiality and thereafter as changes occur. (3.05.a, b, c.)

As can be seen, the ethics codes for mental health professionals all take considerable care to address dual and multiple relationships. Ethical problems often arise when clinicians blend their professional relationships with other kinds of relationships with a client. The ethics codes of most professional organizations currently warn against crossing these boundaries when it is not in the best interests of the client. The emphasis is no longer on an outright prohibition of dual or multiple relationships; rather, the focus has shifted to avoiding the misuse of power and exploitation of the client. Also, it is increasingly acknowledged that some nonprofessional relationships are potentially beneficial.

What Makes Dual or Multiple Relationships So Problematic?

Dual relationships are fraught with complexities and ambiguities, which require counselors to make judgment calls and apply the codes of ethics carefully to specific situations. Dual relationships are problematic for a number of reasons:

- They can be difficult to recognize.
- They can be very harmful, but they are not always harmful, and, in fact, some have argued that they can be beneficial.
- They are the subject of conflicting views.
- They are not always avoidable.

Dual or Multiple Relationships Can Be Difficult to Recognize

Dual relationships are relatively easy to define but much more difficult for us to recognize in our daily practice (Pope & Vasquez, 1998). They can evolve in subtle ways. Some counselors, counselor educators, or supervisors may somewhat innocently establish a form of nonprofessional relationship. They may go on a group outing with clients, students, or supervisees. They may agree to play tennis with a client, go on a hike or a bike ride, or go jogging together when they meet by accident at the jogging trail. Initially, this nonprofessional interaction may seem to enhance the trust needed to establish a good working relationship in therapy. However, if such events continue to occur, eventually a client may want more. The client may want to become close friends with the counselor and feel let down when the counselor declines an invitation to a social event. If a friendship does begin to develop, the client may become cautious about what he or she reveals in counseling for fear of negatively affecting the friendship. At the same time, the counselor may avoid challenging the client out of reluctance to offend someone who has become a friend.

It can be particularly difficult to recognize potential problems when dual relationships are sequential rather than simultaneous. A host of questions present themselves: Can a former client eventually become a friend? How does the relationship between a supervisor and supervisee evolve into a collegial relationship once the formal supervision is completed? What kinds of posttherapy relationships are ever acceptable? These questions are explored in later chapters.

Dual or Multiple Relationships (or Nonprofessional Relationships) Are Not Always Harmful, and There May Be Clinical Benefits

A wide range of outcomes to dual relationships is possible, from harmful to beneficial. Some dual relationships are clearly exploitive and do serious harm to the client and to the professional involved. Others are benign; that is, no harm is done. In some instances, dual relating may strengthen the therapeutic relationship. Moleski and Kiselica (2005) provided a review of the literature regarding the nature, scope, and complexity of dual relationships, which range from the destructive to the therapeutic. They suggested that counselors who begin a dual relationship are not always destined for disaster. They described some therapeutic dual relationships that actually complement and enhance the counseling relationship. For example, in counseling clients from diverse cultures, practitioners may find it necessary to engage in boundary crossing to establish the counseling relationship. Moleski and Kiselica maintained that the positive or negative value of the secondary relationship is determined by the degree to which it enhances the primary counseling relationship. Therapeutic dual relationships are characterized by the counselor's commitment to doing what is in the best interest of the client.

Consider the following two examples. The first is a harmful dual relationship; the second could be described as benign or even therapeutic.

- *A high school counselor enters into a sexual relationship with a 15-year-old student client.*
  All professionals agree that this relationship is exploitive in the extreme. The roles of counselor and lover are never compatible, and the seriousness of the violation is greatly compounded by the fact that the client is a minor.

- *A couple plans to renew their wedding vows and host a reception after the ceremony. The couple invites their counselor, who attends the ceremony, briefly appears at the reception to offer her best wishes to the couple, and leaves. The couple is pleased that the counselor came, especially because they credit the counseling process with helping to strengthen their marriage.* Apparently, no harm has been done. In this case the counselor's blending of a nonprofessional role with her professional role could be argued to be benign or even beneficial to the counseling relationship.

Dual and Multiple Relationships Are The Subject of Conflicting Views

The topic of dual and multiple relationships has been hotly debated in the professional literature. A few writers have argued for the potential benefits of nonsexual dual relationships, or nonprofessional relationships. Lazarus and Zur (2002) asserted that boundary crossings are not unethical and that they often embody the most caring, humane, and effective interventions. Other writers have taken a cautionary stance, focusing on the problems inherent in dual or multiple relationships and favoring a strict interpretation of ethical standards that are aimed at regulating professional boundaries. Persuasive arguments have been made for both points of view.

Welfel (2006) pointed out that many ethics scholars take a stronger stance against multiple relationships than that found in codes of ethics. Perhaps this is because their study of the issues has made them more keenly aware of the risks. Through their work on ethics committees, licensure boards, or as expert witnesses in court cases, they may have direct knowledge of harm that has occurred. Pope and Vasquez (1998) are among those who cautioned against dual relationships. They asserted that counselors who engage in dual relationships are often skillful at rationalizing their behavior as a means of evading their professional responsibility to find acceptable alternatives to dual relationships. They identified the following problems in dual relationships (pp. 193–195):

- Entering into dual relationships with clients, or even considering entering into them after termination, can drastically change the nature of therapy. Counselors could begin using their practices unconsciously to screen clients for their likelihood of meeting the counselors' social, financial, or professional needs.
- Dual or multiple relationships create conflicts of interest and thus compromise the objectivity needed for sound professional judgment.
- There is a danger of exploiting the client because the counselor holds a more powerful position.
- Dual relationships distort the professional nature of the therapeutic relationship, which needs to rest on a reliable set of boundaries on which both client and counselor can depend.
- Dual relationships affect the cognitive processes that benefit clients during therapy and help them maintain these benefits after termination.

- If a counselor were required to give testimony in court regarding a client, the integrity of the testimony might be suspect if a dual or multiple relationship exists.
- Legal complaints can arise from nonsexual nonprofessional interactions, and litigation can be costly or damaging.

Even when practitioners have good intentions, they may unconsciously exploit or harm clients who are vulnerable in the relationship. If the professional boundaries become blurred, there is a strong possibility that confusion, disappointment, and disillusionment will result for both parties.

Although dual relationships are not damaging to clients in all cases, St. Germaine (1993) believed counselors must be aware that the potential for harm is always present. She stated that errors in judgment often occur when the counselor's own interests become part of the equation. This loss of objectivity is one factor that increases the risk of harm.

A number of writers (Gabbard, 1994; Gutheil & Gabbard, 1993; R. I. Simon, 1991, 1992; Sonne, 1994) have warned of the dangers of the slippery slope. They cautioned that when counselors make one exception to their customary boundaries with clients, it becomes easier and easier to make more exceptions until an exception is made that causes harm. Remley and Herlihy (2005) summarized this argument by stating, "the gradual erosion of the boundaries of the professional relationship can take counselors down an insidious path" (p. 177) that could even lead, ultimately, to a sexual relationship with a client.

Other writers believe that codes of ethics should be viewed as guidelines to practice rather than as rigid prescriptions, and that professional judgment must play a crucial role. G. Corey, Corey, and Callanan (2007) reminded us that ethics codes are creations of humans, not divine decrees that contain universal truth. They do not believe that dual or multiple relationships are always unethical, and they have challenged counselors to reflect honestly and think critically about the issues involved.

Bograd (1993) noted that some professionals celebrate multiple connections that cross boundaries among teaching, supervision, therapy, collegiality, and friendship. These helping professionals tend to view multiple relationships as an inevitable and potentially beneficial complexity of interpersonal relationships rather than as evidence of professional indiscretion. For example, Tomm (1993) believed that codes of ethics, in expecting practitioners to maintain their professional distance, imply that all dual relationships are wrong. According to Tomm, actively maintaining interpersonal distance focuses on the power differential and promotes an objectification of the therapeutic relationship. He suggested that dual relating invites greater authenticity and congruence from counselors and that, in fact, counselors' judgments may be improved rather than impaired by dual relationships, making it more difficult to use manipulation and deception or to hide behind the protection of a professional role.

Lazarus and Zur (2002) made the point that none of the codes of ethics of any of the various professions take the position that nonsexual dual relationships are unethical per se. They believe that "dual relationships are neither always unethical nor do they necessarily lead to harm and exploitation, nor are they always avoidable. Dual relationships can be helpful and beneficial to clients if implemented intelligently, thoughtfully, and with integrity and care" (p. 472). According to Jensen (2005), dual relationships are not, in and of themselves, illegal or unethical. Instead, unethical dual relationships are those that are reasonably likely to exploit clients or impair professional judgment.

Hedges (1993), who presented a psychoanalytic point of view, believed that there is an essential dual relatedness in psychotherapy. He argued that transference, countertransference, resistance, and interpretation rest de facto on the existence of a dual relationship. He urged practitioners to remember that, when viewed in this light, all beneficial aspects of therapy arise as a consequence of a dual relationship.

Whatever stance one takes, Tomm (1993) made an excellent point that it is not duality itself that constitutes the ethical problem. Rather, the core of the problem lies in the potential for the counselor to exploit clients or misuse power. Thus, simply avoiding multiple relationships does not prevent exploitation. Counselors might deceive themselves into thinking that they cannot possibly exploit their clients if they avoid occupying more than one professional role. In reality, there are many ways that counselors can misuse their therapeutic power and influence and many ways they can exploit clients without engaging in dual or multiple relationships.

Some Dual or Multiple Relationships Are Unavoidable

It seems evident from the controversy over dual or multiple relationships that not all dual relationships can be avoided and that not all of these relationships are necessarily harmful or unethical. The APA (2002) states that "[m]ultiple relationships that would not reasonably be expected to cause impairment or risk exploitation or harm are not unethical" (3.05. a.). On the subject of nonprofessional relationships (that are nonsexual) ACA (2005) states that "[c]ounselor–client nonprofessional relationships with clients, former clients, their romantic partners, or their family members should be avoided, except when the interaction is potentially beneficial to the client" (A.5.c.). The key is to take steps to ensure that judgment is not impaired and that no exploitation or harm takes place.

Perhaps the clearest examples of situations in which dual relationships may be unavoidable occur in the lives of rural practitioners. In an isolated, rural community the local minister, merchant, banker, beautician, pharmacist, or mechanic might be clients of a particular counselor. In such a setting, the counselor may have to play several roles and is likely to find it more difficult to maintain clear boundaries than it is for colleagues who practice in more densely populated areas. It is worth noting that "small worlds" can exist in urban as well as in rural environments (Herlihy, 2001). In many close-knit communities, nonprofessional contacts and relationships are likely to occur because clients often seek out counselors who share their values and are familiar with their culture. These "small worlds" might include religious congregations, those in recovery from substance abuse, the gay/lesbian/bisexual/transgendered community, some racial or ethnic minority groups, and the military.

The debate over dual relationships has been extensive. At this point, we ask you to consider where you stand.
- What is your stance toward dual or multiple relationships?
- With which of the perspectives do you most agree?
- How did you arrive at this stance?
- What do you see as its risks and benefits?

Boundary Crossings Versus Boundary Violations

The debate on boundary issues has been extensive, and much of it has been enlightening and thought provoking. However, it is important that mental health professionals avoid "painting with too wide a brush" in their attempts to avoid potential boundary problems. Problematic dual relationships arise from the simultaneous taking on of the role of *counselor* and another distinctly different role (such as friend, lover, relative, employer, or business partner) with a client, student, or supervisee. However, some roles that professionals play can be combined without creating a problematic dual relationship. Individuals who choose to enter the helping professions are not expected to sacrifice the multiple roles in which people naturally engage, nor are they expected to restrain themselves from acting as friends, neighbors, relatives, or employers (Glosoff, Corey, & Herlihy, 2006).

Some behaviors in which professionals may engage from time to time have a *potential* for creating a dual relationship but are not, by themselves, dual relationships. Some examples might be accepting a small gift from a client, accepting a client's invitation to a special event such as a wedding, going out for coffee or tea with a client, accepting goods rather than money as payment, making home visits to clients who are ill, or hugging a client at the end of a particularly painful session. Similar types of interactions are listed in the 2005 *ACA Code of Ethics* as examples of "potentially beneficial interactions" (A.5.d.)

Some writers (Gabbard, 1995; Gutheil & Gabbard, 1993; R. I. Simon, 1992; Smith & Fitzpatrick, 1995) have suggested that such interactions might be considered boundary crossings rather than boundary violations. A *boundary violation* is a serious breach that causes harm. When a therapist's actions are harmful to or exploitive of a client, a violation has taken place. In contrast, a *boundary crossing* is a departure from commonly accepted practice that might benefit the client. Crossings occur when the boundary is shifted to respond to the needs of a particular client at a particular moment.

Interpersonal boundaries are not static and may be redefined over time as counselors and clients work closely together. Zur and Lazarus (2002) took the position that rigid boundaries are not in the best interests of clients. They maintained that rigidity, distance, and aloofness are in direct conflict with doing what is therapeutically helpful to clients. We agree with Zur and Lazarus's thoughts on rigid boundaries, but we also believe that even seemingly innocent behaviors can lead to dual relationship entanglements with the potential for exploitation and harm if they become part of a *pattern* of blurring professional boundaries.

Some roles that professionals play involve an *inherent duality*. One such role is that of supervisor. Supervisees often experience an emergence of earlier psychological wounds and discover some of their own unfinished business as they become involved in working with clients. Ethical supervisors do not abandon their supervisory responsibilities by becoming a counselor to a supervisee, but they can encourage their supervisee to view personal therapy with another professional as a way to become more effective as a counselor and as a person. At the same time, although the supervisor and therapist roles differ, personal issues arise in both relationships, and supervisors need to give careful thought as to when and how these issues should be addressed. As another example, counselor educators serve as teachers, as therapeutic agents for student growth and self-awareness, as supervisors, and as evaluators, either sequentially or simultaneously. This role blending can present ethical dilemmas involving conflicts of interest or impaired judgments.

None of these roles or behaviors actually constitutes an ongoing dual relationship of the type that is likely to lead to sanctions by an ethics committee. Nonetheless, each does involve two individuals whose power positions are not equal. Role blending is not necessarily unethical, but it does require vigilance on the part of the professional to ensure that no exploitation occurs. One of the major difficulties in dealing with dual relationship issues is the lack of clear-cut boundaries between roles. Where exactly is the boundary between a counseling relationship and a friendship? How does a counselor educator remain sensitive to the need to promote student self-understanding without inappropriately acquiring personal knowledge about the student? Can a supervisor work effectively without addressing the supervisee's personal concerns that may be impeding the supervisee's performance? These are difficult questions, and any answers must include a consideration of the potential harm to clients, students, or supervisees when a dual relationship is initiated.

The Potential for Harm

Whatever the outcome of a dual or multiple relationship, a *potential* for harm almost always exists from the beginning of the relationship. To illustrate, let's revisit the example given earlier of a behavior that was identified as benign or even therapeutic. No apparent harm was done when the marriage counselor attended the renewal-of-wedding-vows ceremony and reception. But what might have happened if the counselor had simply accepted the invitation without discussing with the couple any potential problems that might arise? What if the counselor had been approached at the reception and asked how she knew the couple? Had the counselor answered honestly, she would have violated the privacy of the professional relationship. Had she lied or given an evasive answer, harm to the clients would have been avoided, but the counselor could hardly have felt good about herself as an honest and ethical person.

One of the major problems with multiple relationships is the possibility of exploiting the client (or student or supervisee). Kitchener and Harding (1990) contended that dual relationships lie along a continuum from those that are potentially very harmful to those with little potential for harm. They concluded that dual relationships should be entered into only when the risks of harm are small and when there are strong, offsetting ethical benefits for the client.

How does one assess the potential for harm? Kitchener and Harding identified three factors that counselors should consider: incompatibility of expectations on the part of the client, divergence of responsibilities for the counselor, and the power differential between the parties involved.

First, the greater the incompatibility of expectations in a dual role, the greater the risk of harm. For example, John, a supervisor, is also providing personal counseling to Suzanne, his supervisee. Although Suzanne understands that evaluation is part of the supervisory relationship, she places high value on the confidentiality of the counseling relationship. John is aware that her personal problems are impeding her performance as a counselor. In his supervisory role, he is expected to serve not only Suzanne's interests but also those of the agency in which she is employed and of the public that she will eventually serve. When he shares his evaluations with her employer as his supervisory contract requires, and notes his reservations about her performance (without revealing the specific nature of her personal concerns), Suzanne feels hurt and betrayed. The supervisory behaviors to which she had agreed when she entered into supervision with John were in conflict with the expectations of confidentiality and acceptance that she had come to hold for John as her counselor.

Second, as the responsibilities associated with dual roles diverge, the potential for divided loyalties and loss of objectivity increases. When counselors also have personal, political, social, or business relationships with their clients, their self-interest may be involved and may compromise the client's best interest. For example, Lynn is a counselor in private practice who has entered into a counseling relationship with Paula, even though she and Paula are partners in a small, part-time mail-order business. In the counseling relationship, Paula reveals that she is considering returning to college, which means that she will have to give up her role in the business. Lynn is faced with divided loyalties because she does not want the business to fold and she does not have the time to take it over. As this example illustrates, it is difficult to put the client's needs first when the counselor is also invested in meeting her own needs.

The third factor has to do with influence, power, and prestige. Clients, by virtue of their need for help, are in a dependent, less powerful, and more vulnerable position. For example, Darla is a counselor educator who is also counseling Joseph, a graduate student in the program. When a faculty committee meets to assess Joseph's progress, Joseph is given probationary status because his work is marginal. Although Darla assures Joseph that she revealed nothing about his personal problems during the committee meeting, Joseph's trust is destroyed. He is fearful of revealing his personal concerns in counseling with Darla because he knows that Darla will be involved in determining whether he will be allowed to continue his graduate studies at the end of his probationary period. He wants to switch to another counselor but is afraid of offending Darla. Counselor educators and counselors must be sensitive to the power and authority associated with their roles. They must resist using their power to manipulate students or clients. Because of the power differential, it is the professional's responsibility to ensure that the more vulnerable individual in the relationship is not harmed.

Risks in Dual or Multiple Relationships

The potential for harm can translate into risks to all parties involved in a dual relationship. These risks can even extend to others not directly involved in the relationship.

Risks to Consumers

Of primary concern is the risk of harm to the consumer of counseling services. A client who believes that he or she has been exploited in a dual relationship is bound to feel confused, hurt, and betrayed. This erosion of trust may have lasting consequences. The client may be reluctant to seek help from other professionals in the future. Clients may be angry about being exploited but feel trapped in a dependence on the continuing relationship. Some clients, not clearly understanding the complex dynamics of a dual relationship, may feel guilty and wonder, "What did I do wrong?" Feelings of guilt and suppressed anger are potential outcomes when there is a power differential.

Students or supervisees, in particular, may be aware of the inappropriateness of their dual relationships yet feel that the risks are unacceptably high in confronting a professional who is also their professor or supervisor. Any of these feelings—hurt, confusion, betrayal, guilt, anger—if left unresolved could lead to depression and helplessness, the antitheses of desired counseling outcomes.

Risks to the Professional

Risks to the professional who becomes involved in a dual relationship include damage to the therapeutic relationship and, if the relationship comes to light, loss of professional credibility, charges of violations of ethical standards, suspension or revocation of license or certification, and risk of malpractice litigation.

From a legal perspective, nonsexual dual relationships are less likely to produce sanctions than are sexual dual relationships, although over the last 10 years or so, state licensing boards seem to be addressing the issue of nonsexual dual relationships more vigorously (Pope & Vasquez, 1998). Malpractice actions against therapists are a risk when dual relationships have caused harm to the client, and the chances of such a suit being successful increase if the therapist cannot provide sound clinical justification and demonstrate that such practices are within an accepted standard of care.

Many dual or multiple relationships go undetected or unreported and never become the subject of an inquiry by an ethics committee, licensure board, or court. Nonetheless, these relationships do have an effect on the professionals involved, causing them to question their competence and diminishing their sense of moral selfhood.

Effects on Other Consumers

Dual or multiple relationships can create a ripple effect, affecting even those who are not directly involved in the relationship. This is particularly true in college counseling centers, schools, hospitals, counselor education programs, or any other relatively closed system in which other clients or students have opportunities to be aware of a dual relationship. Other clients might well resent that one client has been singled out for a special relationship. Because a power differential is also built into the system, this resentment may be coupled with a reluctance to question the dual relationship openly for fear of reprisal. Even independent private practitioners can be subject to the ripple effect. Former clients are typically a major source of referrals. A client who has been involved in a dual relationship and who leaves that relationship feeling confused, hurt, or betrayed is not likely to recommend the counselor to friends, relatives, or colleagues.

Effects on Other Professionals

Fellow professionals who are aware of a dual or multiple relationship are placed in a difficult position. Confronting a colleague is always uncomfortable, but it is equally uncomfortable to condone the behavior through silence. This creates a distressing dilemma that can undermine the morale of any agency, center, hospital, or other system in which it occurs. Paraprofessionals or others who work in the system and who are less familiar with professional codes of ethics may be misled and develop an unfortunate impression regarding the standards of the profession.

Effects on the Profession and Society

The counseling profession itself is damaged by the unethical conduct of its members. As professionals, we have an obligation both to avoid causing harm in dual relationships and to act to prevent others from doing harm. If we fail to assume these responsibilities, our professional credibility is eroded, regulatory agencies will intervene, potential clients will be reluctant to seek counseling assistance, and fewer competent and ethical individuals will enter counselor training programs. Conscientious professionals need to remain aware not only of the potential harm to consumers but also of the ripple effect that extends the potential for harm.

Safeguards to Minimize Risks

Whenever we as professionals are operating in more than one role, and when there is potential for negative consequences, it is our responsibility to develop safeguards and measures to reduce (if not eliminate) the potential for harm. These guidelines include the following:

- Set healthy boundaries from the outset. It is a good idea for counselors to have in their professional disclosure statements or informed consent documents a description of their policy pertaining to professional versus personal, social, or business relationships. This written statement can serve as a springboard for discussion and clarification.
- Involve the client in setting the boundaries of the professional or nonprofessional relationship. Although the ultimate responsibility for avoiding problematic dual relationships rests with the professional, clients can be active partners in discussing and clarifying the nature of the relationship. It is helpful to discuss with clients what you expect of them and what they might expect of you.
- Informed consent needs to occur at the beginning of and throughout the relationship. If potential dual relationship problems arise during the counseling relationship, these should be discussed in a frank and open manner. Clients have a right to be informed about any possible risks.
- Practitioners who are involved in unavoidable dual relationships or nonprofessional relationships need to keep in mind that, despite informed consent and discussion of potential risks at the outset, unforeseen problems and conflicts can arise. Discussion and clarification may need to be an ongoing process.
- Consultation with fellow professionals can be useful in getting an objective perspective and identifying unanticipated difficulties. We encourage periodic consultation as a routine practice for professionals who are engaged in dual relationships. We also want to emphasize the importance of consulting with colleagues who hold divergent views, not just those who tend to support our own perspectives.
- When dual or multiple relationships are particularly problematic, or when the risk for harm is high, practitioners will be wise to work under supervision.
- Counselor educators and supervisors can talk with students and supervisees about balance of power issues, boundary concerns, ap-

propriate limits, purposes of the relationship, potential for abusing power, and subtle ways that harm can result from engaging in different and sometimes conflicting roles.
- Professionals are wise to document any dual relationships in their clinical case notes, more as a legal than as an ethical precaution. In particular, it is a good idea to keep a record of any actions taken to minimize the risk of harm.
- If necessary, refer the client to another professional.

A Contributor's Perspective

Arnold A. Lazarus presents a provocative argument that strict boundary regulations may have a negative impact on therapeutic outcomes. He encourages therapists to avoid practicing defensively and to be willing to think and venture outside the proverbial box.

 ## Transcending Boundaries in Psychotherapy

Arnold A. Lazarus

A prevalent practice that tends to handicap therapists and often leads them to harm rather than to help certain clients or patients is therapists' insistence on maintaining strict boundaries. Thus they practice defensively, guided by their fear of licensing boards and attorneys rather than by clinical considerations. Risk management seminars typically warn therapists that if they cross boundaries, severely negative consequences from licensing boards and ethics committees are likely to ensue. For example, they are warned not to fraternize or socialize with clients and are told to steer clear of any mutual business transactions (other than the fee-for-service). They are advised to avoid bartering and to avoid working with or seeing a client outside the office. Yet those therapists who transcend certain boundaries with selected clients often provide superior help. They rely on their own judgment and refuse to hide behind barriers or to function within a metaphorical straitjacket. Great benefits can accrue when therapists are willing to think and venture outside the proverbial box. Here is a case in point.

> Paul, age 17, required help for some potentially serious drug problems. His parents had tried to find a therapist who could treat and assist him, but to no avail. Paul had initial meetings with four different therapists over a 6-week interval but declared each one "a jerk" and refused to go back. He then reluctantly consulted a fifth therapist (who had been one of my recent postdoctoral students) who quickly sized up the situation. He realized that Paul would regard any formal meeting with a professional therapist as reminiscent of his uptight parents and strict teachers, so he would resist their ministrations. The therapist cleverly stepped out of role and invited Paul to shoot some baskets with him later that day at a nearby basketball court. It took several weeks of basketball playing and informal chatting before adequate rapport and trust were established, at which point Paul was willing to engage in formal office visits and seriously address his problems.

This innovative, freethinking, and creative therapist was willing to take a risk and cross a boundary, and in so doing he gained the trust of a young man who was really hurting emotionally. This enabled Paul to respond to the therapist as a kind and accomplished big brother he could look up to and from whom he could learn a good deal.

Why have psychotherapists found it necessary to form ethics committees, establish a wide range of principled dos and don'ts, and to police, discipline, and penalize those who cross the line? This is probably in response to the extreme laissez-faire climate of therapeutic interaction that prevailed in the 1950s and 1960s in which blatant boundary crossings were openly espoused. For example, at Esalen in California, where Dr. Frederick Perls and his associates established a training and therapy institute, therapists and clients often became playmates and even lovers. It is not far-fetched to look upon many of their dealings as flagrant acts of malpractice. Concerned professionals became aware of the emotional damage that was being wrought in many settings and sought to establish a code of ethics and to lay down basic ground rules for practitioners. Terms such as *boundaries, boundary violation,* and *standard of care* entered the vernacular.

Today, all therapists are expected to treat their clients with respect, dignity, and consideration and to adhere to the spoken and unspoken rules that make up our established standards of care. Many of these rules are necessary and sensible. For instance, it is essential for therapists to avoid any form of exploitation, harassment, harm, or discrimination, and it is understandable that a sexual relationship with a client is considered an ultimate taboo. Emphasis is placed on the significance of respect, integrity, confidentiality, and informed consent. Nevertheless, some elements of our ethics codes have become so needlessly stringent and rigid that they can undermine effective therapy. The pendulum has swung too far in the opposite direction from the era of negligent free-for-all indulgence.

One of my major concerns is that there is a widespread failure to grasp the critical difference between *boundary violations,* which can harm a client, and *boundary-crossings,* which produce no harm and may even enhance the therapeutic connection. For example, what would be so appalling about a therapist saying to a client who has just been seen from 11 a.m. until noon: "We seem to be onto something important. Should we go and pick up some sandwiches at the local deli, and continue until 1 p.m. at no extra fee to you?" Strict boundary proponents would regard such behavior as unethical because it goes outside the therapeutic frame. However, strategic therapists would argue that rigid adherence to a particular frame and setting only exacerbates problems, especially in nonresponsive patients. For example, a patient of mine who had been resistant and rather hostile arrived early for his appointment. I was just finishing lunch and had some extra sandwiches on hand, so I offered him one. He accepted my offer as well as a glass of orange juice. Coincidentally or otherwise, thereafter our rapport was greatly enhanced, and he made significant progress. What became clear during our ensuing sessions was that the act of literally breaking bread led him to perceive me as humane and caring and facilitated his trust in me.

Over the past 40 years, I have seen thousands of clients and have selectively transcended boundaries on many occasions. For example, I engaged in barter with an auto mechanic, who tuned my car in exchange for three therapy sessions. I have accepted dinner invitations from some clients, have attended social functions with others, played tennis with several clients, and ended up becoming good friends with a few. Of course, I do not engage in such behaviors capriciously. Roles and expectations must be clear. Possible power differentials must be kept in mind. For my own protection as well as the client's protection, I don't chance things like this with seriously disturbed people, especially those who are hostile, paranoid, aggressive, or manipulative. But the antiseptic obsession with "risk management" has led far too many therapists to practice their craft in a manner that is needlessly constraining and often countertherapeutic.

Those therapists who rigidly adhere to strict professional boundaries are apt to place risk management ahead of humane interventions. The manner in which they speak to their clients often leaves much to be desired. For example, I recently attended a clinical meeting where a young psychiatrist was interviewing a woman who suffered from an eating disorder, bulimia nervosa. At one point the dialogue continued more or less as follows:

Patient: May I ask how old you are?
Therapist: Why is that important?
Patient: It's no big deal. I was just curious.
Therapist: Why would you be curious about my age?
Patient: Well, you look around 30, and I was just wondering if I am correct.
Therapist: What impact would it have if you were not correct?
Patient: None that I can think of. It was just idle curiosity.
Therapist: Just idle curiosity?

As I watched these exchanges, I grew uncomfortable. It seemed to me that the patient wished she had never raised the issue in the first place and that she was feeling more and more uneasy. It did not seem that the dialogue was fostering warmth, trust, or rapport. On the contrary, it resembled a cross-examination in a courtroom and appeared adversarial.

In psychoanalysis it is deemed important for the analyst to remain neutral and nondisclosing so the patient can project his or her needs, wishes, and fantasies onto a "blank screen." But it makes no sense for this to become a rule for *all* therapists to follow. It has always struck me as ill mannered and discourteous to treat people this way.

I recommend the following type of exchange in place of the aforementioned example:

Patient: How old are you?
Therapist: I just turned 30. Why do you ask?
Patient: I was just curious. It's no big deal.
Therapist: Might you be more comfortable with or have greater confidence
    in someone younger or older?
Patient: No, not at all.

At this juncture, I would suggest that the topic be dropped. Notice the recommended format. First answer the question and then proceed with an inquiry if necessary. In this way, the patient is validated and not demeaned. Why am I dwelling on such a seemingly trivial issue? Because it is not a minor or frivolous point, and I have observed this type of interaction far too often, usually to the detriment of the therapeutic process. I see it as part and parcel of a dehumanizing penchant among the many rigid thinkers in our field who legislate against all boundary extensions. These are the members of our profession (and they are not a minority) who regard themselves as superior to patients and tend to infantilize and demean them in the process.

The purpose of this essay is to alert readers to an issue that is crucial in the field of psychotherapy. I have coedited a book (Lazarus & Zur, 2002) on the subject of boundaries and boundary crossings in which various contributors have addressed the topic from many viewpoints—nonanalytic practice procedures, feminist perspectives, military psychology, counseling centers, deaf communities, legal issues, gay communities, and rural settings (among others). It is generally agreed that the client–therapist relationship is at the core of treatment effectiveness. Yet by adhering to strict boundary regulations, many troublesome feelings are likely to arise and ruptures to emerge that destroy the necessary sense of trust and empathy. Greenspan (2002) aptly described strict boundary adherence as a "distance model" that undermines the true healing potential of the work we do. I fully concur with her opinion that we need an approach of respectful compassion. Safe connection between therapist and client should be the overriding aim because this, not strict boundaries, will protect clients from abuse.

Conclusions

In this introductory chapter, we have examined what the codes of ethics of the major professional associations advise with respect to dual or multiple relationships. We have explored a number of factors that make such relationships problematic, as well as factors that create a potential for harm and the risks to parties directly or not directly involved in multiple relationships. Some strategies for reducing risks were described.

It is critical that counselors give careful thought to the potential complications before they become entangled in ethically questionable relationships. The importance of consultation in working through these issues cannot be overemphasized. As with any complex ethical issue, complete agreement may never be reached, nor is it necessarily desirable. However, as conscientious professionals we need to strive to clarify our own stance and develop our own guidelines for practice within the limits of codes of ethics and current knowledge.

2
Sexual Dual Relationships

Sexual dual relationships with clients are among the most serious of all boundary violations. In a general sense, boundaries define who we are, what is ours and what is not ours, and what is intimate and what is separate (Rutter, 1989). In a professional relationship, boundaries are a kind of frame around the therapeutic dyad that defines the roles of the participants (Smith & Fitzpatrick, 1995). Sexual violations of these boundaries involve an abuse of power and a betrayal of trust that can have devastating effects on clients. Later in this chapter, we describe in some detail the harm to clients that such violations can cause. The consequences for counselors who engage in sexual intimacies with their clients also can be severe: They may have their licensure or certification revoked, be expelled from professional associations, be restricted in or lose their insurance coverage, be fired from their jobs, be sued in civil court for malpractice, or be convicted of a felony.

Sexual improprieties also undoubtedly have a negative impact on the profession. Publicity about such occurrences is likely to make potential consumers more reluctant to seek counseling services and certainly does not help mental health professionals to persuade legislators, government regulators, and health insurance companies of the value of our services (Welfel, 2006). Because sexual relationships with clients are such serious violations, they deserve careful attention. In this chapter, we focus specifically on sexual dual relationships and address these questions:

- How do professional codes of ethics address sexual intimacies with clients?
- What are the ethics of sexual relationships with former clients?
- How widespread is the practice of engaging in sex with current or former clients?
- Is there a "typical" offending therapist?
- What are the legal sanctions against these behaviors?
- What makes sexual dual relationships particularly harmful to clients?

- How can counselors deal with sexual attraction to clients?
- What steps can our profession take to increase awareness of problems involved in sexual misconduct and prevent their occurrence?
- What are some legal perspectives pertaining to nonsexual dual relationships? to sexual dual relationships?

A Contributor's Perspective

To frame the discussion of topics to be explored in this chapter, we begin with Mary A. Hermann's perspective on the legal issues surrounding dual relationships. She makes it clear that if clients can prove that they were emotionally harmed because of a dual relationship, they could prevail in a malpractice lawsuit against the counselor.

 Legal Perspectives on Dual Relationships

Mary A. Hermann

Counselors' legal liability related to dual relationships emanates from legal responsibilities associated with the counselor–client relationship. Courts have characterized the counselor–client relationship as fiduciary in nature (Douglass, 1994), a relationship in which one party places trust and confidence in another party who has power or influence (Black, 1983). In counselor–client relationships, counselors have the power or influence and clients place their trust and confidence in the counselors. Setting and maintaining appropriate boundaries with clients supports the fiduciary relationship and protects clients.

From a legal perspective, it is significant that dual relationships exist on a continuum ranging from boundary crossings for the benefit of the client to sexual dual relationships that can cause major trauma to the client. The legal implications of engaging in dual relationships vary, depending on the nature of the relationship and whether the client suffers harm. Thus, the mere existence of a dual relationship does not, in itself, constitute malpractice. If a dual relationship is managed effectively, it may have no negative impact on the counseling relationship and no cause of action against the counselor would exist. However, if the client suffered harm because of a dual relationship, the client could file a malpractice lawsuit against the counselor.

In a malpractice case, the client has the burden of establishing by a preponderance of the evidence that the counselor had a duty to the client, the counselor breached the duty, and the client suffered harm. The client would have little difficulty establishing the duty element of malpractice because, as previously noted, the very nature of a counseling relationship establishes a counselor's fiduciary duty to clients.

In a malpractice action, the client also has to show that the counselor breached his or her duty to the client by not adhering to the standard of care in the community. The standard of care can be described as acting like other similarly trained counselors would act under the circumstances. This standard would be established by expert testimony and reference to codes of ethics. A court would apply this standard of care to the case at bar to determine whether a counselor breached his or her professional duty to the client.

Finally, the client has to establish that the client suffered harm because the counselor breached the duty to the client. Emotional harm is a compensable injury in a malpractice case against a mental health professional. Therefore, if a client could prove that his or her mental health was negatively affected by a dual relationship or a nonprofessional interaction, the client could prevail in a malpractice lawsuit.

Nonsexual dual relationships can cause counselors legal problems, but counselors are more likely to incur legal sanctions if they engage in sexual dual relationships. The *ACA Code of Ethics* (2005) clearly forbids counselors from having sexual relationships with clients and from counseling clients with whom they have had sexual relationships, and courts have found mental health professionals were negligent by engaging in sexual relationships with clients.

Unfortunately, the legal system was slow to respond to clients' claims of sexual exploitation. When clients first began alleging that therapists were sexually exploiting them, many mental health professionals discounted the claims (Welfel, 2006). Before the mid-1970s, some mental health professionals even defended sexual relationships with clients by alleging that they had therapeutic value (Welfel, 2006). In the landmark case of *Roy v. Hartogs* (1975), a court finally acknowledged that a psychiatrist caused harm by engaging in sexual intercourse with a client and that such action was not in accordance with acceptable professional procedures. Welfel (2006) credited the courage of victims in pursuing their legal claims, and the persistence of scholars who demonstrated that sex with clients is harmful, for the resulting ban on sexual relationships with clients.

Currently, the inappropriateness of engaging in sexual relationships with clients is universally recognized (Remley & Herlihy, 2005). Such behavior is considered unethical and illegal (G. Corey et al., 2007). Yet one of the most common allegations in malpractice lawsuits against mental health professionals remains sexual misconduct. Courts now recognize that clients are vulnerable in a counseling relationship and have refused to consider consent of the client to be a defense for the counselor (G. Corey et al., 2007). Courts have also acknowledged that clients are likely to suffer serious emotional distress when they have engaged in a sexual relationship with their therapist. Thus, clients who sue their counselors for sexual impropriety are likely to be victorious in a lawsuit.

Legal sanctions for sexual intimacy between a counselor and client vary by state. An increasing number of state statutes have criminalized therapist–client sexual intimacy. G. Corey et al. (2007) noted that in California, Colorado, Florida, Georgia, Idaho, Maine, Michigan, Minnesota, Missouri, New Hampshire, New Mexico, North Dakota, Rhode Island, Texas, Washington, and Wisconsin a counselor who is sexually involved with a client is committing a felony. Kane (1995) found that sexual intimacies between counselors and clients are a violation of criminal law in California, Colorado,

Connecticut, Florida, Georgia, Iowa, Maine, Michigan, Minnesota, New Mexico, North Dakota, South Dakota, and Wisconsin. Remley and Herlihy (2005) explained that some states take even tougher positions such as allowing prosecutors to file injunctions against counselors, forcing them to discontinue their practice even before they are found guilty of engaging in sexual relations with clients if the prosecutors can show that the professional could harm clients if the counselor continues to practice.

In addition to filing criminal charges or malpractice lawsuits against counselors engaged in harmful dual relationships with clients, counselors can also be expelled from professional organizations and lose their insurance coverage, especially if they engage in sex with clients. Furthermore, clients can file complaints against counselors with their state licensure board. Licensure boards are responsible for enforcing codes of ethics. These boards can impose sanctions or even have a counselor's license to practice suspended or revoked if the counselor engages in inappropriate dual relationships. Many state licensure boards have revoked the licenses of mental health professionals who have had sex with clients (G. Corey et al., 2007).

Recent research seems to indicate that tough civil and criminal law penalties and the possibility of losing one's license to practice counseling have reduced the incidence of sexual impropriety with clients. In Neukrug, Milliken, and Walden's (2001) 1999 survey of ethical complaints reported to state licensure boards in the previous year, only 7% of the complaints were related to having a sexual relationship with a client. In an earlier similar study, Neukrug, Healy, and Herlihy (1992) found that 20% of complaints since the establishment of the existing licensure boards were for having a sexual relationship with a client. Interestingly, in the 2001 study, 24% of the ethical complaints related to inappropriate dual relationships, whereas in the 1992 study only 7% of the complaints were for engaging in dual relationships. Thus, although the incidence of sexual relationships with clients seems to be declining, complaints for inappropriate dual relationships have increased.

Dual relationships are frequently problematic. Although not all dual relationships will lead to legal liability, even occasional boundary crossings can lead to a pattern of boundary violations. This pattern of boundary crossings could be used in a licensure board proceeding or a lawsuit as evidence that a counselor risked harm to clients by not maintaining appropriate boundaries with clients (Remley & Herlihy, 2005). Accordingly, counselors are wise to avoid dual relationships to the extent possible and to document precautions taken to protect clients when dual relationships are unavoidable.

Ethical Standards

Virtually all professional codes of ethics prohibit sexual intimacies with current clients. Many of the codes also specify that if therapists have had a prior sexual relationship with a person, they do not accept this person as a client. Relevant ethical standards for counselors, psychologists, social workers, and marriage and family therapists include the following:

- Sexual or romantic counselor–client interactions or relationships with current clients, their romantic partners, or their family members are prohibited. (ACA, 2005, A.5.a.)
- Psychologists do not engage in sexual intimacies with current therapy clients/patients. (APA, 2002, 10.05.)
- Psychologists do not accept as therapy clients/patients persons with whom they have engaged in sexual intimacies. (APA, 2002, 10.07.)
- Social workers should under no circumstances engage in sexual activities or sexual contact with current clients, whether such contact is consensual or forced. (NASW, 1999, 1.09.a.)
- Social workers should not provide clinical services to individuals with whom they have had a prior sexual relationship. Providing clinical services to a former sexual partner has the potential to be harmful to the individual and is likely to make it difficult for the social worker and individual to maintain appropriate professional boundaries. (NASW, 1999, 1.09.d.)
- Sexual intimacy with clients is prohibited. (AAMFT, 2001, 1.4.)

There is clear consensus among the professional associations that concurrent sexual and professional relationships are unethical, and many of the associations agree that a sexual relationship cannot later be converted into a therapeutic relationship. Is there similar consensus regarding the issue of converting a therapeutic relationship into a sexual one once the professional relationship has been terminated? We examine this issue next.

Sexual Relationships With Former Clients

In the previous edition of this book we indicated that codes of ethics of the professional associations had been silent for a long time on the issue of whether sexual relationships with former clients are ever acceptable. That situation has changed. Today the various associations specifically address this topic:

Sexual or romantic counselor–client interactions or relationships with former clients, their romantic partners, or their family members are prohibited for a period of 5 years following the last professional contact. Counselors, before engaging in sexual or romantic interactions or relationships with clients, their romantic partners, or client family members after 5 years following the last professional contact, demonstrate forethought and document (in written form) whether the interaction or relationship can be viewed as exploitive in some way and/or whether there is still potential to harm the former client; in cases of potential exploitation and/or harm, the counselor avoids entering such an interaction or relationship. (ACA, 2005, A.5.b.)

Counsellors avoid any type of sexual intimacies with clients and they do not counsel persons with whom they have had a sexual relationship. Counsellors do not engage in sexual intimacies with former clients within a minimum of three years after terminating the counselling relationship.

This prohibition is not limited to the three year period but extends indefinitely if the client is clearly vulnerable, by reason of emotional or cognitive disorder, to exploitative influence by the counselor. Counsellors, in all such circumstances, clearly bear the burden to ensure that no such exploitative influence has occurred, and to seek consultative assistance. (Canadian Counselling Association [CCA], 1999, B12.)

(a) Psychologists do not engage in sexual intimacies with former clients/ patients for at least two years after cessation or termination of therapy. (b) Psychologists do not engage in sexual intimacies with former clients/ patients even after a two-year interval except in the most unusual circumstances. Psychologists who engage in such activity after the two years following cessation or termination of therapy and of having no sexual contact with the former client/patient bear the burden of demonstrating that there has been no exploitation, in light of all relevant factors, including (1) the amount of time that has passed since therapy terminated; (2) the nature, duration, and intensity of the therapy; (3) the circumstances of termination; (4) the client's/patient's personal history; (5) the client's/patient's current mental status; (6) the likelihood of adverse impact on the client/patient; and (7) any statements or actions made by the therapist during the course of therapy suggesting or inviting the possibility of a posttermination sexual or romantic relationship with the client/patient. (APA, 2002, 10.08.)

Rehabilitation counselors will not engage in sexual intimacies with former clients within a minimum of 5 years after terminating the counseling relationship. Rehabilitation counselors who engage in such relationships after 5 years following termination will have the responsibility to examine and document thoroughly that such relations do not have an exploitative nature, based on factors such as duration of counseling, amount of time since counseling, termination circumstances, client's personal history and mental status, adverse impact on the client, and actions by the counselor suggesting a plan to initiate a sexual relationship after termination. Rehabilitation counselors will seek peer consultation prior to engaging in a sexual relationship with a former client. (Commission on Rehabilitation Counselor Certification [CRCC], 2001, A.5.b.)

Social workers should not engage in sexual activities or sexual contact with former clients because of the potential for harm to the client. If social workers engage in conduct contrary to this prohibition or claim that an exception to this prohibition is warranted because of extraordinary circumstances, it is social workers—not their clients—who assume the full burden of demonstrating that the former client has not been exploited, coerced, or manipulated, intentionally or unintentionally. (NASW, 1999, 1.09.c.)

Sexual intimacy with former clients is likely to be harmful and is therefore prohibited for two years following the termination of therapy or last professional contact. In an effort to avoid exploiting the trust and dependency of clients, marriage and family therapists should not engage in sexual intimacy with former clients after the two years following termination or last professional contact. Should therapists engage in sexual intimacy with former clients following two years after termination or last professional contact, the burden shifts to the therapist to demonstrate that there has been no exploitation or injury to the former client or to the client's immediate family. (AAMFT, 2001, 1.5.)

The American Psychological Association (APA, 2002) and the American Association for Marriage and Family Therapy (AAMFT, 2001) agree that sexual contact before 2 years after termination is unethical. The Canadian Counselling Association (CCA, 1999) specifies a ban on sexual intimacies for a minimum of 3 years after termination of therapy. The American Counseling Association (ACA, 2005) and the Commission on Rehabilitation Counselor Certification (CRCC, 2001) have a minimum waiting period of 5 years following termination. The National Association of Social Workers (NASW, 1999) prohibits its members from engaging in sexual relationships with former clients but does not specify a time period after termination. Most of the professional organizations state that in the exceptional circumstance of sexual relationships with former clients—even after a 2- to 5-year interval—the burden of demonstrating that there has been no exploitation clearly rests with the therapist. The factors that need to be considered include the amount of time that has passed since termination of therapy, the nature and duration of therapy, the circumstances surrounding termination of the professional–client relationship, the client's personal history, the client's competence and mental status, the foreseeable likelihood of harm to the client or others, and any statements or actions by the therapist suggesting a plan to initiate a sexual relationship with the client after termination. Gary Schoener, interviewed for an article in *Counseling Today* (Foster, 1996), discussed some useful questions that practitioners can ask themselves when they are considering a posttermination romantic relationship:

- What was the length and level of therapeutic involvement?
- How much transference, dependency, or power inequity remains after termination?
- Was there any deception or coercion, intentional or unintentional, by the therapist indicating that sex is generally acceptable after termination of therapy?
- Was there an actual termination? Was the decision to terminate a mutual one? Did the therapist end the professional relationship to make it possible to enter into a romantic or sexual relationship?
- Who initiated posttermination contact?
- What kind of consultation, if any, took place?

Despite the consistency shown by the professional *organizations*, there remains disagreement among *practitioners* about whether a sexual relationship initiated after termination is ever ethical. Some maintain that "once a client, always a client." They contend that the transference elements of the therapeutic relationship persist forever; therefore, romantic relationships with former clients are always unethical. They also point out that a 2- or 5-year time limit is artificial and arbitrary and that it is nonsensical to assume that what was unethical for several years becomes ethical after a specific time period has elapsed. Others contend that the probability for harm is not high in some cases and that each case should be considered individually.

The majority of therapists who have been surveyed regarding this issue viewed posttermination sexual relationships as unethical (Borys, 1988; Lamb, 1992). However, substantial minorities, ranging from 23% (Borys, 1988; Gibson & Pope, 1993) to 33% (Salisbury & Kinnier, 1996), believed they could be ethical under some circumstances. Interestingly, Salisbury and Kinnier found that counselors who believed such relationships could be acceptable also believed, on average, that the appropriate waiting time should be slightly more than 5 years.

Those who argue that a blanket prohibition of all sexual intimacies with former clients is too extreme also argue that there is a real difference between an intense, long-term therapy relationship and a less intimate brief-term one. What should be the appropriate response, for instance, by Ellen to Craig's invitation in the following scenario?

> Ellen served her counseling internship at her university's counseling center. One of her clients was Craig, a graduate student who was a businessman returning to college for his MBA. Craig sought counseling because he was having second thoughts about committing himself to a lifelong career in the cut-throat competitive field he was in. During five counseling sessions with Ellen, he completed a series of inventories, weighed his values, and decided to switch majors. A little more than 2 years later, Craig and Ellen ran into each other at a social event. Craig asked her out on a date.

> Assume that Ellen approaches you for consultation. She tells you that she does not want to be unethical, yet she also wants to accept Craig's offer for a date. Because Ellen had only five sessions with him, because the focus was on career counseling, and because the counseling took place more than 2 years ago, Ellen does not think that accepting a date with Craig is unethical. However, she wants to get your opinion and wants to know if she is overlooking some important issues.
> - What might you say to Ellen?

If Ellen consults with us, we will first ask her to state what she sees as the pros and cons of each decision. We will explore with her the reasons she is seeking consultation. Although she does not think that accepting the date is unethical, she seems uncertain. Can she see potential problems in accepting? We will ask her if there is a pattern here. Has she dated other former clients? We will not flatly tell Ellen that accepting the date is either appropriate or inappropriate, although we will explore with her any possible consequences. We will ask her to consider carefully the factors listed by her professional association and questions such as those posed by Schoener. Our goals for the consultation are to have Ellen understand her reasons for choosing whatever course of action she may follow and be aware of and take responsibility for the possible consequences of her decision.

The counseling profession is clearer than it once was about sexual relationships with former clients. Still, whether sexual relationships with former clients are ever acceptable, even after more than 2 or 5 years, probably will be a subject of continuing discussion. On one hand, we need to remain aware of the harm that can result from sexual intimacies that occur after termination, of the aspects of the therapeutic process that continue after termination including residual transference, and of the continuing power differential. On the other hand, it seems reasonable to consider the wide range of circumstances that could arise, especially the differences between long-term, intense, personal counseling relationships and brief, career-oriented, or other types of counseling. Under the present codes, if a counselor does consider entering into a romantic relationship with a former client after 5 years have passed, some safeguards should be followed. These include consulting with a colleague, documenting carefully, and going for a therapy session conjointly with the former client to examine mutual transferences and expectations. As a general rule, we agree with Welfel (2006) that counselors who consider entering into a sexual relationship with a former client should be extraordinarily cautious about taking such a step. They are wise to refrain from doing so except under the most unusual or exceptional circumstances.

Incidence

It is difficult to determine the actual incidence of sexual intimacies between therapists and clients—or between counselor educators and students or supervisors and supervisees. Various studies have shown clearly, however, that male therapists are significantly more likely to approve of and engage in sexual activities with a client than are female therapists (Gabbard, 1989; Gibson & Pope, 1993; Pope, Keith-Spiegel, & Tabachnick, 1986; Pope & Vetter, 1991). Other studies have indicated that from 9% to 13% of male therapists and 2% to 3% of female therapists report engaging in sex with current or former clients (Akamatsu, 1988; Borys, 1988; Pope & Bouhoutsos, 1986; Pope, Sonne, & Holroyd, 1993; Pope, Tabachnick, & Keith-Spiegel, 1987; Salisbury & Kinnier, 1996). One study found that a significant number of cases involve clients who are minor children (Bajt & Pope, 1989). It appears that the typical offender is a repeat offender: Holroyd and Brodsky (1977) found that 80% of psychologists who reported sexual contact had engaged in it with more than one client.

These estimates are probably conservative. Survey data may be distorted because there are compelling reasons for offending therapists to withhold information or to make false claims (Smith & Fitzpatrick, 1995). Sexual misconduct is thought to be grossly underreported (Gartrell, Herman, Olarte, Feldstein, & Localio, 1987), and R. I. Simon (1989) estimated that the real percentage of therapists who have engaged in sexual intimacies with current or former clients may be as high as 25%. Incidence rates may vary depending on the variables considered. Thoreson, Shaughnessy, Heppner, and Cook (1993) surveyed male ACA members and found that only 1.7% reported sexual contact with *current clients*. However, when the additional factors of sexual contact after termination and sexual contact with *students or supervisees* were considered, the prevalence rate rose to 17%. If there is any good news in all this information, it is that S. K. Anderson and Kitchener (1996) reviewed studies that were conducted since 1977 and concluded that the frequency of sexual intimacy between therapists and current clients was decreasing. They suggested that therapists are becoming increasingly sensitive to this issue.

The Offending Therapist

As we have seen, male therapists are far more likely to engage in sexual relationships with clients than are female therapists. Although systematic research on offending therapists is scant, the most typical profile that emerges is that of a middle-aged male therapist who is "burned out," professionally isolated, and currently experiencing some personal distress or midlife crisis (S. Simon, 1987; Smith & Fitzpatrick, 1995). This "lovesick therapist" often begins by sharing his own personal problems and vulnerabilities with a younger female client (Twemlow & Gabbard, 1989). This typical offender also appears to share many of the characteristics of the impaired professional who has personal problems and attempts to meet his own needs through his clients.

Of course, not all offending therapists fit this profile, and other writers have suggested that there may be a wide range of types of professionals who become involved in sexual relationships with clients. Golden, interviewed in a *Guidepost* article (Schafer, 1990), suggested that they generally fall into one of three categories: professionals who are ignorant of the standards; those who are aware of the standards but are blinded by what dual relationships can offer romantically; and sociopathic individuals who know the standards but willfully and repeatedly violate them.

Schoener and Gonsiorek (1988) described six categories of perpetrators. *Uninformed and naive* therapists are led into sexual relationships through ignorance. They genuinely lack knowledge of ethical standards and professional boundaries and have difficulty distinguishing between personal and professional relationships. *Healthy or neurotic* counselors are aware that sexual relationships are unethical, are typically involved in limited or isolated instances, are experiencing situational stressors, and are remorseful about their behavior. They often terminate sexual intimacy on their own and may self-report and request help. *Severely neurotic* counselors have longstanding and significant emotional problems, especially depression, feelings of inadequacy, low self-esteem, and social isolation. Typically, they begin by becoming emotionally or socially involved with a client, and professional boundaries disintegrate as intimacy grows. These counselors may feel guilt and remorse, but they are less able to terminate the inappropriate behavior and may deny, distort, or rationalize their behavior.

Counselors with *character disorders and impulse control problems* have longstanding problems and a history of legal difficulties. They are often caught due to their multiple violations and poor judgment. When consequences are pending, they show guilt and remorse, but they rarely have a true appreciation of the impact of their behavior on others. *Sociopathic or narcissistic character disordered* individuals have characteristics similar to the previous group but are more cunning and detached. They are adept at manipulating clients and colleagues into helping them avoid the consequences of their acts. Finally, *psychotic or borderline personality disordered* counselors have in common poor social judgment and impaired reality testing. Therapists who fall into these last three categories are poor candidates for rehabilitation.

Legal Sanctions

One of the major causes of malpractice suits is sexual misconduct. Pope and Vasquez (1998) reported that 20% of the total number of malpractice claims are due to sexual impropriety. Sexual dual relationships account for the largest share of formal complaints against psychologists, whether these complaints are filed with licensing boards, ethics committees, or the civil courts.

Austin, Moline, and Williams (1990) reviewed relevant court cases and concluded that few, if any, arguments in defense of therapists who have sex with clients are likely to succeed in court. In particular, courts have rejected claims that the client consented, determining that consent was not voluntary or informed because it was affected by transference.

Malpractice suits are tried in civil court. Increasingly, charges of sexual misconduct against mental health professionals can also be brought in criminal court. Exploitation by practitioners is so damaging to clients that it is being criminalized in some states. Foster (1996) noted that state legislatures throughout the United States are working to increase the criminal sanctions for sexual misconduct.

Harm to Clients

As Bates and Brodsky (1989) have noted, problems in love relationships are frequently the impetus for clients to enter therapy. These authors contended that it is unforgivable for therapists to contaminate and de-objectify their role in helping to resolve these clients' problems. Therapy is not "a mating game, or a place for lovers to meet" (p. 133).

Kenneth S. Pope has produced an impressive body of research into sexual dual relationships. He has provided a clear and comprehensive picture of the harm that may be done to clients by sexual relationships with their therapists. In an excellent article describing a therapist–patient sex syndrome, Pope (1988) noted that clients may have reactions similar to those of victims of rape, battering, incest, child abuse, or posttraumatic stress. Ten general aspects commonly associated with the syndrome are ambivalence, guilt, emptiness and isolation, identity/boundary/role confusion, sexual confusion, impaired ability to trust, emotional lability, suppressed rage, cognitive dysfunction, and increased suicidal risk. We believe it is worth examining each of these indicators in more depth.

- *Ambivalence.* Clients who are sexually involved with their therapist may experience a sense of deep ambivalence, fearing separation or alienation from the therapist yet longing desperately to escape from the therapist's power and influence. Loyalty to the therapist may prevent clients from acting to protect themselves (resisting sexual advances or reporting the abuse) for fear that their action could destroy the therapist's personal or professional life. This ambivalence and misplaced loyalty help to explain why the behavior can go unreported completely or for a number of years.

- *Guilt.* Clients may feel guilty, as though they are somehow to blame for what has happened. Their reactions may be similar to those of incest victims. They may have a sense of guilt that they did not do more to stop the sexual activity or that they enjoyed the relationship or that they did something to invite such a relationship with a person they deeply trusted.

- *Emptiness and isolation.* Sexual activity between a therapist and client can seriously erode the client's sense of self-worth. Clients may feel emotionally isolated, alone, and cut off from the world of "normal" human experience.

- *Identity/boundary/role confusion.* A phenomenon often involved in a patient–therapist sexual relationship is a reversal of roles. As the therapist becomes more self-disclosing, and as meeting the therapist's needs becomes more important in the relationship, the client becomes responsible for taking care of the therapist. Clients become confused, not knowing where safe and appropriate boundaries lie, and this adds to the erosion of their sense of identity and worth.

- *Sexual confusion.* Many clients seem to manifest a profound confusion about their sexuality. Lingering outcomes can take two forms: Some clients will be threatened by any sexual activity, and others may be trapped into compulsive or self-destructive sexual encounters.

- *Impaired ability to trust.* Because therapy involves such a high degree of trust, violations can have lifelong consequences. When therapists abuse this trust, they are taking advantage of their clients in the most fundamental way. This is perhaps the core issue in sexual violations, and the consequences can extend far beyond the therapeutic relationship in question. Client victims are likely to mistrust other helping professionals, particularly therapists, and the damage may reverberate outward to other, less intense relationships.

- *Emotional lability.* This can be a long-term consequence. Clients who have been sexually involved with a therapist often feel overwhelmed by their emotions, both during the relationship and afterward. Even with subsequent therapy, victims may reexperience traumatic emotions when they become involved with a new and appropriate sexual partner. Pope (1988) cautioned counselors who work with these victims to keep these setbacks in perspective so that clients will not lose hope.

- *Suppressed rage.* Victims may feel a justifiable, tremendous anger at the offending therapist. But this rage may be blocked from awareness or expression by feelings of ambivalence and guilt and by manipulative behaviors of the therapist. Offending therapists may use threats and intimidation to prevent clients from reporting the behavior and can be adept at eliciting compliance, hero worship, and dependency. As is true of feelings of guilt, this anger needs to be identified, expressed, and worked through in later therapy with another therapist. If the anger is bottled up, it is likely to affect clients' relationships with significant others in their lives and with any other therapists from whom they might later seek treatment.
- *Cognitive dysfunction.* The trauma caused by sexual involvement with a therapist can be so severe that clients may experience cognitive dysfunction. Attention and concentration may be disrupted by flashbacks, nightmares, and intrusive thoughts.
- *Increased suicidal risk.* Finally, suicide risk is increased for clients who feel hopelessly trapped in ambivalence, isolation, and confusion. These feelings, coupled with an impaired ability to trust, may prevent victims from reaching out for help.

It should be clearly understood that even if clients behave in seductive ways, it is always the *therapist's* responsibility to maintain a professional distance in the relationship. Therapists can help clients to understand such behavior on their part as a manifestation of transference. The therapist, not the client, has the responsibility to evaluate the therapeutic situation and to monitor the boundaries of the relationship. Therapists who have trouble keeping clear boundaries in the professional relationship are often guilty of poor judgment in other areas of their practice. Clearly, the effects on clients can be profound and violate one of our most fundamental moral principles: to do no harm.

Sexual Attraction to Clients

The existing codes are explicit with respect to sexual relationships with clients. However, they do not, and maybe they cannot, define some of the more subtle ways that sexuality may be part of professional relationships. For example, sexual attractions between counselors and clients do occur, and it is not the attraction per se that is problematic. It is acting on the attraction that is inappropriate and becomes an ethical problem. It may be inevitable that most counselors will at some time feel a sexual attraction to a client. Barbara, a counselor in private practice, related this anecdote:

> The client was my prototype of the physically attractive man. He was tall, lean but muscular, and very good looking. As counseling progressed, it became apparent that he was sensitive to others, had a solid sense of personal integrity, and had a great sense of humor—all qualities that I admire. I realized that I found him attractive but wasn't particularly

concerned about it. After all, I had it in awareness and certainly didn't intend to act on my feelings. Then, during one session he began to relate a lengthy story, and my attention wandered. I drifted off into a sexual fantasy about him, I don't know for how long, probably only a few seconds. I snapped back to reality, and as I refocused on his words I realized he was now talking about sex. I nearly panicked: Had I somehow telegraphed my thoughts? I felt my face begin to redden, and compounded my discomfort by wondering if he saw me blushing and thought I was embarrassed about the subject of sex. With real effort I directed my concern away from myself and back to him and got through the rest of the session. But I was so shaken by the incident that I immediately sought consultation.

Assume you are the person to whom Barbara turns for consultation. She wonders whether she should continue counseling this man or whether she should make a referral. Barbara tells you that she worries about the effect of her attraction on the counseling process. Yet she also wonders what she might tell him if she decided to suggest a referral to another professional.

- What might you suggest to Barbara?
- If you found yourself in a situation similar to hers, what course of action might you take?

In *Sexual Feelings in Psychotherapy*, Pope et al. (1993) suggested that not only is it difficult to acknowledge sexual feelings toward a client but that it is even more difficult to talk about these feelings with colleagues or in supervision. Despite the likelihood that sexual attraction is a common occurrence, there has been a lack of systematic research into the topic. Most practitioners reported that their graduate training and internships provided no coverage whatsoever about sexual attraction and characterize their graduate training on therapists' sexual feelings as poor or virtually nonexistent (Pope et al., 1986; Pope & Tabachnick, 1993). The profession's silence on the topic has left practitioners to manage feelings of attraction by trial-and-error methods (Gill-Wigal & Heaton, 1996).

Pope et al. (1993) specified the conditions necessary for learning how to recognize and deal with feelings of attraction to a client. They believed that exploration of sexual feelings about clients is best done with the help, support, and encouragement of others. They maintained that practicums, internships, and peer supervision groups are ideal places to raise this topic and list some common reactions to sexual feelings in therapy, which include surprise and shock, guilt, anxiety about unresolved personal problems, fear of losing control, fear of being criticized, frustration at not being able to speak openly or at not being able to make sexual contact, anger at the client's sexuality, fear or discomfort at frustrating the client's demands, and confusion about tasks, boundaries, roles, and actions.

The tendency to treat sexual feelings as if they were taboo has made it difficult for therapists to recognize, acknowledge, and accept attractions to clients. It is not surprising that many therapists are at a loss as to how to deal with their sexual feelings in therapy. In light of these findings, we recommend that counselor education programs place more emphasis on the issue of sexual attraction. Prospective counselors need to be reassured that their feelings are a common manifestation of countertransference, that these feelings are natural, and that with awareness and preparedness they can still counsel effectively with clients to whom they feel attracted. The importance of consultation should also be emphasized, in both preservice and inservice education, to help prevent sexual attraction from crossing the boundary into an inappropriate dual relationship.

Gill-Wigal and Heaton (1996) offered some useful suggestions to therapists for managing their feelings of attraction to a client:

- Never act out feelings of attraction. Avoid actions that could foster the attraction, such as sitting close to or hugging the client, prolonging sessions, or increased self-disclosure.
- Acknowledge feelings of attraction.
- Seek to understand these feelings through conversations with supervisors, colleagues, and personal therapists.
- Take responsibility for feelings and any psychopathology. Be alert to factors such as work stress and tendencies to rationalize or make the client responsible for the attraction.
- Monitor boundaries by setting clear limits on physical contact, self-disclosure, and client requests for personal information about the therapist.
- Seek help.

Pope and Vasquez (1998) have summarized the issue of sexual attraction. They stated that "to feel attraction to a client is not unethical; to acknowledge and address the attraction promptly, carefully, and adequately is an important ethical responsibility" (p. 173). They suggested consulting with colleagues, obtaining supervision, and seeking personal therapy in dealing with sexual attraction. An excellent resource for further understanding is *Sexual Feelings in Psychotherapy: Explorations for Therapists and Therapists-in-Training* (Pope et al., 1993).

Consider, for a moment, how this subject applies to you.
- Have you had to struggle with the matter of sexual attraction in counseling relationships?
- If so, how did you deal with your feelings and the feelings of your clients?
- What would you do if you found yourself attracted to a client, or a client to you?
- What do you want to see included in training programs about issues of sexual attraction?

Prevention and Remediation

Sexual dual relationships are one of the most harmful types of unethical behavior. We have seen how destructive they can be for clients, counselors, and the profession as a whole. Because violations are common—and probably occur more frequently than we realize—we need to make concerted efforts toward awareness and prevention. Steps that can be taken include consumer education, support for the victims, improved counselor training, and monitoring professional practice.

Consumer Education

As professionals, we seem to be communicating well with each other regarding sexual dual relationships, as is evidenced by the large number of articles in our professional journals. However, it is equally important that we communicate clearly to consumers that they have the right to services that are free from sexual exploitation. Statements of client rights should include this information and be routinely distributed. An important step in prevention is to educate the public so that they have clear expectations about the counseling process and knowledge of the boundaries of the relationship.

As Hotelling (1988) has noted, many clients do not know what avenues of redress are available to them when they have been victimized. Information about the ethical, administrative, and legal options available to clients who have had a sexual relationship with their counselors needs to be routinely shared with consumers. One excellent example of how this might be accomplished is the booklet titled *Professional Therapy Never Includes Sex* (California Department of Consumer Affairs, 2004), which was specifically designed to help victims of sexual exploitation by therapists. It describes warning signs of unprofessional behavior and presents the rights of clients. Another helpful resource for clients is a brochure titled *If Sex Enters Into the Psychotherapy Relationship* (American Psychological Association, 1987).

Support for Victims

Many counselors may feel unprepared to help clients, students, or others who have had sexual relationships with their therapists. It is important to remember that clients who have been sexually exploited tend to be exceptionally vulnerable to revictimization when counselors fail to recognize their clinical needs (Pope & Vasquez, 1998). An abused client can be empowered by taking action against the offending therapist. As Hotelling (1988) has aptly stated, "The reality of what happened and its inappropriateness and destructiveness is affirmed; the burden of responsibility can be shifted to its rightful owner" (p. 233). Despite the potential for healing, it is extremely difficult for an abused client to pursue a complaint. In addition to the emotional toll that the process takes, it requires perseverance and some sophistication about the ethical complaint process and the legal system.

Counselors who work with these clients need to have a high degree of preparedness. They may need to deal with their own feelings of discomfort at being involved in a complaint against a colleague. They need to know all the possible avenues of redress and the advantages and disadvantages of each, so that these can be communicated accurately to the client. Finally, counselors need to keep in mind that the decisions—whether to pursue a complaint, what avenue(s) to take—rest with the client.

Women report great reluctance to file complaints that could lead to disciplinary action against their therapists or trainers (Gottlieb, 1990; Hotelling, 1988; Riger, 1991). These women often have ambivalent feelings about reporting their therapists, but they also encounter institutional barriers within the profession that contribute to their feelings of intimidation and deter them from following through with the complaint process. Gottlieb (1990) suggested that there is a need for an organizational structure within the profession that will reach out to these women and assist them in the complaint process.

Counselor Education

Counselor education is discussed more fully in Chapter 4, but at this point we want to note some concerns specific to sexual dual relationships. We have the impression that, generally, counselor education programs are not giving much emphasis to the topic. Whether this is due in part to erotophobia, as Vasquez (1988) has suggested, or to an assumption that there is no need to belabor the obvious, it creates a serious omission in the counselor training process. Counselor education programs have a dual responsibility: to train prospective counselors and to protect the public whom they eventually will serve. Vasquez (1988) described some training strategies to prevent counselor–client sexual contact, including knowledge, self-awareness, program climate, and faculty behavior. This is an excellent resource for counselor educators who want to assess or strengthen their programs.

Bartell and Rubin (1990) contended that education can play an important role in helping trainees first to recognize sexual attraction and then to take the necessary steps to avoid acting on the attraction. They suggested that the injunctions against sexual relationships be emphasized in training programs and be well publicized as a way to eliminate dangerous liaisons. Syme (2003) also recommended that graduate programs examine in detail the likelihood of erotic transference and countertransference in therapy and that they teach prospective therapists how to handle both of these phenomena.

On the matter of providing trainees with education on this subject, we think issues of attraction to clients ideally should be introduced in a beginning class in counseling, then dealt with in more depth in an ethics course, and further addressed in seminar sessions attached to students' fieldwork or internship experiences. Students are bound to encounter attractions as a part of their fieldwork, and instructors can encourage them to bring up these concerns for discussion. Individual supervision sessions provide an excellent venue for exploring these issues. We agree with Syme's (2003) observation that trainees may be very reluctant to publicly talk about feeling attracted to clients, but they will often do so privately in the safety of a supervision session. Some students may need to consider seeking therapy for themselves to explore their countertransferences and sexual attraction to clients.

Before attempting to educate others, instructors must gain their own clarity. Counselor educators who lack clarity will pass along their confusion to future generations of helping professionals, and counselor educators who behave in ethically questionable ways imply that those behaviors are acceptable. Counselor educators have a special obligation to be role models for what constitutes ethical behavior.

Tabachnick, Keith-Spiegel, and Pope (1991) acknowledged that numerous social and other types of activities exist for both students and faculty on and off campus, so that "little boundary blurrings" seem almost to be built into the academic system. Thoreson et al. (1993) suggested that issues of sexual contact between counselor educators and students and between supervisors and supervisees are more complex than issues of sex between client and therapist. Conflicting principles emerge, in that consenting adults have the right to establish consensual relationships, but because of the power differential involved, the notion of voluntary decision making is clouded with coercion. They recommended that education address the difficult issues of conflicting ethical principles, intimacy needs, the complexities of dual relationships, power inequities between "consenting adults," and gender-role stereotypes.

Monitoring Professional Practice

Professionals have been reluctant to report their colleagues who engage in sexual relationships with clients, students, or supervisees. Tabachnick et al. (1991) reported that 79% of psychology faculty who responded to their survey had ignored unethical behavior by colleagues. There may be a combination of explanations for this reluctance. In large measure, our sense of professional identity depends on the interpersonal bonds we form with our colleagues. We may fear being criticized or ostracized by colleagues for speaking out against "one of our own." The possibility of a defamation suit could also contribute to our hesitancy to take action. Many of us are reluctant to stand in judgment of others, particularly when we recognize our own fallibilities.

Consider what you might do in this situation: You become aware that a student intern in a counseling center has dated several of his clients. You and the student intern are in the same graduate program and are serving as interns in the same center. You approach him and inform him that you have heard from one of his former clients that they were involved in a sexual relationship. He tells you that he has no problem with this because *both* he and his client are consenting adults, and that because he is not a licensed professional he is not bound by a set of ethics codes. In essence, he informs you that you are interfering in his personal business.

- Where would you go from here?

It is difficult for professionals to take action against colleagues. However, despite our reluctance, we clearly have an ethical responsibility to act when we have reason to believe that a colleague has engaged, or is engaging, in sex with clients. As Syme (2003) has so aptly stated, "if a therapist does not report suspected sexual abuse of a client by a fellow therapist, this is false loyalty and a derogation of their duty of care to the general public" (p. 16). Keep in mind that it is not our role to investigate, judge, or punish. These responsibilities belong to ethics committees, licensing boards, and the courts.

It may also help to remember that, sometimes, sexually exploitive behavior may be a symptom of impairment (Emerson & Markos, 1996). Characteristics of counselors who have become sexually involved with their clients parallel in many ways the characteristics of the impaired professional. Here are some of the similarities:

- Fragile self-esteem, possibly manifested in a narcissistic style
- Difficulty establishing intimacy in one's personal life
- Professional isolation
- A need to rescue clients
- A need for reassurance about one's attractiveness or potency
- Abuse of alcohol or other drugs

Because one of the most common mechanisms of impairment is denial, responsibility for confronting the problem is likely to fall on the professional colleagues of an impaired counselor. One ethical course of action is to confront the counselor and to do so with sensitivity, respect, and preparedness (Herlihy, 1996). If the counselor is receptive, options such as seeking help, suspending or limiting practice, working under supervision, or self-reporting can be explored. Although the counseling profession has yet to address the rehabilitation of impaired professionals systematically, there is at least one model program for treating counselors who have sexually exploited their clients (Schoener & Gonsiorek, 1988). It is important to know whether such a program is available in the counselor's local area, and if not, to be able to provide the names of colleagues who are willing to counsel their impaired peers. However, if the impaired counselor denies, rationalizes, or justifies his or her behavior, there may be no other option than to report him or her to a supervisor, an ethics committee, or a licensing board. Although some offending therapists who are experiencing burnout or impairment can be restored to healthy functioning, there may be others who should not be allowed to practice. The high rate of recidivism and the difficulty of ensuring that an offender has been "cured" are factors that support this stance. The first and highest obligation must be to protect clients from harm.

Conclusions

Having a sexual relationship with a client is one of the most serious of all ethical violations. All codes of ethics of the professional associations prohibit sexual intimacies with current clients and with former clients until a specified amount of time has passed. The effects of sexual exploitation can be profound for the client, and the consequences can be severe for the counselor and for the profession.

Sexual attraction to clients is not unethical, but acting on that attraction creates problems. This topic has not been fully addressed in counselor training programs and is deserving of more attention.

The most productive future efforts will focus on prevention and remediation. The counseling profession needs to make a systematic effort to address sexual exploitation among its ranks and to educate clients about what they can rightfully expect from the professionals whose help they seek.

The Client's Perspective

The beliefs and behaviors of mental health professionals regarding dual relationships have been extensively studied, but surprisingly little literature exists to describe the client's or consumer's perspective or experiences, particularly with respect to nonsexual dual relationships. We believe it is essential to consider the client's perspective. In this chapter we discuss the few studies that have been conducted on consumer beliefs and attitudes toward dual relationships and present some anecdotes in which clients speak in their own words about their experiences. We raise questions about the implications of our profession's focus on our own point of view. Our guest contributor to this chapter, Susan L. Walden, presents a rationale and offers strategies for creating a counselor–client partnership in ethical decision making. These questions frame our discussion:

- How do clients and potential clients view dual or multiple relationships?
- How do clients describe their experiences with dual relationships, both sexual and nonsexual?
- Have the mental health professions taken a paternalistic approach to dealing with dual relationships, and if so, how can we make clients active partners in the decision-making process?

Attitudes and Beliefs of Consumers

Nerison (1992) studied the attitudes of both therapy consumers and potential consumers toward dual relationships, as well as consumers' actual experiences with sexual and nonsexual dual relationships. More than half of the 259 participants in her study were themselves professional therapists or psychologists, so her sample was not representative of consumers in general. However, the study does provide some information about the consumer's perspective. Survey participants rated sexual activity with a current client as the least acceptable type of dual relationship, with 99% rating it as never acceptable. Sexual activity with former clients was also viewed as inappropriate, with 70% rating it as never acceptable. It appears that clients' attitudes toward sexual relationships with current and former clients are very similar to therapists' attitudes as reported by Borys (1988), Gibson and Pope (1993), and Salisbury and Kinnier (1996).

Interestingly, Nerison (1992) found a high degree of ambivalence about whether a therapist's sexual attraction toward a client is ethical. This item received the highest number of "unsure" responses, and ratings were spread evenly along all acceptability ratings. As we discussed in Chapter 2, many therapists feel unprepared to deal with their feelings of sexual attraction. It appears that this issue may be equally confusing for clients.

With respect to nonsexual dual relationships, a majority of Nerison's respondents rated the following behaviors as never acceptable: providing therapy to a current employee (78%), inviting a client to a party or social event (65%), accepting a gift worth more than $50 (60%), providing therapy to a current student (59%), going out to eat with a client after a session (56%), and offering employment to a client (55%). These results are similar to those obtained by Borys (1988) in her survey of therapist attitudes, with the exception that client attitudes toward counseling an employee seem to be more strongly negative.

Walden (1996) studied the general public's knowledge of ethical counselor behavior, including nonsexual and sexual dual relationships. Her questionnaire was constructed from vignettes taken from the fifth edition of the *ACA Ethical Standards Casebook* (Herlihy & Corey, 1996). Participants were uncertain about the ethics of the behavior of a counselor in one vignette who conducted business and social relationships with clients. Only 41.5% "thought" or "strongly believed" this behavior was unethical. A second vignette described a sexual dual relationship between a counselor and a former client slightly more than a year after termination of the professional relationship. Again, respondents were uncertain, with 41.5% judging it unethical. Walden also found that there was no significant relationship between experience as a client in counseling and knowledge of counselor ethics. She recommended that counselors work to educate the public about the ethical standards of our profession and that we take steps to include the client's perspective in formulating and adjudicating our codes.

Clients' Experiences With Dual Relationships

Women are often reluctant to take action against offending professionals (see Chapter 2). Even when sexual advances are unwanted and sexual feelings are unreciprocated, reporting an offender can be a painful experience. Not all instances involve a client and therapist. Other relationships involving a power differential, such as the relationship between student and professor, are potentially as harmful. Anonymous (1991) has written about her experiences with Professor X, a charismatic professor of counseling. Although Professor X singled out this student for special attention, praise, encouragement, and hugs, she trustingly failed to consider that he was "coming on to her" sexually until she learned that he had had affairs with other students. After much soul searching, she filed sexual harassment charges with the university and the ethics committees of professional associations. A lengthy process followed, filled with frustrations and disappointments for her, but in the end Professor X was found in violation and disciplined. Although this student successfully resisted the professor's attempted seduction and her complaints were successfully resolved, the experience was traumatic for her, as is evident in the following passages (Anonymous, 1991):

> I sat for hours, staring off into space, unable to focus. I saw Professor X as two images that refused to meld . . . his well-meaning, kind, and caring persona as opposed with a lustful and menacing one. I wondered if I had inadvertently given him some signal that I was approachable sexually. (p. 503)

> My anger grew as the week wore on. It emanated from deep within me—I felt consumed by it, and I felt that I would not be able to stop myself from expressing it the next time I saw Professor X. I avoided having any contact with him. (p. 505)

> I felt obsessed by the experience—it drew attention away from every area of my life. To keep myself going, I read about sexual harassment and about research regarding sexual intimacy between therapists and clients. . . . These activities helped me to combat the worst aspect of this problem—the loneliness. (p. 506)

It can be helpful for those who have been sexually exploited to read about experiences similar to their own. First-person accounts of sexual relationships with therapists include *Betrayal* (Freeman & Roy, 1976), *A Killing Cure* (Walker & Young, 1986), *Sex in the Therapy Hour: A Case of Professional Incest* (Bates & Brodsky, 1989), *Therapist* (Plaisel, 1985), and *You Must Be Dreaming* (Noel & Watterson, 1992).

Nerison's (1992) study included client experiences with nonsexual dual relationships. Among her survey participants, 27% reported that they had become friends with their former therapists. Those who were interviewed tended to express ambivalent feelings. Despite positive outcomes, they felt a diminished sense of respect for the therapist.

Implications

Most counselors aspire to have fiduciary relationships with their clients. In a fiduciary relationship, the client's viewpoints are recognized and respected although the client's less powerful position in the relationship is acknowledged (Nerison, 1992). Counselors are likely to be uncomfortable with the notion of practicing paternalistic relationships with their clients. Nonetheless, the position taken by professionals with respect to dual relationships, as reflected in our codes of ethics and our professional literature, has tended to be paternalistic. Mental health professionals seem to have assumed that it is up to the *professional* to determine the boundaries of the relationship. Nerison described the assumptions underlying paternalism this way: (a) Therapists have the power to harm clients through dual relationships, (b) therapists are in a better position than clients to know what is best for the client, and (c) therapists are therefore obligated to protect clients from dual relationships regardless of clients' beliefs or feelings on the matter.

We do not argue that mental health professionals should abdicate their responsibility to maintain therapeutic boundaries in the interests of avoiding paternalism. Nonetheless, we do agree with Nerison's point that loss of autonomy is the price exacted by paternalistic relationships. To us, this underscores the importance of involving the client in ongoing discussions about relationship boundaries and potential dual relationship problems. It is important that we strive to balance our responsibilities for maintaining appropriate boundaries with our commitment to making our clients active partners in the therapeutic relationship.

Bringing the Client Into the Therapeutic Process as a Collaborator

A number of theories of counseling emphasize including the client in the therapeutic process as a collaborative partner. Theories that emphasize the collaborative nature of the therapeutic endeavor include Adlerian therapy, cognitive behavior therapy, narrative therapy, solution-focused brief therapy, feminist therapy, and social constructionism.

Adlerian therapists strive to establish an egalitarian therapeutic alliance with their clients. They consider an effective therapeutic relationship to be one between equals that is based on cooperation, mutual trust, respect, confidence, and alignment of goals. From the beginning of therapy, the relationship is a collaborative one, characterized by two persons working equally toward specific, agreed-on goals.

Cognitive behavior therapy encourages clients to take an active role in the therapy process. Clients are expected to bring up topics to explore, identify the distortions in their thinking, summarize important points in the session, and collaboratively devise homework assignments that they agree to carry out. Cognitive therapists are continuously active and deliberately interactive with clients; they also strive to engage clients' active participation and collaboration throughout all phases of therapy.

Narrative therapists place great importance on the qualities a therapist brings to the therapy venture. Some of these attitudes include optimism and respect, curiosity and persistence, valuing the client's knowledge, and creating a special kind of relationship where power is shared. Collaboration, compassion, reflection, and discovery characterize the therapeutic relationship. If counseling relationships are to be truly collaborative, therapists need to be aware of how power manifests itself in their professional practice. Therapists treat clients as experts on their own lives.

Similarly, in solution-focused brief therapy, the emphasis is on creating collaborative therapeutic relationships. Although therapists have expertise in creating a context for change, clients are viewed as experts on their own lives and often have a good sense of what has or has not worked in the past, and what might work in the future. In short, collaborative and cooperative relationships tend to be more effective than hierarchical relationships in therapy.

Feminist therapists view the therapeutic relationship as being based on empowerment and egalitarianism. The very structure of the client–therapist relationship models how to identify and use power responsibly. Feminist therapists clearly state their values to reduce the chance of value imposition and to allow clients to choose whether to work with the therapist. Feminist therapists actively focus on the power clients have in the therapeutic relationship. They encourage clients to take charge of their lives and relationships by making choices that increase the possibility for experiencing mutuality in their relationships. Feminist therapists work to demystify the therapeutic relationship. They do this by sharing with the client their own perceptions about what is going on in the relationship, by making the client an active partner in determining any diagnosis, and by making use of appropriate self-disclosure. Feminist therapy has also been applied to ethical decision making. In their discussion of a feminist model for ethical decision making, Hill, Glaser, and Harden (1995) contended that the client's perspective provides valuable information that the practitioner cannot afford to ignore. Although clients should be included in the ethical decision-making process as much as possible, it is the therapist who is responsible for the ultimate decision. Later in this chapter, Susan L. Walden addresses the feminist model for ethical decision making and the importance of including the client's voice in ethical practice.

In social constructionism, the therapist disavows the role of expert, preferring a more collaborative or consultative stance. Clients are viewed as experts about their own lives. The principles of social constructionism can be applied to ethics as well as to the therapeutic process. The social constructionist model of ethical decision making shares some aspects of the feminist model but focuses primarily on the social aspects of decision making in counseling (Cottone, 2001). This model redefines the ethical decision-making process as an interactive rather than an individual or intrapsychic process and places the decision in the social context itself, not in the mind of the person making the decision. This approach involves negotiating, consensualizing, and, when necessary, arbitrating. In dealing with an ethical dilemma or concern, Cottone (2001) stated that

> the ethically sensitive professional operating from a social contructivism mode would take several steps: (a) obtain information from those involved, (b) assess the nature of the relationships operating at that moment in time, (c) consult valued colleagues and professional expert opinion (including ethics codes and literature), (d) negotiate when there is a disagreement, and (e) respond in a way that allows for a reasonable consensus as to what should happen or what really occurred. Every relationship involved must be examined for potential linkage to another

(possibly adversarial) system of thought. In addition, every relationship must be assessed for a potential conflict of opinion over what should or did happen. If consensus is not possible, further negotiation, interactive reflection, or arbitration may be necessary. (p. 43)

Other approaches to therapeutic practice also emphasize the collaborative nature of the therapeutic endeavor. Many theoretical orientations are built on principles that involve the client as an active and involved partner in the therapeutic process; these orientations also favor including the client in making decisions that will affect his or her therapeutic work.

A Contributor's Perspective

Susan L. Walden suggests that important therapeutic benefits can result from inclusion of the client in the ethical decision-making process. She offers some strategies for accomplishing this goal at both the organizational and the individual level.

 Inclusion of the Client's Voice in Ethical Practice

Susan L. Walden

Numerous studies have investigated the knowledge, judgment, and experiences of counselors, psychologists, and social workers with respect to dual relationships and other ethical issues (Borys & Pope, 1989; Gibson & Pope, 1993; Gottlieb, Sell, & Shoenfeld, 1988). We have data reflecting practitioners' opinions on appropriate ethical actions as well as their self-reported practices when faced with ethical dilemmas. Although such studies certainly contribute greatly to our understanding, they tell only part of the story. The literature is scant concerning the other party in the counseling dyad, the client. Although it is true that both the professional and the field of counseling suffer when unethical practice occurs, in many cases the party who stands to incur the greatest harm is the client. Injury to clients resulting from dual relationships, especially sexual dual relationships, has been well investigated. Pope (1994) and Nerison (1992), among others, have documented the negative effects of dual relationships on clients.

Because of the potential for harm to clients, more attention must be given to understanding the client's perspective and to educating and empowering clients. Inclusion of the client in ethical considerations is not an attempt to "victim blame" or to shift the responsibility for ethical practice onto the client—the professional *always* bears the onus for maintaining professionalism and ethical practice—rather, inclusion of the client can be a strong asset to the counselor in resolving ethical dilemmas and can be a source of empowerment for the client.

Why has so little attention been accorded to the client's perspective? There are numerous possible responses to this question. First, perhaps tradition has dictated that we, as the professionals in counseling relationships, have the knowledge and training required to create and enforce the standards needed for best practice. Yet if we judge our clients as uninformed about the nature of counseling, we also deny them the potential for participation in the processes of understanding and resolving ethical dilemmas. Another potential explanation for the exclusion of the client perspective is the fear that telling a client too much about standards of practice might intimidate a client. For example, haven't we all occasionally worried that explaining all the limits of confidentiality to a client might frighten the client into silence?

A third possible hesitation in involving the client in ethical considerations is that an educated consumer base might result in an increase in ethics complaints. We are charged with the responsibility of monitoring ourselves and our profession. Most of the time we do a good job, as evidenced by the fact that only a small percentage of mental health professionals are named in complaints to ethics boards. Perhaps we might do a better job, not by turning over the responsibility for monitoring practice to the consumers or by blaming the victims of unethical practice, but by engaging the consumers of our services and empowering them in the process. We must remember that the client is the most important person in the counseling relationship.

Perhaps none of the aforementioned suggestions are accurate. It is possible that turning our focus to the client's perspective is simply a paradigm shift of sorts. We have espoused a somewhat paternalistic model of practice in the profession of counseling and in the creation and enforcement of ethical standards. We, as the professionals, create a set of standards that we believe will protect the client's welfare and best interests, yet we do this without the input or presence of the consumers of our services. I suggest that involving the client represents a natural step from a therapeutic benefits stance as well as a genuine move toward the aspirational level of ethical practice.

Therapeutic Benefits

Potential therapeutic benefits may be derived from the inclusion of the consumer perspective in ethics. First, when we make decisions concerning a client *for* the client rather than *with* the client, we rob the client of power in the counseling relationship. Conversely, when we create collaboration between counselor and client, the client is empowered. The concept of collaboration emphasizes the importance and essential nature of both parties in the relationship. Although counselor and client each bring different contributions to the collaboration—the counselor's training and professional experience and the client's strengths, hard work, and life experiences—both contributions are essential for the success of the counseling endeavor.

Client empowerment through inclusion in ethical considerations is a good fit with current thinking in the mental health professions. Newer therapies, particularly social constructivism and solution-focused brief therapies, emphasize the collaboration between counselor and client. The aim is to work toward goals determined by the client, drawing on the successes and strengths of the client. Why not extend this way of thinking into the arena of ethics? Bringing the client into ongoing dialogue regarding a potential dual relationship or other ethical concern should be a continuous process if we are truly to work within the client's frame of reference, respecting the client's views. We cannot pretend to understand fully the client's view of a situation or gauge the potential ramifications of certain decisions for the life and well-being of the client accurately. What we may hope to communicate is a genuine regard for the impact of a situation on the client and respect for the client's welfare in working to find the solution that best protects and respects the client. By soliciting the client's perspective, we may ultimately achieve better counseling results and the best resolution for any ethical questions that arise.

Let's examine the case of a client who presents with complaints of social isolation. She and the counselor work for several sessions reframing her sense of isolation, highlighting her strengths, and building strategies for connecting with others in social situations. When she invites the counselor to accompany her to a party, the counselor is concerned about the dual relationship implications but fears hurting the client. Rather than just turning down the client's offer or making excuses of previous plans, the counselor might engage the client in a discussion of the ramifications of such a venture, eliciting the client's thoughts and feelings about potential situations that might occur, including the impact on the client and the counseling relationship. Some clients may be unable to see the potential risks involved in the situation, and in those cases the ultimate decision rests with the counselor. However, in many cases, the counselor and client working together may arrive at a solution that allows the counselor to preserve the counseling relationship and helps the client feel a part of the decision-making process.

A second therapeutic benefit derived from the inclusion of the client perspective may be more culturally appropriate practice. The counseling profession is growing in its understanding of the demands of counseling in a culturally pluralistic society. Our codes of ethics may reflect primarily Western values and certain cultural biases, but they do not have to be applied in a culturally encapsulated manner. The 2005 *ACA Code of Ethics* addresses culturally appropriate practice, for example, in the provisions made for bartering and the giving of gifts, which have important cultural implications for some clients. When the counselor has strict beliefs or policies regarding accepting gifts, misunderstandings may occur. However, if counselors are willing to understand the client's perspective and share their own perspectives, a solution may be reached by working together. Without such an exchange of views, the client may be offended by the counselor's behavior. With an exchange, client empowerment and the selection of a solution more in keeping with the client's cultural values are possible. Garcia, Cartwright, Winston, and Borzuchowska (2003) proposed integrating multicultural theory and competencies into the process of ethical decision making. They emphasized the significance of a client's and counselor's worldviews in influencing the resolution of ethical issues in counseling. We can be culturally inclusive in the application of ethical standards, and the inclusion of the client perspective may be an important step toward this goal.

Aspirational Level of Ethical Practice

Not only are there potential therapeutic benefits to be gained by including the client's perspective in ethics, but such practices also speak to the attainment of the aspirational level of ethical practice. At the aspirational level, the practitioner is concerned with the spirit of the code and the moral principles on which the code rests (Remley & Herlihy, 2005). Functioning at the aspirational level of ethics means that the counselor's concern is for the welfare of the client. The inclusion of the client's voice in ethical matters speaks to this higher level of ethical functioning.

When a practitioner has decisions to make or ethical dilemmas to resolve, certainly the responsible professional consults the appropriate standards and is mindful of the impact of potential decisions on the welfare of the client. However, even the most well-meaning and skilled practitioner cannot fully understand the client's perspective or investment in the situation without the input of that client. Although we may see a situation as being relatively low risk for a client, the client may view the situation differently. I also question whether it is truly possible to attain the aspirational level of ethical functioning *without* including the client in the decision-making process. In order fully to prize and value a client and best represent what is in the client's best interests, should we not involve the client in the process? Only by asking the client can we really know what a situation looks like through the client's eyes.

The potential benefits of including the client perspective in ethics issues are many. Numerous therapeutic advantages may be gained, and a practitioner has moved closer to the aspirational level of ethical practice. Ultimately, such genuine regard for the client's welfare may bring about benefits for the counselor, for the profession, and, most important, for the client.

Operationalized Client Inclusion

With the rationale in place for the inclusion of the client perspective in ethics, the question becomes how to put this process into practice. Infusion of the client perspective begins on two major levels: the organizational level and the individual level. At the organizational level, professional counseling organizations can use several strategies to promote the client perspective. First, we must continue and strengthen our efforts at educating members of the public in general and our clients in particular regarding ethical practice. Frequent reference has been made in the literature to the benefits of educating consumers of counseling services regarding ethical considerations (Allen, 1986; Herlihy & Corey, 1994; Shimberg, 1986; Vinson, 1987).

In addition, most state licensure boards and other ethics bodies have begun to require that practitioners provide professional disclosure statements and use informed consent procedures. These developments are much needed and provide a useful source of information for our clients.

A second strategy for client inclusion at the organizational level involves client participation in the creation and adjudication of ethics codes. Rather than the paternalistic model currently in place in which we (the professionals) create and adjudicate our codes of ethics without the voice of the consumers, we might include representation by members of the general public. There is precedent for consumer participation in an ethics committee of a professional organization. In 1987 the Ethics Committee of the American Psychological Association added a nonpsychologist member of the general public to its committee (APA, Ethics Committee, 1987). No report was found to indicate how this public member was selected or to document the success or implications of this endeavor. Given the vast human resources we have in ACA, it does seem that the logistical aspects of appointing a consumer member to the ACA Ethics Committee could be managed if the membership and leadership of the organization supported such a move. By adding the voice and unique perspective offered by a consumer, we might be better able to formulate standards that protect our clients, better understand the implications of ethical and unethical practice for the client, and also indicate to the public that we as a profession are interested in protecting the rights and welfare of those who use our services.

A third component of client inclusion at the organizational level is to develop ethical decision-making models that include the client's voice in the resolution of ethical dilemmas. The ethical decision-making model described in *A Practitioner's Guide to Ethical Decision Making* (Forester-Miller & Davis, 1995) is a useful tool for the resolution of ethical dilemmas; however, the model does not call for consultation with the client as a part of the decision-making process. Hillerbrand and Stone (1986) suggested that the client is an integral part of the "ethical community of the counseling relationship," capable of participating in determining appropriate actions in ethical dilemmas. The feminist model for ethical decision making (Hill et al., 1995) calls for consultation with the client at every stage of the decision-making process. More recent models for decision making have been proposed, including the social constructivism model (Cottone, 2001), which is based on the systemic-relational service models, and the collaborative model (Davis, 1997), which values inclusion and multiple perspectives and goals. Both models acknowledge that multiple parties are affected by practice and ethical decision making and emphasize a collaborative approach to the resolution of issues.

The transcultural integrative model (Garcia et al., 2003) rests on the essential influence of both client and counselor cultural perspectives. Finally, Herlihy and Watson (2006) proposed a new paradigm for ethical decision making based on ethics, cultural identity development, and collaboration between counselor and client. This approach emphasizes the essential components of promoting social justice based on the client's worldview, the understanding by the counselor of the influence of culture on the counseling process, and the value of the client's participation in all aspects of the counseling relationship. These models all represent significant steps away from the individual perspective and influence common in earlier models.

Most ethical decision-making models share many common steps or procedures in the resolution process. The feminist model (Hill et al., 1995), which emphasizes the importance of including the client throughout the process, applies the following steps:

1. Recognize a problem
2. Define the problem (collaboration with the client is essential at this stage)
3. Develop solutions (with client)
4. Choose a solution
5. Review the process
6. Implement the solution and evaluate the result (with client)
7. Continued reflection

In the fifth step, which calls for consideration of the consequences of all options, readers are reminded to "ponder the implications of each course of action for the client" (p. 13). The authors of the feminist model specifically state that consultation with the client "as fully as is possible and appropriate" is an essential step in ethical decision making (p. 27). The inclusion of the client in the decision-making process is a stated component of several steps of the feminist model, and the authors suggest that the client may and should be included throughout the process whenever possible. The decision-making model presented in the final chapter of this book provides an excellent model for the resolution of ethical dilemmas involving dual relationships, and the model includes consultation with the client.

The feminist model and the earlier model presented by Forester-Miller and Davis (1995) are not that different; however, the latter does not reflect the importance of collaboration with the client in ethical matters that are often of great consequence to the client. A guide for ethical decision making published by the ACA Ethics Committee that reflects current thinking in the resolution of ethical dilemmas, with an emphasis on the inclusion of the client's voice, would be welcomed at this juncture. Such a step at the organizational level certainly would both instruct practitioners about the importance of including the client perspective and give them concrete strategies to use. The support of such practices from the professional organization would surely impress upon the membership the importance of the client perspective and should ultimately lead to fewer misunderstandings and healthier relationships between counselors and their clients.

At the individual level numerous strategies may be employed to involve the client in ethical matters. Informed consent is the process that most commonly includes the client in discussions of ethics, and practitioners can discuss potential dual relationship and other boundary issues at the outset. A good practitioner will revisit areas of informed consent periodically and especially as ethical concerns arise. Because informed consent by nature necessarily involves the client, perhaps reframing it as a process rather than an event will help counselors be more inclusive of the client as the counseling relationship progresses. Another strategy for the individual practitioner involves using a professional decision-making model when ethical dilemmas arise. This model should include consultation with the client at any and all possible stages during the process.

One final suggestion for infusing the client perspective involves the counselor educator. As counselor educators, we teach ethical principles to our students through our courses and through our deeds. If we teach students the process of informed consent and how to include the client in ethical decision making, we are equipping them from the beginning with a client-oriented philosophy and strategies. In addition, we can model these practices through our dealings with them in the teacher–student relationship.

Summary

The inclusion of the client's voice in ethical matters may not be appropriate in all situations, and some clients may not be able to participate fully or objectively in the resolution of ethical dilemmas. Nonetheless, I believe that the client perspective is an essential component of sound ethical practice. There are therapeutic benefits to be gained in terms of client empowerment and culturally appropriate practice. We strive toward the aspirational level of ethical practice when we value the client's perspective. There are few risks involved in bring the client into ethical matters, and the benefits are many, not only for the professionals and for the profession but also, and primarily, for the client. When we value our clients, we do all that is possible to understand the world through their eyes. When we listen to our clients, we teach them that their voice is important and is heard. When we include our clients in the process of ethical decision making, we empower them. When we include our client's perspective, we decrease the likelihood of harm to clients and increase the opportunities for positive results in counseling.

Conclusions

This chapter on the client's perspective concludes our introduction to dual or multiple relationships. In Chapter 1, we provided a foundation by defining dual relationships and discussing relationship boundary issues. We looked at risks and the potential for harm and offered some safeguards to minimize risk. In Chapter 2, we explored sexual dual relationship issues. In this chapter, we focused on the client's perspective and suggested a rationale and strategies for including clients in ethical decision making. In the next three chapters, we turn to boundary issues in counselor education and training.

Issues in Counselor Education

Numerous dual relationship issues present themselves in the counselor education and training process. Some of these issues involve subtle and complex questions about where boundaries should be drawn when counselor educators play multiple roles and have multiple responsibilities with their students. In this chapter we explore relationship boundary concerns that commonly arise in counselor education programs and present the thoughts of two guest contributors. Holly A. Stadler presents a faculty perspective. She identifies potential areas of conflict in the various roles taken by counselor educators and students and suggests that prudence and ethical reasoning are essential in creating an ethically congruent training environment. Michelle C. Muratori presents a student perspective on dual relationships between faculty and students, reflecting on her experiences in her bachelor's, master's, and doctoral programs.

The focus questions that guide us through our discussion include the following:

- What are the implications for counselor educators and students of the 2005 revisions to the *ACA Code of Ethics* (2005)?
- What kinds of conflicts do counselor educators face in the multiple roles they fulfill in their work?
- Can some forms of role blending in the professor–student relationship be beneficial?
- What are the responsibilities of counselor educators in teaching students about dual and multiple relationships? How can the issues best be raised and explored, and how can students be prepared to deal with dual or multiple relationship dilemmas?

The 2005 *ACA Code of Ethics* addresses the issue of relationship boundaries between student and professor and between student and student more extensively than did the previous code (ACA, 1995). In the Introduction to

Section F, the need to establish and maintain appropriate and effective boundaries in teaching, training, and supervision is stated as follows: "Counselors aspire to foster meaningful and respectful professional relationships and to maintain appropriate boundaries with supervisees and students."

Clearly, there are parallels between the counselor–client relationship and the professor–student relationship. In both types of relationship, it is the responsibility of the person in the more powerful position to define and maintain appropriate boundaries, and to engage the person who is in the less powerful, more dependent position in ongoing discussion and explanation to prevent problems when possible and resolve them when they do arise.

Two standards address different aspects of nonprofessional relationships between counselor educators and students. One standard addresses the risk of potential harm to the student, whereas the other addresses the potentially beneficial aspects of such relationships:

> Counselor educators avoid nonprofessional or ongoing professional relationships with students in which there is a risk of potential harm to the student or that may compromise the training experience or grades assigned. In addition, counselor educators do not accept any form of professional services, fees, commissions, reimbursement, or remuneration from a site for student or supervisee placement. (F.10.d.)

> Counselor educators are aware of the power differential in the relationship between faculty and students. If they believe a nonprofessional relationship with a student may be potentially beneficial to the student, they take precautions similar to those taken by counselors when working with clients. Examples of potentially beneficial interactions or relationships include, but are not limited to, attending a formal ceremony; hospital visits; providing support during a stressful event; or mutual membership in a professional association, organization, or community. Counselor educators engage in open discussions with students when they consider entering into relationships with students outside of their roles as teachers and supervisors. They discuss with students the rationale for such interactions, the potential benefits and drawbacks, and the anticipated consequences for the student. Educators clarify the specific nature and limitations of the additional role(s) they will have with the student prior to engaging in a nonprofessional relationship. Nonprofessional relationships with students should be time-limited and initiated with student consent. (F.10.f.)

Sexual Dual Relationships

The 2005 *ACA Code of Ethics* explicitly forbids counselor educators from engaging in sexual or intimate relationships with students or subjecting them to sexual harassment of any kind:

> Sexual or romantic interactions or relationships with current students are prohibited. (F.10.a.)

> Counselor educators do not condone or subject students to sexual harassment. (F.10.b.)

For some time, the codes of ethics of other professional associations also have had prohibitions against sexual dual relationships between students and educators: the APA code has included such a provision since 1992, and the AAMFT since 1988. The current APA (2002) code states that "psychologists do not engage in sexual relationships with students or supervisees who are in their department, agency, or training center or over whom psychologists have or are likely to have evaluative authority" (7.07.).

The American Psychiatric Association (2001) provides a rationale for avoiding sexual involvement in education and training:

> Sexual involvement between a faculty member or supervisor and a trainee or student, in those situations in which an abuse of power can occur, often takes advantage of inequalities in the working relationship and may be unethical because:
>   a. Any treatment of a patient being supervised may be deleteriously affected.
>   b. It may damage the trust relationship between teacher and student.
>   c. Teachers are important professional role models for their trainees and affect their trainees' future professional behavior. (3.14.)

Despite these clear statements in codes of ethics of professional associations, faculty–student sexual relationships do occur, although it is difficult to estimate the incidence rate. Two decades ago, 17% of Glaser and Thorpe's (1986) sample of female psychologists reported having had sexual contact with faculty members or clinical supervisors during their graduate training. Studies conducted a decade later found that 5% to 6% of female counselors and about 4% of male counselors experienced sexual contact with their professors or supervisors while they were students (Miller & Larrabee, 1995; Thoreson, Shaughnessy, & Frazier, 1995; Thoreson et al., 1993).

It may be that the incidence of faculty–student sexual relationships has actually decreased, or it may be that professionals have become more reluctant to admit to such relationships. It does seem clear that male counselors are more likely to have engaged in sexual contact while in the high-power role (professor or supervisor) and female counselors are more likely to have had these experiences while in the low-power role as students (Thoreson et al., 1995). Several studies (Glaser & Thorpe, 1986; Hammel, Olkin, & Taube, 1996; Miller & Larrabee, 1995) have indicated that women's attitudes toward their experiences change over time. In retrospect, they believe their sexual contacts with professors were more coercive, more of a hindrance to the working relationship, and more damaging to their professional careers than they believed at the time. These studies raise questions about students' ability to consent freely to such relationships and about how prepared students are to deal with the ethics of such intimacies at the time. Moreover, it seems clear that educators and supervisors tend to have professional power and authority long after direct training ends.

Both Miller and Larrabee (1995) and Hammel et al. (1996) have taken the position that engaging in sexual behavior with students is highly inappropriate and contrary to the spirit of the codes of ethics of most professional organizations. Miller and Larrabee (1995) emphasized that educators and supervisors function as role models for the profession and occupy positions of power. In addition, because of the detrimental impact of sexual involvements during training, they believed educators and supervisors ought to refrain from any sexual involvements with students or supervisees.

In their study of psychologists who reflected on their sexual relationships with clients, supervisees, and students, Lamb, Catanzaro, and Moorman (2003) found that 1% of the total sample reported a sexual boundary violation with a supervisee and 3% of the total sample reported a sexual boundary violation with a student. The majority of these violations occurred after the professional relationship had ended (100% after supervision and 54% after teaching). The respondents in the study were asked to identify the circumstances or reasons that influenced their decisions to pursue these sexual relationships. Three general types of reasons and circumstances were given:

- "No harm, thus I proceeded" (40% of the responses).
- "Consulted and/or negotiated" (32% of the responses).
- "Continued although I knew the behavior was problematic and/or unethical" (28% of the responses).

Approximately half of the respondents indicated that they had terminated the professional relationship (therapist, supervisor, teacher) so that they might initiate or continue the sexual relationship.

Concern about the harm caused by sexual relationships between students and professors is not limited to faculty in counseling or psychology programs in university communities. The University of Iowa, California State University, the University of Virginia, and the University of Oregon have implemented policies that forbid all professors and administrators from dating students they teach, mentor, or supervise (James, 1996; Leatherman, 1993). The president of the University of Oregon described the policy at that institution as "an essential ethical statement we must make . . . to counter anyone's capacity for the illusion that the exploitation of others in a power relationship is acceptable" (James, 1996, p. 1).

Role Conflicts for Counselor Educators

Self-Growth Experiences

Counselor educators confront some nonsexual relationship boundary issues that are inherent in the very nature of counselor training. It is a well-accepted assumption in the profession that the counselor's personal characteristics influence therapeutic outcomes. This assumption makes it incumbent on counselor training programs to focus on counselors-in-training as persons as well as on their academic performance. Students need to develop a strong sense of self-awareness along with an understanding of interpersonal dynamics if they are to become effective counselors (Glosoff &

Herlihy, 1995). Thus, counselor training programs blend academic study and experiential or personal learning, and counselor educators are expected to use sound professional judgment when they conduct training experiences that require student self-growth or self-disclosure. The *ACA Code of Ethics* (2005) states that training programs must provide safeguards so that students are aware of the ramifications their self-disclosure may have on professors who function in a variety of roles:

> Counselor education programs delineate requirements for self-disclosure or self-growth experiences in their admission and program materials. Counselor educators use professional judgment when designing training experiences they conduct that require student and supervisee self-growth or self-disclosure. Students and supervisees are made aware of the ramifications their self-disclosure may have when counselors whose primary role as teacher, trainer, or supervisor requires acting on ethical obligations to the profession. Evaluative components of experiential training experiences explicitly delineate predetermined academic standards that are separate and do not depend on the student's level of self-disclosure. Counselor educators may require trainees to seek professional help to address any personal concerns that may be affecting their competency. (F.7.b.)

As counselor educators, we are challenged with some key questions. Even when we consciously adhere to our pledge to keep self-growth experiences nongraded, can we avoid unintentionally incorporating knowledge gained through students' self-disclosures into our evaluations of their performance? When student limitations are personal or interpersonal rather than academic, what are the most effective ways to address those limitations? Can we require students to seek personal counseling when their personal problems are interfering with their ability to provide services? How can we encourage students to be alert to signs of potential impairment and seek professional assistance for themselves to remediate problems that are interfering with their ability to provide services to others? (See ACA, 2005, F.8.b.)

Gatekeeper Role

One of the major goals of counselor education programs is to promote and facilitate competence and professional behavior of their students. A problem faced by counselor educators is identifying, dealing with, and possibly dismissing students who are not making satisfactory progress toward professional competence (Oliver, Bernstein, Anderson, Blashfield, & Roberts, 2004). Counselor educators serve as gatekeepers to the profession. They protect consumers by identifying and intervening with graduate students who exhibit problematic behaviors (Vacha-Haase, Davenport, & Kerewsky, 2004).

Role conflicts can occur because we encourage personal growth and, at the same time, also serve as gatekeepers to the profession. As counselor educators, we are challenged to balance our mentoring role with our evaluative role. As mentors, we encourage students to develop personally and professionally by taking risks, and we support students in the process of accomplishing their goals. As evaluators, we sometimes are required to challenge students to take action when they exhibit problematic interpersonal behavior. Not only are we concerned about assisting our students in acquiring knowledge and skills, but we also are invested in helping them to assess their personal strengths and limitations that will affect their professional work. It is essential to evaluate trainees' professional behavior, clinical performance, and psychological fitness and to identify those interpersonal behaviors and personality characteristics that are likely to influence trainees' ability to effectively deliver mental health services. At times, conflicts may arise as we try to manage the dual roles and responsibilities of mentoring and evaluating.

Evaluation of Personal Factors

According to the *ACA Code of Ethics* (2005), counselor educators are responsible for ongoing evaluation of students' didactic and clinical competencies (F.9.a.) and are aware of any personal limitations of students that might impede performance (F.9.b.). When students are unable to provide competent service due to these limitations, counselor educators are expected to assist students in securing remedial assistance when it is needed. If remediation efforts are unsuccessful, counselor educators may be required to dismiss students from the program or refuse to endorse them for completion of the program (F.9.b.). When dismissal is a course of action, it is essential that counselor educators seek professional consultation, document their decision, and provide students with due process.

Certainly, if counselor educators do not attempt to help students become aware of personal factors that could impede their functioning as counselors, they are neither doing them a service nor helping their future clients. As personal problems or limitations of students become evident, faculty members have an ethical duty to encourage and even challenge students to face and deal with these issues lest these issues impede their performance as helpers. If students who have unresolved personal issues or who hold rigid and dogmatic attitudes, values, or prejudices are allowed to graduate from training programs, then it can hardly be said that the welfare of the consumer is being considered seriously. We think that programs should provide, as part of the curriculum, opportunities for students to examine their personal lives, with special emphasis on their needs, motivations, and life experiences that may affect their abilities to function effectively as practitioners.

Ethical quandaries sometimes arise when instructors become aware of personal problems or limitations of students through a nongraded experiential component of a course. It might be a dyadic practice session between two students in which one is serving as the counselor and the other as the counselee; it might occur in an experiential portion of a group counseling class; or it might emerge in exploring the student's difficulties in working with a certain client in practicum. If instructors raise their concerns with these students in a way that leads to a negative evaluation or an administrative action, students may feel that their trust was betrayed, no matter how carefully instructors have explained in advance any possible repercussions. Yet counselor educators cannot ignore their serious concerns about students; they have an ethical responsibility to monitor the profession.

Sometimes students who have personal characteristics or problems that interfere with their ability to function effectively may deny the feedback they receive. A program has an ethical responsibility to take action rather than simply pass on a student with serious academic or personal problems. Training programs need to establish written policies regarding the way that personal psychotherapy might be either recommended or required to remediate a student's problems (Elman & Forrest, 2004).

Informed Consent and Orientation to a Program

The preceding discussion underscores the importance of providing informed consent for students in counselor training programs. Students need to know that becoming an effective counselor entails more than mastering a body of knowledge and acquiring counseling skills. They also need to be made aware of the importance of their personal characteristics and their ability to function effectively in the interpersonal realm. Students must understand how their personal qualities are directly related to their ability to competently perform in the clinical area. The personal growth aspects of a program need to be made known to prospective students prior to their entrance into a program. Because many of us challenge students to think about their personal lives and their values and invite them to explore a range of feelings, students have a right to know where there may be potential problems. We ought to tell our students what we are doing to ensure that we are keeping their interest and welfare in mind, and we should talk about the procedures and practices we use to minimize the potential negative consequences of any role blending. The *ACA Code of Ethics* (2005) provides a range of topics about which students have a right to be informed before they decide to enter a particular training program:

> Counselor educators recognize that orientation is a developmental process that continues throughout the educational and clinical training of students. Counseling faculty provide prospective students with information about the counselor education program's expectations:
>
> 1. the type and level of skill and knowledge acquisition required for successful completion of the training;
> 2. program training goals, objectives, and mission, and subject matter to be covered;
> 3. bases for evaluation;
> 4. training components that encourage self-growth or self-disclosure as part of the training process;
> 5. the type of supervision settings and requirements of the sites for required clinical field experiences;
> 6. student and supervisee evaluation and dismissal policies and procedures; and
> 7. up-to-date employment prospects for graduates. (F.7.a.)

Relationship Boundaries Between Students and Professors

In the first edition of this book (Herlihy & Corey, 1992), we raised the question of whether a counselor educator should ever counsel a student. At that time, we noted that this was one of the most controversial questions pertaining to dual role relationships of counselor educators, and two guest contributors presented contrasting points of view. Today, with the revised *ACA Code of Ethics* (2005), we have a clear answer to this question:

> If students request counseling or if counseling services are required as part of the remediation process, counselor educators provide acceptable referrals. (F.9.c.)

> Counselor educators do not serve as counselors to current students unless this is a brief role associated with a training experience. (F.10.e.)

Although counselor educators should not enter into formal therapeutic relationships with students, this does not mean that we must remain aloof and distant from our students as persons. In the first edition, Lloyd (1992) raised a concern that counselor educators might be developing a "dual relationship phobia." He cautioned that no constituency (institution, student, or profession) is well served when counselor educators avoid the struggles of making responsible decisions by hiding behind a prohibition against multidimensional relationships. His concern was that opportunities for live demonstrations of individual and group counseling, and for supervision with a personal focus, might be lost if counselor educators approach dual relationship issues too conservatively.

We agree that it is as possible to err on the side of caution as it is to err on the side of carelessness about relationship boundaries. We hope the 2005 *ACA Code of Ethics* guidelines will be helpful to counselor educators and students alike who are searching for an appropriate middle ground. Mentoring relationships, as we noted in Chapter 1, are not dual relationships of the type that the code is intended to discourage. A mentor serves as adviser, confidant, friend, teacher, and supervisor—and the mentee can benefit a great deal from this special relationship. Mentoring often involves collaborative research efforts, and conflicts can arise around such issues as giving credit for publication of research findings. Unfortunately, most of us know of students who have felt pressured to have their work presented under the first authorship of their major professors.

Two standards in the *ACA Code of Ethics* provide safeguards to ensure that counselor educators do not take unfair advantage of their more powerful positions. The first requires that students be given adequate credit for their contributions to research: "Counselors who conduct joint research with colleagues or students/supervisees establish agreements in advance regarding allocation of tasks, publication credit, and types of acknowledgment that will be received" (G.5.e.). The second addresses students as principal authors: "For articles that are substantially based on students' course papers, projects, dissertations or theses, and on which students have been the primary contributors, they are listed as principal authors" (G.5.f.). For mentoring relationships to work as they are intended, it is essential that professor and student talk candidly beforehand to establish clear working guidelines and that an open dialogue be maintained.

Other types of role blending occur in the counselor training process. Live class demonstrations of counseling can enhance student learning and fall within the ethically permissible bounds of "a brief role associated with a training experience." Counselor educators certainly can remain ethical and relate to students on an unstructured and personal level, making themselves available to students beyond class time and office hours. Issues raised during a class session are often continued over a cup of coffee after class, professors attend graduation parties of their doctoral students to extend their congratulations, and graduate student associations sponsor social events as well as lectures and other educational opportunities. None of these or other, similar situations need be problematic. A key factor, as guest contributor Michelle C. Muratori comments later, is the counselor educator's level of comfort and aptitude in moving among formal and informal roles.

Bowman, Hatley, and Bowman (1995) assessed both faculty and student perceptions of dual relationships in mentoring, friendships, monetary transactions, informal social interactions, and romantic/sexual relationships. They observed that certain dual relationships are unavoidable in most training programs and suggested that dual relationships may be more accurately evaluated when viewed from the perspective of how the faculty member and student *behave* within the relationship, rather than concluding that the mere existence of a dual role is necessarily unethical.

According to Burian and O'Connor Slimp (2000), multiple-role relationships may at first appear benign, and sometimes even beneficial, yet they pose some risks. For example, the mentoring that occurs between faculty and students may include social elements, which can be beneficial to the student. However, Burian and O'Connor Slimp suggested ending or postponing the social relationship if more than a minimal risk of harm exists. The ultimate ethical responsibility rests with the individual with the greatest power, in this case, the counselor educator.

Biaggio, Paget, and Chenoweth (1997) observed that faculty–student relationships are not static and that some multiple roles and overlapping relationships are to be expected. Students progress from the beginning stages, to graduation, and eventually to becoming colleagues with faculty members. Biaggio and her colleagues presented three general guidelines for faculty in maintaining ethical relationships with students. First, faculty need to recognize the potential for harm in dual relationships with their students and that they hold a position of power and authority over students. Second, they need to have a framework for evaluating appropriate and inappropriate conduct and to monitor contact carefully so that students are not harmed or exploited. Third, faculty need to model appropriate and ethical relationships with other professionals, students, and clients.

Above all, counselor educators must not exploit students and trainees or take unfair advantage of the power differential that exists in the context of training. Managing multiple roles ethically is primarily the counselor educator's responsibility. Counselor educators who are able to establish appropriate personal and professional boundaries are in a good position to teach students how to develop appropriate boundaries for themselves.

Dual Relationships Between Students

In doctoral programs, advanced students are often involved in the supervision of students who are seeking their master's degrees. The supervision of students by students raises a potential for problematic dual relationships, even though such an arrangement has many potential benefits. When students are involved in leading counseling groups or providing clinical supervision for their peers, counselor educators are required to take steps to ensure that "the rights of peers are not compromised when students or supervisees lead counseling groups or provide clinical supervision" (ACA, 2005, F.6.e.). Careful supervision and monitoring are needed to ensure that problematic dual relationships between students are avoided whenever possible and that they are resolved when they do occur.

A Contributor's Perspective

Holly A. Stadler provides a thoughtful discussion of the various roles played by counselor educators and students. She discusses the importance of prudence in ethical decision making and offers suggestions for managing ethical dilemmas in the training environment.

 ## Dual Relationships in Counselor Education

Holly A. Stadler

Educators and students in counseling programs engage in a wide variety of roles and relationships as a function of their program-related activities as well as their participation as members of the larger society. For the most part, these roles and relationships do not converge in ways that elicit ethical concerns. Occasions do arise, however, in which such convergences could be seen as ethically problematic. Over the years, professional groups such as ACA have recognized the need to offer increasingly explicit guidance with regard to dual role relationships. For example, a counselor educator might be asked to join the board of directors of an agency employing one of her current students. Or a practicum student could find out that one of his clients at the university counseling center plans to attend a self-help group of which the student is a member. Herlihy and Corey have noted earlier in this chapter that there is sufficient evidence of ineffective management of these relationships. If the counseling profession is to enjoy the public trust, counselor educators, supervisors, and counselors-in-training must manage dual relationships prudently and reasonably.

I will address dual relationships in counselor education, leaving to others the topic of such relationships in supervision. To underscore the theme of R. Brown and Prager (1985) that "developmental growth can occur optimally in an ethically congruent environment" (p. 403), I will focus on the training environment as a necessary locus of instruction, supervision, and modeling of prudence and reason in dual relationships. I begin with a review of the 2005 ACA *Code of Ethics* with special attention to dual relationships in counselor education. Then I identify a number of types of multiple roles and relationships and associated concerns that occur in counselor education, and conclude with a call for sound ethical reasoning and the exercise of prudence in dual role situations.

Dual Relationships and the 2005 *ACA Code of Ethics*

Along with evidence of failure on the part of some professionals successfully to negotiate dual relationships has come increased specificity in codes of ethics about the boundaries of such relationships. With respect to counselor education, the 2005 *ACA Code of Ethics* takes special note of these issues, highlighting them in specific sections and going beyond general statements characteristic of previous codes to articulate positions on dual relationships that directly and indirectly relate to counselor education. Section F (Supervision, Training, and Teaching) takes on potential dual role concerns in counselor education such as close relatives of faculty as students in counselor education programs, peer relationships among students, counselor educators leading student self-growth experiences, and relationships with previous students.

These standards draw attention to two of the most frequent and troubling dual relationships between faculty and students: counseling relationships and sexual relationships. I have written elsewhere (Stadler, 1986b, 1992) about ethical perspectives on counseling relationships between educators and students. It is not necessary to revisit that issue here other than to note "the inherent inadvisability of pursuing options that involve conflicting obligations" (Stadler, 1992, p. 56).

In addition, numerous others (Bersoff, 2003; Glaser & Thorpe, 1986; Miller & Larabee, 1995; Pope, Levenson, & Schover, 1979; Robinson & Reid, 1985) have engaged the topic of sexual relationships between educators and students, and I encourage you to pursue those sources. In both areas—boundaries regarding counseling relationships and sexual relationships—Kitchener's (1988) guideline that these relationships should be considered a priori unethical can be applied because the "conflict of interests is great, the power differential large, and the role expectations incompatible" (p. 220).

Multiple Roles and Relationships

Rest (1982) has noted that one of the chief attributes of effective ethical decision making is the ability to recognize the existence of an ethical dilemma. Thus, it is useful to anticipate some of the possible role and relationship conflicts (excluding the already discussed sexual or counseling relationships) that could develop as counselor educators fulfill their academic responsibilities in multiple roles that include educator, researcher, colleague, administrator, and consultant.

Consider that the objectivity of the selection and evaluative aspects of the educator role (such as admission decisions or assignment of grades) can be compromised by noneducational roles that involve, for example, business, social, or familial relationships. These noneducational dual relationships can be cause for concern. The 2005 *ACA Code of Ethics* is specific about prohibiting close family relatives, romantic partners, or friends from being supervised by a counselor educator (see F.3.d.).

To recognize a common dual relationship for faculty in the *researcher* role, reflect on the faculty member conducting research on counselor education who directly solicits students in counselor education classes to participate in a study. This scenario frequently comes to the attention of institutional review boards at universities. For our purposes, however, it is important to note that students in this situation might either feel that they could gain some advantage over other students or feel coerced to participate in a faculty study. A similar situation can occur with clients whose therapist requests their participation in dissertation or other research. Strategies for soliciting research participants should incorporate procedures that avoid placing potential participants in dual role conflicts.

Dual roles in *collegial* and *administrative* relationships are also potential sources of conflicting interests and obligations. For example, consider colleagues who are in a business partnership or who are intimate partners. Serving together as members of a curriculum committee might not produce any inordinate conflicts beyond those that already take place in such a committee. But if one of the partners is in a position to evaluate the other for tenure or merit pay, there could be serious ethical implications. Concerns about the objectivity of the evaluator and the interests being served in the evaluation could overshadow the actual record of the person under review. Conflicting interests may deter candor and cloud judgment when untenured faculty members are in selection or evaluation roles regarding an applicant, student, or colleague who has a dual relationship with a tenured faculty member.

With respect to the *consulting* role, many universities expect that faculty members will offer their expertise to the community. Here questions of selection and evaluation are likely to cause the most difficulty. For example, personnel in a consultee agency might be enrolled or be seeking enrollment in the program with which the faculty member is associated.

Counselor education students may also face role and relationship conflicts because of their multiple roles, including student, teacher, researcher, and peer. Several of these roles entail concerns similar to those discussed previously. The 2005 *ACA Code of Ethics* makes it clear that students are responsible for their own ethical conduct. With respect to the *student* role, this includes not initiating dual relationship entanglements with faculty members, supervisors, or clients.

With regard to *teaching* and *research* roles, the concerns and potential conflicts for students are also similar to those of faculty members. Issues of objectivity in student evaluation and selection and of noncoercive solicitation of research participants apply equally to students who teach and serve as research assistants.

Students also must take responsibility for not creating dual relationships with clients and for avoiding turning peer or friend relationships into therapeutic relationships. The 2005 *ACA Code of Ethics* makes reference to one aspect of *peer* role relationships: "Counselor educators make every effort to ensure that the rights of peers are not compromised when students or supervisees lead counseling groups or provide clinical supervision" (F.6.e.). Counselors-in-training must guard against engaging in therapeutic relationships with peers, friends, and family (Davenport, 2004). Counselor educators are familiar with the counseling student who, unable to set boundaries on relationships, is exhausted by the multiple demands of one-sided, quasi-therapeutic friendships with others seeking "professional advice."

Managing Ethical Quandaries in the Training Environment

My observation, based on having participated on and chaired state and national counseling ethics committees, is that many complaints that come before those bodies are due to imprudence and lack of sound ethical reasoning. As mentioned earlier, the training environment is a necessary locus of instruction, supervision, and modeling of prudence and reason in dual relationship situations. Ethical sensitivity in professional life requires both the intellectual tools to formulate justifications for conduct and the disposition to do good. Counselors-in-training can learn to make informed ethical choices based on a reasoned account of the nature of the circumstance, the application of ethical principles as action guides, and the development of a course of action (Kitchener, 1984; Stadler, 1986a). Ethics course work and practicum/internship supervision are typical opportunities for instruction and modeling in ethical decision making (Urofsky & Sowa, 2004). These opportunities also prepare students to anticipate common ethical concerns such as child abuse reporting (Stadler, 1989) and to use ethical reasoning strategies to articulate justifications for possible courses of action. Infusion of topics of ethical concern in all aspects of the curriculum and in research projects further alerts students to the various manifestations of ethical dilemmas and the operation of ethical principles while modeling ethical sensitivity.

Ethical decisions based on application of moral principles help to answer the question, What should I do? Virtue ethics help in reflection on the question, What kind of person should I be? "A moral virtue is a fixed disposition, habit, or trait to do what is morally commendable" (Beauchamp, 1982, p. 150). Prudence is one of a group of virtues or traits of character that augment principle-based decision making. Pellegrino and Thomasma (1993) have described prudence as the "indispensable connection between cognition of the good and the disposition to seek it in particular acts" (p. 84). Prudence moves us from thought to action in the moral domain. Some writers (Meara, Schmidt, & Day, 1996; Pellegrino & Thomasma, 1993) believed that prudence is the defining virtue of professional moral life. Meara et al. (1996) have described prudence as "appropriate restraint or action, deliberate reflection upon which moral action to take, an understanding of the long-range consequences of choices made, acting with due regard for one's vision of what is morally good, and a knowledge of how present circumstances relate to that good or goal" (p. 39).

Students usually enter counselor education programs with their character traits well formed. Careful selection procedures have been used to identify applicants who are best suited for the profession. If the profession is concerned about monitoring ethically troublesome dual relationships, then the virtue of prudence might be one character trait to look for in the candidate selection process. During the course of training, faculty can support, model, and habituate (J. Wilson, 1993) this character trait through reinforcement and demonstration of the general practice of prudence (e.g., clinical prudence), not merely prudence in ethical matters. Discussions of situations that might test a student's prudence (such as crisis intervention) can augment general reflections on the question, Who do I want to be as a counselor?

Summary

In an ethically congruent training environment, counselor educators and counselors-in-training are guided by a sense of mutual respect and respect for the counseling profession and for those served by the profession. We acknowledge the conflicts and complexities of dual relationships. Through the exercise of prudence and ethical reasoning, the boundaries of multiple roles and multiple relationships can be managed effectively so as to respect all those engaged in and served by the counseling profession.

Teaching Students About Boundary Issues

We agree with Stadler's contentions and believe that multiple roles frequently come into play in counselor education. Apart from sexual relationships with students, which are clearly unethical, a wide range of dual and multiple relationships exist that are part and parcel of the training process. Rather than lumping all these nonsexual multiple relationships as unethical along with sexual relationships, professional training ought to focus on teaching students how to manage situations involving multiple roles and relationships. We conclude our portion of this chapter with a look at these questions: What is the responsibility of counselor educators in teaching students about dual relationships and boundary issues? How can the issues best be raised and explored, and how can students be prepared to deal with dual relationship dilemmas?

In the ethics courses we teach, we spend considerable time discussing dual and multiple relationships. Our students show a great deal of interest in discussing these issues. Many students have never really considered the potential risks of dual relationships, so the discussions serve to increase their awareness of potential ethical dilemmas. We examine dual and multiple relationship standards contained in the codes of ethics of the various professional organizations. We use case vignettes to introduce ethical dilemmas, frequently role-playing a vignette and then discussing possible courses of action. Students are encouraged to think about their values as these pertain to a host of dual relationship issues. The combination of reading codes and articles, enacting case situations, participating in debates, and being challenged to defend a position typically results in an increased awareness of the pervasiveness of dual relationships. Students begin to develop sensitivity to the subtlety and complexity of the topic.

Through careful attention to program planning and evaluation, students can be helped to increase their sensitivity to dual and multiple relationships that are unethical and harmful. Recommendations for training programs include the following:

- Programs should present literature in which the nature, causes, and consequences of dual relationships are explored.
- The ethical and clinical implications of both sexual and nonsexual dual relationships need to be reflected in virtually all clinical course work and supervision. Real-life dilemmas that surface during students' practica and internships should be addressed in the individual and group supervision sessions that accompany them.
- When programs include a separate ethics course, ample time should be devoted to examination of dual relationship issues.
- The issue of sexual attraction needs to be addressed, initially in didactic course work and then in supervision throughout students' field experiences.
- In course work containing experiential components, the relevant dual or multiple relationship issues can be specified at the outset and carefully worked through as they occur on a case-by-case basis.
- Institutions and programs within institutions need to develop clear and explicit standards regarding potential dual relationships between students and educators.
- Written, operationally defined procedures need to be developed for avoiding conflicts of interest in monitoring and enforcing institutional standards regarding dual relationships.

A Contributor's Perspective

Michelle C. Muratori presents a student perspective on boundaries in the relationship between faculty and students. She reflects on her experiences in an undergraduate human services program, her master's program, and a doctoral program, each at different universities, and identifies important variables in managing dual relationship questions.

 Dual Relationships in Counselor Education Programs: Reflections of a Recent Doctoral Graduate

Michelle C. Muratori

I recently celebrated an important achievement in my life: I successfully defended my doctoral dissertation and brought closure to my formal training in counselor education. Upon being granted the right to put the letters "PhD" following my name, I immediately felt an overwhelming sense of responsibility. I have spent the past few weeks contemplating how my educational experiences as an undergraduate, master's student, and doctoral student have shaped my professional identity. One thought that has come to mind repeatedly is that I have had the good fortune of experiencing diverse training methods in programs that viewed the counseling enterprise from different philosophical perspectives. In comparing how the issue of dual relationships was approached in the three programs I attended, I will illustrate how diverse educational experiences have enhanced my training.

The sharpest contrast I experienced was in the fundamental differences in views on dual relationships between the faculties of the undergraduate and master's programs I attended. The two programs shared a deep respect for clients and a reverence for the process of psychotherapy; however, they were structured dissimilarly, which may have been due to their ideological differences. One program emphasized experiential learning far more heavily than the other program.

In the undergraduate human services program I attended, professors and clinical supervisors strongly encouraged students to engage in deep self-reflection through a number of experiential courses to augment their personal and professional development. Given this program's structure, dual relationships could hardly be avoided. Because the faculty seemed to wear different hats effectively and to be skilled in the roles of teacher, evaluator, clinical supervisor, and therapeutic agent, students could trust that they were not being graded on the basis of the quantity or quality of the personal material they self-disclosed during the experiential activities. Faculty members did an outstanding job of creating a safe climate in which students could freely explore the gray areas associated with dual relationships that were inherent in the program as well as the range of dual relationships that could conceivably develop between therapists and clients. I partially attribute my ability to tolerate ambiguity and work through ethical dilemmas to my early training experiences in that program. In my view, it was the optimal learning environment for a beginning counselor trainee.

The master's program in counseling psychology that I attended clearly endorsed a more conservative view of dual relationships. Although students were provided with ample opportunities for intellectual challenge and professional growth, the implicit rule within the context of the graduate program was to avoid dual relationships if at all possible. Faculty members encouraged trainees to seek professional help from a therapist in the community if their work with clients triggered unresolved personal issues. I suspect their rationale might have been that there were abundant resources in the community to facilitate the resolution of personal problems and that an academic setting was not the most appropriate environment in which to address such issues due to the hazards of dual relationships. Opportunities did exist within the structure of the program to examine the impact of personal experiences on professional development (e.g., via clinical supervision); however, there appeared to be a more distinct separation or boundary between the academic and clinical components in my master's program than in my undergraduate program.

Both programs were effective largely because the professors truly subscribed to the ideologies that guided their respective programs. I am convinced that professors in my undergraduate program believed in the power of experiential learning and, thus, were quite effective in their roles. They seemed comfortable with student self-disclosure, which created a safe environment for students to engage in deep self-exploration. By the same token, I think it was an ethically sound decision for professors in my master's program to adhere to the boundaries they established with students. The administrators and faculty of this program created safety by clearly drawing the parameters between behaviors that were deemed acceptable and those that were unacceptable.

When I began my doctoral training a few years ago, I did not expect that my relationships with faculty would gradually become more collegial. Although I was always cognizant of the power differential that existed between me and my professors, I was also aware that I was being groomed to be an academician and was afforded professional opportunities that previously had not been available to me. For example, as a doctoral student, I was employed as a teaching assistant and had opportunities to teach courses independently and to coteach courses with my professors. I also had an opportunity to gain experience and hone my skills as a clinical supervisor. Because these opportunities were part of my doctoral education, my performance was constantly evaluated by faculty members who, in some cases, served multiple roles in my training. To illustrate this, one professor served as my adviser and chaired all of my committees. Because I held a clinical position in a center on campus where he served as director, he also was my employer and supervisor. In my current postdoctoral position at a different university, I recently coauthored a chapter with two of my adviser's esteemed colleagues that will be published in a book he is editing. My role has shifted in relation to his role in each of these situations. The power differential between us has never ceased to exist, but there have been times when the gap was wider and times when it was narrower.

Reminiscent of my undergraduate experience, dual relationships in my doctoral training could not be avoided. Because I have encountered dual relationships so often in my training, I have reached the conclusion that students pursuing careers in counseling and counselor education should be taught how to successfully manage dual relationships when they cannot be avoided. We should all be mindful of the fact that today's students will be tomorrow's counselors and counselor educators. As one who is making the transition from student to professional, I can attest to the fact that my ability to handle dual relationships successfully has been influenced by the role models I have had. If I had worked with professors who misused their power, I suspect that I would not feel adequately prepared to one day negotiate dual relationships with my students. Fortunately, that has not been my experience. My professors have had an ethical awareness and have been positive role models who could easily adapt to different roles in relation to their students.

In my short history of college teaching, I already have encountered a dual relationship with one of my students. As a doctoral trainee, I once needed to complete a master's-level course to fulfill a requirement for licensure. A student who had taken a group process course that I had taught was enrolled in the class. I was now a classmate of an individual who had formerly been my student. Aware of the power differential inherent in the instructor–student relationship that had been established earlier, I felt an ethical obligation to proceed cautiously in my interactions with the student. Although my demeanor was friendly, I was always mindful of the previous relationship that had existed between us.

On the basis of my clinical and teaching experiences, I believe that counselors and counselor educators can expect to encounter situations that are far from clear-cut. Consequently, it is important that we establish clear boundaries that will help us to navigate ethically through nebulous situations. Fortunately, my diverse training experiences have broadened my perspective sufficiently to enable me to approach novel situations (e.g., dual relationships) in a flexible yet ethical manner. One major lesson I have learned after gaining exposure to varied educational practices is that one's comfort level has to be taken into account when defining boundaries. The professors I have admired the most have adapted almost seamlessly to their various professional roles and have established boundaries that are appropriate given their personalities, theoretical orientations, and comfort levels with self-disclosure.

Faculty members need to carefully consider potential problems in managing dual or multiple relationships. Counselor educators, like therapists, need to be mindful that their roles are inherently powerful and that they are in a position to abuse that power. Just as clients tend to imbue their therapists with omnipotence, a parallel process occurs between counselor trainees and their professors. With this in mind, it is important that counselor educators consider the ramifications of entering into dual relationships with students. I believe there are instances in which dual or multiple relationships in counselor education programs can be productive without being harmful. However, the potential pitfalls should not be glossed over. In the final analysis, counselor educators must feel comfortable with the choices they make regarding this issue. Because faculty members typically have more than one function, role blending does seem inevitable. However, it is crucial that no dual relationship be developed at the student's expense.

In conclusion, I have come to recognize that just as there often is not a single pathway to any given destination, there are multiple ways to approach counseling as well as the training of counselors. As is true of so many things in life, "the fit" makes a tremendous difference—the fit between student and program as well as the fit between counselor educator and program.

Conclusions

In concluding this chapter, we are reminded that actions speak louder than words, and that counselor trainees learn by observing the conduct of their professional role models. Therefore, it behooves counselor educators to model ethical *behavior*, including maintaining clear boundaries and being open to discussing any potential problems that might arise. One key to fostering ethical management of dual relationships also lies in the *awareness* of counselor educators. If we are unaware of the potential problems, we are likely to find ourselves involved in relationships that are harmful to both student and professor. Another key lies in carefully and systematically teaching our students about the dual relationships and potential dual relationships they may encounter while they are our students and later as practitioners. If we—and our students—are clearly aware of the potential for conflicts of interest, for exploitation, or for misusing power, then these situations are much less likely to occur.

5

Issues in Supervision and Consultation

We have seen how subtle and complex boundary issues can emerge in the dyadic relationships between counselor and client and between faculty member and student. These issues can be even more complicated when a relationship is tripartite, as in the relationship among supervisor, supervisee, and client, or among consultant, consultee, and client or client system. In this chapter, we first explore multiple roles and relationships in supervision. Guest contributor L. DiAnne Borders adds a supervisor's personal and thoughtful perspective, and Jamie Bludworth shares his experiences as a supervisee. We then look at issues in consultation, with input from guest contributor A. Michael Dougherty.

Supervision

Supervisors play a critical role in helping counselors-in-training and novice counselors to understand and manage dual relationships. Students may learn about dual and multiple relationships during their academic course work, but it is during their internships and other field experiences that they come face-to-face with these issues. The professionals responsible for supervising counselors-in-training must take the initiative in examining dual relationship concerns so that novice practitioners are prepared to respond appropriately when such relationships begin to develop, not only during internships but throughout their professional careers (Slimp & Burian, 1994).

There is an inherent duality in the supervisory relationship, and the complexity of the supervisory role can create some unique boundary issues. In this section of the chapter, we review some of the literature on these issues, share our own views, and present the guest contribution of L. DiAnne Borders. These are the questions that will guide our discussion:

- What guidance do codes of ethics and specialty guidelines offer supervisors?
- How prevalent is sexual contact in the supervisory relationship, and what are its effects?

- What are the ethical issues in social and business relationships between supervisors and supervisees?
- How can supervision include exploration of the supervisee's personal issues and remain within ethical boundaries? What is the appropriate balance for supervisors between attending to the professional development and the personal development of the supervisee?
- How can informed consent procedures help to prevent problematic dual and multiple relationships, as well as nonprofessional relationships?
- How can supervisor countertransference best be dealt with in supervision?
- What are the ethical and legal ramifications when the supervisee does not perform competently? How can this create role conflicts for the supervisor?

Ethics Codes and Guidelines

In the *ACA Code of Ethics* (2005), Section F (Supervision, Training, and Teaching) Standards F.1. through F.5. focus on the supervisory relationship. In addition, the "Ethical Guidelines for Counseling Supervisors" (Association for Counselor Education and Supervision [ACES], 1993) clarify and give specific guidance regarding multiple relationships and relationship boundaries in supervision.

The central issue pertaining to multiple-role relationships in the supervisory process is the potential for abuse of power. Like clients in counseling relationships, supervisees are in a vulnerable position and can be harmed by a supervisor who exploits them, misuses power, or violates boundaries. Supervisors must not exploit students and trainees or take unfair advantage of the power differential that exists in the context of training.

It is the responsibility of the supervisor to "clearly define and maintain ethical professional, personal, and social relationships with their supervisees" (ACA, 2005, F.3.a.). When supervisors have multiple role functions (such as clinical and administrative supervisor, or instructor and supervisor), they strive to minimize potential conflicts and explain expectations and responsibilities associated with each supervisory role to their supervisees. Supervisors are aware of the power differential in the relationship and explain to supervisees how this differential creates a potential for exploitation. Supervisors avoid any nonprofessional relationship that might negatively influence the supervisory relationship.

The *ACA Code of Ethics* also addresses potentially beneficial relationships:

> Counseling supervisors are aware of the power differential in their relationships with supervisees. If they believe nonprofessional relationships with a supervisee may be potentially beneficial to the supervisee, they take precautions similar to those taken by counselors when working with clients. Examples of potentially beneficial interactions or relationships include attending a formal ceremony; hospital visits; providing support during a stressful event; or mutual membership in a professional association, organization, or community. Counseling supervisors engage in open discussions with supervisees when they consider entering into relationships with them outside of their roles as clinical and/or administrative supervisors. Before

engaging in nonprofessional relationships, supervisors discuss with supervisees and document the rationale for such interactions, potential benefits or drawbacks, and anticipated consequences for the supervisee. Supervisors clarify the specific nature and limitations of the additional role(s) they will have with the supervisee. (F.3.e.)

The *ACA Code of Ethics* prohibits supervisors from accepting close relatives, romantic partners, and friends as their supervisees (F.3.d.), and explicitly states that sexual relationships and sexual harassment are prohibited (F.3.b; F.3.c.).

The ACES (1993) "Ethical Guidelines for Counseling Supervisors" also caution against dual relationships that might cause harm to the supervisee and suggest remedies.

> Supervisors should not engage in any form of social contact or interaction which would compromise the supervisor–supervisee relationship. Dual relationships with supervisees that might impair the supervisor's objectivity and professional judgment should be avoided and/or the supervisory relationship terminated. (2.10.)

> Supervisors who have multiple roles (e.g., teacher, clinical supervisor, administrative supervisor, etc.), with supervisees should minimize potential conflicts. Where possible, the roles should be divided among several supervisors. Where this is not possible, careful explanation should be conveyed to the supervisee as to the expectations and responsibilities associated with each supervisory role. (2.09.)

Competence Issues for Supervisors

Mental health professionals often are expected to assume the role of clinical supervisor. To carry out these roles ethically and effectively, they must have proper training for their supervisory responsibilities. The skills used in counseling are not necessarily the same as those needed to adequately supervise trainees; thus, there is a need for specific training in how to supervise. Supervision is becoming a specialized field that requires specific course work in supervision:

> Prior to offering clinical supervision services, counselors are trained in supervision methods and techniques. Counselors who offer clinical supervision services regularly pursue continuing education activities including both counseling and supervision topics and skills. (ACA, 2005, F.2.a.)

Recently the standard for qualifying to be a clinical supervisor has come to include formal course work and supervision of one's work with supervisees. Currently, most psychology and counselor education programs offer a course in supervision at the doctoral level, and some programs provide training for supervisors at the master's level (Polanski, 2000). Training in supervision for master's-level counselors will most likely include course work in which students conduct practice sessions to develop their supervisory skills. In doctoral programs, advanced students learn to supervise by supervising master's students, and the doctoral students are in turn supervised by the course instructor. The complexity of managing boundary issues can be challenging when the relationship is tripartite, involving a client, a supervisee, and a supervisor. When relationships involve clients, a supervisee, a novice supervisor, and the supervisor of the supervisor, sorting out the roles and responsibilities can be a daunting task.

Sexual Dual Relationships in Supervision

Of course, if a sexual relationship becomes a part of the supervisory relationship, this confounds the entire process. Both the *ACA Code of Ethics* (2005) and the ACES (1993) "Ethical Guidelines for Counseling Supervisors" state clearly that sexual intimacies between supervisors and supervisees are prohibited. In addition, the *ACA Code of Ethics* (2005) prohibits supervisors from engaging in or condoning sexual harassment of supervisees (F.3.c.).

The ethics codes of other professional organizations also take a clear position on sexual intimacies in the supervisory relationship:

> Rehabilitation counselors will not engage in sexual relationships with students or supervisees and will not subject them to sexual harassment. (CRCC, 2001, G.1.b.)

> Social workers should not engage in any dual or multiple relationships with supervisees in which there is a risk of exploitation of or potential harm to the supervisee. (NASW, 1999, 3.01.c.)

> Marriage and family therapists do not engage in sexual intimacy with students or supervisees during the evaluative or training relationship between the therapist and student or supervisee. Should a supervisor engage in sexual activity with a former supervisee, the burden of proof shifts to the supervisor to demonstrate that there has been no exploitation or injury to the supervisee. (AAMFT, 2001, 4.3.)

> Marriage and family counselors who provide supervision respect the inherent imbalance of power in the supervisory relationship. They do not use their potentially influential positions to exploit students, supervisees, or employees. Supervisors do not ask supervisees to engage in behaviors not directly related to the supervision process, and they clearly separate supervision and evaluation. Supervisors also avoid multiple relationships that might impair their professional judgment or increase the possibility of exploitation. Sexual intimacy with students or supervisees is prohibited. (International Association of Marriage and Family Counselors [IAMFC], 2005, F.2.)

> Psychologists do not engage in sexual relationships with students or supervisees who are in their department, agency, or training center or over whom psychologists have or are likely to have evaluative authority. (APA, 2002, 7.07.)

As we have noted in previous chapters, actual prevalence of sexual misconduct is difficult to determine. Miller and Larrabee (1995) surveyed female ACES members, 6% of whom reported sexual experiences with educators or supervisors during their graduate training. Over half of the sexual contacts were with course instructors, and 28% were with clinical supervisors. A similar ratio was found for sexual advances. Miller and Larrabee cautioned that findings on perceptions of coercion imply that sexual involvements with supervisees are detrimental. For this reason, sexual relationships between supervisors and supervisees are expressly forbidden.

The Boundary Between Counseling and Supervision

Clinical supervisors operate in multiple roles including teacher, mentor, consultant, sounding board, adviser, administrator, evaluator, recorder, and empowerer (Haynes, Corey, & Moulton, 2003). Although supervisors have a responsibility to clarify their roles, the boundaries are not always clear. It can be particularly difficult to discern where to draw the line between the roles of counselor and supervisor. Herlihy (2006) has suggested that confusion over the roles may stem in part from the terminology used in some of the popular models of supervision. For example, Bernard's (1979) discrimination model identifies three supervisor roles as counselor, teacher, and consultant. Yet ethical guidelines state clearly that supervisors should not function as counselors to their supervisees.

Some of the professional codes of ethics have provided guidelines for distinguishing between counseling and supervision. The *ACA Code of Ethics* (2005) states that although supervisors have the responsibility to help supervisees understand how their personal issues may interfere with working effectively with clients, it is not appropriate for supervisors to change the supervisory relationship into a counseling relationship.

> If supervisees request counseling, supervisors provide them with acceptable referrals. Counselors do not provide counseling services to supervisees. Supervisors address interpersonal competencies in terms of the impact of these issues on clients, the supervisory relationship, and professional functioning. (F.5.c.)

The ACES (1993) "Ethical Guidelines for Counseling Supervisors" are in agreement and also describe the extent to which personal issues should be addressed in supervision:

> Supervisors should not establish a psychotherapeutic relationship as a substitute for supervision. Personal issues should be addressed in supervision only in terms of the impact of these issues on clients and on professional functioning. (2.11.)

ACES also recommends that supervisors take care to eliminate or minimize potential role conflicts. When a supervisor recommends that a supervisee participate in remedial activities involving personal growth or self-disclosure, the supervisor should not be the direct provider of these activities.

Several of the focus questions that we asked at the beginning of this chapter are so interrelated that they cannot be discussed separately. Is it ever appropriate to integrate both counseling and supervision in the same relationship? What are the problems involved in blending the two roles? How can supervision include exploration of the supervisee's personal issues as well as cases? The following vignette illustrates how some of these issues may arise:

Andrew is a counselor educator and supervisor who regularly teaches an internship seminar. Andrew makes it clear to students at the initial class meeting that he conducts his seminar using a group supervision format that focuses on the counselor as a person. He informs his students that "the main emphasis will be on your own dynamics and reactions to your clients—not on an analysis of your clients, counseling skills and techniques, or case management strategies. Of course, you will learn various alternatives for working with your clients, but our primary concern will be on how your attitudes and behaviors may be influencing your clients. Thus you will be expected to examine your needs, motivations, and most of all your potential sources of countertransference in these group supervision sessions."

Andrew's chairperson questions the appropriateness of his style of teaching the seminar. Other instructors focus on teaching specific skills and interventions and do a great deal of case management work. The chairperson thinks that Andrew is opening himself to the possibility of blurring his role as an educator by focusing on the personal dimensions of his supervisees. She suggests that he recommend to his students that they seek personal counseling apart from the program and that he focus his course more on skill development.

In his defense, Andrew claims that he is not conducting group therapy; rather, he is asking his students to look at how their own dynamics influence their interventions with their clients. He deals with personal problems of his supervisees only to the extent that these problems appear to be influencing their work. He sees it as his job to help supervisees become aware of the ways their personal dynamics are affecting their clients.

- Do you think Andrew's chairperson has legitimate reasons for her concern that he is getting involved as both educator and therapist with his supervisees?
- What do you think of Andrew's approach to group supervision?
- What is the appropriate balance between teaching supervisees about their own dynamics and the dynamics of their clients?
- What is the balance between focusing on supervisee self-awareness and teaching skills?
- What are some potential benefits and risks to Andrew's supervisees?
- Would you want to be a student in the class?

Although a dual relationship occurs when a supervisor becomes the supervisee's counselor, the distinction between the therapeutic aspect of the supervisor's role and the role of the counselor is not well defined (Whiston & Emerson, 1989). It can be difficult to determine when a supervisory relationship has become a counseling relationship. When supervisees have personal problems, supervisors may be tempted to counsel them. However, because the primary goal of supervision is to protect the welfare of the client, the personal growth of the supervisee cannot become the primary focus of supervision. When supervisors agree to counsel their supervisees, these dual relationships model dangerously inappropriate behavior for supervisees, who may later perpetuate the behavior when they become supervisors themselves (Tyler & Tyler, 1994).

If supervisors overextend the boundaries of supervision into a therapeutic relationship, there is the potential that the supervisor's objectivity will be impaired and that the supervisee will be inhibited from making full use of the supervision process. It has been argued that, because of the power differential and evaluative components in the relationship, supervisees cannot give true informed consent to a therapeutic relationship with their supervisor (Miller & Larrabee, 1995; Sherry, 1991). Any therapy is likely to be compromised because supervisees will be concerned that their self-disclosures will have a negative impact on their evaluations. Instead of entering into a counseling relationship with a supervisee, the supervisor should make a referral to another professional.

When a supervisor recommends personal counseling for a supervisee, this may infuse an emotionally charged issue into the relationship. The supervisee may feel threatened and believe he or she has been judged to be incompetent. The supervisory relationship could become strained, and the supervisee might be less open about his or her own experiencing in discussing cases with the supervisor. Wise, Lowery, and Silverglade (1989) have noted that whether the student receives the suggestion of personal counseling as a criticism or as a helpful aspect of supervision depends on the supervisor's tact, attitude, and timing in making the recommendation.

- If you were a supervisor faced with the need to recommend counseling for a supervisee, how might you go about it?
- What factors might you consider in making your recommendation, and what might you tell the supervisee?
- If you were a supervisee, how would you react if your supervisor made such a recommendation to you?
- Might this change the nature of the supervisory relationship from your perspective?

From our perspective, effective supervision includes a focus on the impact of the counselor on the counseling process. When supervision focuses exclusively on client cases or problem-solving strategies for working with clients, some opportunities for positive experiences are lost. The results of a study by Sumerel and Borders (1996) seemed to indicate that a supervisor who is open to discussing personal issues with supervisees in an appropriate manner does not necessarily affect the supervisor–supervisee relationship negatively. Ladany and Friedlander (1995) found that the stronger the emotional bond between supervisor and supervisee, the less role conflict experienced by the supervisee. Usher and Borders (1993) found that counselors preferred a supervisor who is collegial and relationship oriented over one who is task oriented.

Supervision can be useful in helping students become aware of personal limitations or unresolved problems that intrude into effective helping. However, there is a difference between helping students identify and clarify those concerns they need to explore versus converting supervision into an in-depth personal therapy session. For instance, if a student becomes aware of an unresolved issue with his mother that is being played out in his counseling sessions with "motherly" women, it is appropriate to focus on how his personal limitations are blocking effective counseling, but it is not appropriate to abandon the supervisory focus for a therapy experience. In such cases, students should be encouraged to find a resource where they can get the therapy they need for themselves personally and professionally.

Distinguishing the appropriate boundary between supervision and counseling can be difficult.

- If you are a counseling supervisor, where do you stand on these issues?
- Do you believe that the supervisory and counseling roles are separable? Or do you think that some role blending is inevitable?
- How might you defend your position if a colleague challenged your views?
- If you are a graduate student working under supervision, or a counselor working under supervision toward your licensure or certification, from your point of view do you believe supervisory and counseling roles are separable?
- Where do you want your supervisor to draw the line in dealing with any personal concerns you may be facing?

Social and Business Relationships With Supervisees

Another boundary issue concerns social relationships. It is inevitable that supervisors will encounter trainees in social settings and at community activities. Hararr, VandeCreek, and Knapp (1990) suggested that a supervisor need not avoid supervisees on such occasions, unless the supervisor believes the professional relationship will be compromised. However, they caution against attempting to supervise relatives, spouses, friends, former clients, or others with whom the supervisor might find it difficult to be candid about performance.

It can be tempting to relax the boundaries as supervisees near completion of their training programs or their postmaster's supervision. At this stage, interactions with their supervisors often take on a collegial tone, and supervision becomes more consultative in nature. The social relationships that might develop out of a sense of collegiality and common interests may help to mark the supervisee's transition to becoming a professional peer. Nonetheless, Slimp and Burian (1994) noted that the supervisor is still in a position to evaluate supervisees and to recommend them for future employment and that a social relationship could compromise the supervisor's ability to make an objective evaluation. Yet some relaxing of boundaries may be both inevitable and appropriate. Bernard and Goodyear (2004) acknowledged this reality and suggested that supervisors need not be overly concerned about dual relationships that occur within the "positive context of a maturing professional relationship" (p. 60).

There is a difference between client–counselor and supervisee–supervisor relationships in considering postprofessional relationships. Some have argued that "once a client, always a client," but that claim is not made about supervisees. Our supervisees evolve into our professional colleagues. It is important to remember, though, that the perception of change in role relationships does not necessarily accompany the fact of the change. The end of formal supervision does not automatically mean that a supervisee perceives that he or she is now on equal footing with the former supervisor.

Regarding business relationships with supervisees, Slimp and Burian (1994) believed it is not uncommon for interns in field placements to be hired as staff members' employees. They cited examples ranging from babysitting to assisting staff members in research or consulting activities and note that it could be quite difficult for an intern to resist staff members' requests for paid services. Such situations place the supervisee in double jeopardy, and if the babysitting, research, or consulting activities do not go well, the negative consequences are compounded. Trust, respect, and a sense of safety are damaged; the reputations of both individuals may be diminished if the problems come to light; the quality of training is likely to be affected; and the staff member's evaluation of the supervisee will almost certainly be influenced. In addition, others within the training agency are affected because fellow interns may feel left out of what they perceive to be preferential treatment, and staff members may become fractionalized as they develop opinions about the relationship. Such dual relationships have implications for the profession as well, because supervisees who learn that such relationships are acceptable may engage in them with their clients. For all these reasons, Slimp and Burian recommended that these types of relationships be avoided.

A Contributor's Perspective

Some boundaries in the supervisory relationship are clearly demarcated: Supervisors should not enter into sexual or romantic relationships with their supervisees, supervision should not be converted into therapy, and business relationships with supervisees should be avoided. There are, however, some much more subtle boundary issues in supervision. L. DiAnne Borders offers a thoughtful personal perspective on these issues.

 Subtle Boundary Issues in Supervision

L. DiAnne Borders

To the best of my knowledge, I have not violated the two ethical "rules" regarding dual relationships (ACA, 2005; ACES, 1993). I have not knowingly taken the counselor role with a supervisee, although I've explored personal issues affecting supervisees' work many times, and I've never had an intimate or sexual relationship with a supervisee. However, I have had a dual relationship with all of my supervisees. In fact, I have had triple and quadruple relationships with some of them.

As department chair, I hire, evaluate, and supervise all the graduate assistants in the department, so I am the employer of some of my supervisees. For some, I am the chair of their doctoral and dissertation committees. For these and others, I serve in mentoring roles that create dual relationships (e.g., coauthor, copresenter). At the least, most of my supervisees are students in my classes. In addition, a few have been my babysitter at one time or another (when I was in a real pinch). All have heard numerous stories about my son, and a few have been valued consultants regarding their areas of expertise related to his development. Usually these multiple relationships are not particularly problematic or particularly challenging. At other times, I have had to give deliberate thought to putting boundaries around my varied roles with a supervisee, and I have even ended a role with a few.

At times, then, I've concluded that I was in a dual role that was affecting my ability to provide adequate supervision, thus overstepping a guideline in our profession's ethics codes. But how am I to know when I've crossed the line? How does any supervisor accurately evaluate the impact of a dual role on a supervisory relationship? In particular, how does a supervisor evaluate the situation from the *supervisee's* perspective? The more subtle boundary issues in supervision may go unnoticed whether they have positive or negative effects.

Clearly my supervision is colored by my knowledge about my supervisees from our other interactions. On the positive side, I sometimes can predict those situations in which the student will need extra help, and often I already have some sense of how feedback is most easily heard. In addition, the context of the supervisory relationship frequently provides the needed vehicle for bringing to light issues that I need to address with a student. There are negative consequences also, however. Recently, for example, I did not push an observation as far as I could (or should) have because I thought it would be too much on top of the feedback I'd just given her regarding her dissertation the day before. She graduated without the assumed benefit of this particular feedback.

My broader knowledge of and interactions with these students also often brings to light how our personal and interpersonal dynamics can or do affect our supervisory work together. In one supervisory session I realized this was the third time that week that I had urged a supervisee to urge his client to break free of constraints, act outside the norm, and explore an untapped aspect of self. Was this perhaps a theme of my own rather than some coincidence of supervisee (or client) issues? And there are those times that I realize I am allowing too much supervision time to be spent in philosophical discussions that the supervisee and I enjoy, or when I am aware of how much I rely on a supervisee's sense of humor (being overly prone to seriousness myself), both in and outside of our supervision sessions. With other supervisees, I must refuse to stand on the pedestal, even though they need me (or any other supervisor) to be there, but wonder if I might so quickly recognize the dynamics and respond the same way if it was one of those times in my life when I needed to be appreciated or admired. Such dynamics challenge the boundaries of the supervisory relationship, even though they also may enrich it at times. Nevertheless, I struggle with how to be human without being overly familiar or inappropriately self-revealing.

It could be easy to become good friends with many of my supervisees. We have similar interests, they are often good cooks, and we have some understanding of each other's professional pressures and goals. Over the years, however, I have learned to be cautious. Social relationships and friendships tend to interfere with two priorities: to be consistent and fair with all supervisees, and to feel free to say whatever I need to say in supervision. The more relaxed atmosphere created by sharing a good meal or another social event seem to blur the boundaries for both supervisor and supervisee. I find it somewhat uncomfortable to confront a supervisee shortly after we have been in each other's homes, and I have seen confusion on a supervisee's face when I did confront. I have heard supervisees, my own and others, wonder what academic benefits a peer might be getting because of his or her social relationship with a supervisor. In addition, certainly my experiences on the ACA Ethics Committee have made me more sensitive to the potential problems in even well-intentioned acts of friendship. As cochair of the Ethics Committee, I learned details of clear abuses of power, often rationalized as a "natural" outgrowth of the multiple roles a counselor educator and supervisor plays with students, and I tried to sort out what seemed to be supervisees' unfortunate misunderstandings of a supervisor's benign overtures of friendship and support.

As a result, I more and more have limited my social encounters with students to officially sanctioned events (such as departmental picnics) and more frequently address these issues up front with supervisees (and students in similar roles). In particular, I ask students to share their perspectives on our dual roles and relationships and make clear that I don't assume their perspective will be the same as mine. As needed, we can make a plan together that respects their feelings as well as mine. As the ethical guidelines make clear, it is always *my* responsibility to maintain appropriate boundaries and monitor dual or multiple roles with supervisees and students. Given the power differential, which exists in whatever relationships we have with students, supervisees are at a great disadvantage in terms of bringing to my attention that they feel uncomfortable or unsure about such issues.

Clearly, such issues need to be addressed in supervisor training programs. In fact, doctoral students often encounter boundary and multiple role issues *before* they graduate. "I just realized," a recent note from one student indicated, "that I'm in the same class with one of my supervisees. Do we need to do something about this?" Recognition of potential problems is a critical first step, to be followed by discussions of how to handle the situation, thus providing an important learning opportunity for supervisees and their peers. I can have hope that they will recognize similar dilemmas in the future.

The many gray areas and potential hazards also suggest to me that we supervisors always have need of supervision or consultation regarding our work with supervisees. The need will vary not only by supervisee but also by the relevant circumstances in a supervisor's life. We are more vulnerable in terms of our own needs and motivations at various points in time. Just as we seek additional monitoring of our work with clients during these times, we also must consider how our circumstances and personalities may affect the supervision process.

Interestingly, there is very little research on the gray areas and more subtle issues regarding boundaries and multiple roles presented in this chapter. Even less attention has been given to the *supervisor's* dynamics alluded to here. This may be because typically the supervisors are conducting the research or because the relevant variables are difficult to identify, let alone operationalize. We should not continue to pretend, however, that we become objective, neutral supervisors simply via having earned a diploma.

Although I have written primarily about my boundary and role confusion in an academic setting, I would be surprised if similar issues were not found in supervisory relationships in employment settings and for private practitioners working with counselor licensure applicants. Guidelines for assessing these situations and determining how to respond would be helpful for all, so that we can avoid problematic boundary violations and, when necessary, appropriately negotiate how to handle such situations. (For a more complete discussion of ethical issues in supervision, see Borders & Brown, 2005.)

A Contributor's Perspective

In the preceding contribution, we learned about boundary and role issues from a supervisor's and counselor educator's perspective. In the following article, Jamie Bludworth, a doctoral student in counseling psychology, shares how his experiences in supervision addressed his personal concerns in a way that helped him to work more effectively with clients.

A Doctoral Student's Reflections on His Supervision

Jamie Bludworth

Although the supervision literature tends to draw a clear distinction between supervision that emphasizes a supervisee's personal issues as they relate to working with clients and supervision that focuses primarily on clinical or client issues, my experience with a variety of supervisors has taught me that the two are intricately related. Throughout my training I have always valued supervision that integrates personal and professional development. Nevertheless, managing the boundary between supervision that appropriately explores the ways in which my personal issues influence aspects of my work with clients (such as case conceptualization or choice of intervention) and supervision that crosses over into personal counseling has required vigilance and sensitivity from my supervisors and me. Here is how one of my supervisors and I successfully navigated the nebulous boundary between supervision and personal counseling to help a client work through her personal concerns while fostering my personal and professional development.

During the first year of my doctoral studies, my father died of alcoholism. I experienced many confusing and painful emotions around his death. I found solace in the unwavering support of my wife and new friends in my cohort. During the ensuing summer, I focused on what his passing meant to me as a person and as a psychologist in training. An intensive group experience during that time made a profound difference in the way I thought and felt about my relationship with my father.

As the fall semester began, I wondered how the death of my father might affect my work with clients in my first doctoral practicum. My supervisor was a faculty member who was aware of what had happened in my life during the past year. In our first meeting we both communicated our hopes and expectations for our work together. She was very clear and direct with me about her theoretical orientation and how she viewed the purposes and methods of counseling and supervision. I expressed my hope that we would be able to find a way to balance our focus between my development as a person and my development as a professional. She responded by affirming the value I placed on the integration of personal and professional issues in supervision.

She then did something that would prove to be pivotal to our work together over the course of the next year. She addressed the boundary issue with me directly. She expressed her concern that I might try to use our supervision sessions as a sort of proxy for personal counseling. Moreover, she also expressed her concern that I might use the focus on my personal development as it related to my work with clients as a means to avoid the sometimes difficult task of facing and remediating any clinical growth areas I may have. She then collaborated with me to establish and define boundaries of our supervisory relationship. Together we decided how we would know if our sessions had veered into the realm of personal counseling. We also agreed upon how we would proceed if this should occur. At the end of our first session, I had very few questions about how we would be working together or what the focus of our work would be.

During the course of the semester, I had many opportunities to explore the ways in which my personal history influenced my reactions to clients. Throughout this time my supervisor assisted me in challenging the negative judgments I had about my clinical efficacy and worked with me in finding ways of turning my personal experiences to therapeutic advantage in sessions with clients. This became especially salient for me in working with clients who had substance abuse issues. How could I possibly work effectively with such clients given my history with my father? Through my deepening collaboration with my supervisor and her ability to negotiate the complex interaction between personal and professional development, I began to have an experiential understanding that my reactions to clients did not have to "run the show." Rather, they could serve as important pieces of information in understanding clients from an interpersonal perspective, provided I remained committed to my personal awareness and did not allow such reactions to cloud my clinical judgment.

As the spring semester and the anniversary of my father's death approached, my supervisor and I anticipated possible difficulties I might have. Nevertheless, my work with clients continued to improve and, although I was somewhat concerned about the upcoming anniversary, I felt a new sense of confidence in my clinical abilities and an increasing capacity to recognize the ways in which my personal issues served as both impediments and as facilitative factors in my work with clients. Beyond that, I experienced supervision as a place where I was safe to disclose my honest reactions to clients and use my supervisor's expertise to help my clients move toward their goals.

The anniversary of my father's death passed without any noticeable impact on my work with my clients. I had been working with a client who was dealing with issues of impulse control that were not substance related. She had used therapy efficiently and had made remarkable strides over the course of the semester. I was very happy with her progress. As we prepared to terminate our counseling sessions, however, I felt a strange sense of pessimism regarding her prognosis. I was confused by this because it did not fit with how I experienced her commitment to her work.

I brought my concern into supervision. The safety I felt in the relationship with my supervisor created a space that allowed me to honestly look at my reactions to this client. Although it seems obvious to me now, I was surprised then to see that my experience of disappointment with my father's failed attempts at recovery was affecting my judgment about a client who was nothing like my father. My supervisor helped me to separate my historical issues with my father from the task of providing a therapeutic termination experience for my client. Our termination session turned out to be one of our most powerful and effective sessions, and my client reported that she felt empowered to move forward in a healthy and hopeful way.

Reflecting on this supervision experience, I recognize that my supervisor and I could have easily slipped into a personal counseling mode during our supervision sessions. We were able to successfully traverse the boundary between supervision that integrates clinical and personal issues and supervision that merges with personal counseling through a clear, collaborative, and direct exploration and definition of that boundary. We continually evaluated our work together with the expressed intent of assessing our relationship and the various boundaries contained within it. In this way, my experience of supervision provided room for me to grow professionally and personally while simultaneously helping my clients work toward their goals therapeutically. Moreover, this experience helped me to better see the ways that personal issues can influence my perceptions of clients (even if I am committed to my personal awareness) and highlights the importance of supervision that allows for some personal exploration on the part of the supervisee.

Decision-Making Models for Supervisors

Several writers have offered models to assist supervisors in working though the supervision process with their boundaries intact. Wise et al. (1989) suggested a stage-oriented approach. In the *self-focus* stage, supervisees begin to see clients but lack knowledge and experience. Supervision is most helpful when it concentrates on skill development, clarifying concerns and providing structure. In the *client focus* stage, supervisees have increased interaction with clients, and they typically increase their initiative and become less dependent on their supervisors. The supervisor continues to concentrate on skill development and case conceptualization. Personal counseling might be recommended only if the supervisee remains too dependent on the supervisor or is not making adequate progress due to personal issues. In the *interpersonal focus* stage, supervisees become more comfortable with their skills and shift their focus from issues of competence to issues of self-awareness. This may be the most appropriate time to recommend personal counseling to promote supervisee openness and awareness. In the final *professional focus* stage, supervisees have begun to develop a therapeutic personality and a sense of professional identity. A consultation model of supervision is most appropriate, and personal counseling should be recommended only to deal with "blind spots" in specific areas or life stressors that are impeding performance.

Whiston and Emerson (1989) have taken a somewhat different approach. They suggest that Egan's (2007) three-stage model provides a practical method for distinguishing between supervising and counseling. They believe supervisors should limit their work to Egan's first stage: exploring and clarifying a supervisee's personal problems when those problems are impeding his or her work. After the supervisor has identified the personal issues, the supervisee then has the responsibility for resolving them. If the supervision process moves into Egan's second and third stages—establishing goals and taking action regarding the personal problem—supervision has become counseling and should be provided by an independent counselor rather than the supervisor.

Informed Consent in Supervision

Informed consent regarding supervision is as essential as informed consent in counseling. It is beneficial to discuss the rights of supervisees from the beginning of the supervisory relationship in much the same way as the rights of clients are addressed early in the therapy process. If this is done, the supervisee is empowered to express expectations, make decisions, and become an active participant in the supervisory process.

Informed consent is also essential for the clients of supervisees. Supervisors are responsible to see that trainees provide the information to clients that they need to make informed choices. Supervisees' clients certainly should be informed that the counselor is working under supervision and what this involves.

One way to clarify the multiple roles of supervisors is to provide a written informed consent document that can be given to all supervisees at the outset of the relationship (Sutter, McPherson, & Geeseman, 2002). Such contracts may not be legally binding, but they do serve to inform the supervisee of expectations and responsibilities of both parties in the supervisory relationship and to benefit both the supervisor and supervisee.

If there is a frank discussion at the beginning about the mutual responsibilities of supervisors and supervisees, conflicts are less likely to develop at a later time. As a part of the informed consent discussion, supervisors can explain that supervision is a complex process and that supervisors are required to function in multiple roles. They can take this opportunity to be clear from the outset that personal issues might be activated in supervision, and that if these issues affect performance, the supervisee will be asked to work them through with another professional (Bernard & Goodyear, 2004). The risks and safeguards of multiple relationships can be explored. This not only can lead to more effective supervision sessions, but it can also model the importance of informed consent in therapy. Supervisees can learn firsthand how to convey information to their clients that will enable them to become active partners in the therapeutic process.

The "Ethical Guidelines for Counseling Supervisors" (ACES, 1993) mandate that informed consent be a basic part of the supervisory relationship. Ladany and Friedlander (1995) found that supervisees experienced less role ambiguity when their supervisors made expectations clear. McCarthy et al. (1995) contended that informed consent should be clearly articulated through written documents and a discussion between the supervisor and supervisee. Accountability can be increased with a written contractual agreement for supervision. When expectations are discussed and clarified from the beginning of a supervisory relationship, the relationship is likely to be enhanced and quality client care will be promoted. McCarthy and her colleagues recommended that the contract include statements concerning ethical and legal parameters of the supervisor–supervisee relationship. Topics should include dual relationship issues, structuring of the supervisory relationship, limits to confidentiality, and professional guidelines for ethical treatment of clients.

Countertransference Issues

Supervisor countertransference is bound to occur in some supervisory relationships when supervisors have intense reactions to certain supervisees. We hope that supervisors monitor their countertransference and that when these issues arise they seek their own supervision, or at least consult regularly with colleagues. To help ensure that evaluation remains fair, Bernard and Goodyear (2004) recommended getting a second opinion about a supervisee's abilities.

Countertransference does not have to be viewed negatively. Indeed, by monitoring our countertransference in the supervisory process, we can learn some important lessons about supervisees. Our reactions to supervisees can tell us something about them as well as ourselves. We suggest that supervisor countertransference be dealt with in a manner similar to therapist countertransference. First, it is important to be aware of our countertransference reactions. It is crucial that we understand our needs and how they may be triggered by certain supervisee behaviors. This is especially true when a supervisor is sexually attracted to a certain type of supervisee. It is crucial that supervisors do not exploit supervisees for the purpose of satisfying their needs and that they do not misuse their power over supervisees. When a supervisor has unmet needs that interfere with effective supervision, the supervisee is placed in a difficult position. As supervisors, it is important that we recognize our countertransference issues and seek consultation. We also have an obligation to take further measures to protect our supervisees if we are unable to successfully resolve our issues. These measures might include seeking personal therapy, referring the supervisee to another supervisor, or inviting a colleague to cosupervise sessions if the supervisee agrees to this.

Supervisee Incompetence: Ethical and Legal Considerations

Supervisors are both ethically and legally responsible for the actions of those they are supervising. For example, if a client of a supervisee commits suicide, the supervisor is likely to be more vulnerable than the supervisee from a legal standpoint. The reality of the fact that supervisors are responsible for all of the cases of their supervisees does place special pressures on the supervisor that could create a conflict. If the supervisor becomes aware that the supervisee lacks basic relationship skills or lacks personal maturity, what is the supervisor to do? Is it appropriate to bring this to the attention of the faculty? A determination must be made regarding whether the supervisee is personally qualified to remain in the training program. The legal ramifications of the supervisor's responsibilities when the supervisee is not functioning competently underscore the importance of clearly defining the nature of the supervisory relationship from the outset. Students should know about the consequences of not competently fulfilling their contracts. To be sure, supervisors have a duty to do what is in the best interest of the supervisee, yet they also have a responsibility to the welfare of the clients who are being seen by the supervisee. As gatekeepers of the profession, supervisors cannot ethically ignore dealing with supervisees who cannot competently carry out their training role because of some personal limitations. This matter deserves full discussion at the outset of the supervisory relationship.

Monitoring the competency of students in training has long been viewed as an essential component in training programs. In addition to evaluating a supervisee's academic ability, knowledge, and clinical skills, it is essential to identify and evaluate a supervisee's personal characteristics, interpersonal behaviors, and professional behaviors that will likely influence his or her ability to effectively deliver mental health services.

It is critical that supervisees do not hear from their supervisors that their performance is substandard when it is too late for them to take corrective measures. Supervisors have an obligation to provide their supervisees with regular, specific, and ongoing feedback. If there are problems regarding supervisees' performances, they must be given opportunities to take remedial steps in correcting such problems. Of course, due process is essential and dismissal from a training program should be the last resort after other interventions have failed to produce any change in supervisees who exhibit deficiencies.

Consultation

Consultation, like supervision, is a complex, tripartite process. It involves at least three parties: a consultant, a consultee, and a client system. The client system can consist of an individual, a group, an organization, or a community. Consultation has been defined as "a process in which a human services professional assists a consultee with a work-related (or caretaking-related) problem with a client system, with the goal of helping both the consultee and the client system in some specified way" (Dougherty, 2005, p. 11).

Although counselors are often the service providers for consultation, consultation is not the same as counseling. In fact, consultation deals exclusively with the consultee's work-related problems, and thus by definition does not deal with the personal concerns of the consultee. Nevertheless, in actual practice it can be difficult to determine where to draw the line between consultation and counseling. When this line is crossed, a dual relationship is created. Dual role conflicts also occur when a consultant functions as a supervisor to a consultee. Consultants may ponder these questions in their work:

- How can consultants set clear boundaries to distinguish between work-related and personal concerns of their consultees?
- How can consultants best avoid potential role conflicts?

Role conflicts often occur when a consultant blurs the boundaries between the professional and personal concerns of the consultee. The following example illustrates how this can occur.

Willene contracts with a community mental health agency to provide consultation for volunteers who work with people who are dying and their family members. Willene has been hired as a consultant by the agency director to teach people basic helping skills (listening, attending, and some crisis intervention strategies). Willene is working with these volunteers as a group, and many of the participants express a need to talk about how they are affected personally by working with those who are dying. Their work is opening up feelings of helplessness, fears of dying, and unfinished business with grieving their own losses. Willene decides that it is more important to attend to the needs being expressed by the volunteers than to focus on teaching them helping skills. Her interactions with the volunteers focus more and more on helping them explore their personal issues, and only secondarily on teaching skills.

- To what extent do you think Willene's shift in focus can be supported? On what basis?
- What potential dual relationship issues do you see in this situation?

A Contributor's Perspective

Conflicts can occur when a consultant maintains two professional roles in the consultation relationship, such as serving as both counselor and consultant or supervisor and consultant. A. Michael Dougherty presents a rationale for avoiding these types of dual relationships.

 Dual Role Conflicts in Consultation

A. Michael Dougherty

Do the conflicts that might occur when a consultant maintains two professional roles in the consultation relationship outweigh the benefits that serving in the two roles may create? I believe counselors should be extremely cautious before they engage in two professional roles in the consultation relationship. As a general rule of thumb when providing these services, counselors should take a conservative stance and avoid maintaining multiple professional roles. My rationale for this stance is based on seven considerations.

First, the complexity of the consultation process has contributed to disagreement among authorities in the field as to the boundaries of the consultant's role. This disagreement makes it difficult to ascertain what is ethical or unethical in many situations. Because of their tripartite nature, consultation relationships are more complex than the counseling relationship, and an additional professional role only increases the complexity of already intricate processes. For example, when does the feedback of consultation become the evaluation of supervision? When does acknowledgment of the negative emotions of a fellow consultee cross the boundary into counseling concerning those emotions?

Second, there is disagreement in the field concerning the definition of consultation, which makes it difficult to define the appropriate roles the consultant can assume when providing these services. An additional professional role only complicates these difficulties. For example, how does a consultant differentiate a work-related from a personal concern of a consultee and then go about contracting to consult regarding the work-related concern and counsel regarding a personal concern? Because work-related and personal concerns are typically intricately intertwined and consultation is so difficult to define, it is best to limit contact with the consultee to one professional role.

Third, when they consult, counselors should be wary of multiple roles that might create conflicts of interest that could in turn reduce their efficacy. When providing these services, counselors should be wary of being drawn into any roles that are incompatible with their stated purposes and contract. Counselors should decline to take on additional roles when these roles reduce freedom of expression or objectivity, or limit the consultant's commitment to the consultee organization. By engaging in dual relationships when consulting, counselors may easily jeopardize their commitment to the consultee organization. For example, when a consultant takes on the additional role of supervisor, the consultant may be placed in the position of being expected to share information with parties-at-interest about a supervisee and yet maintain the confidentiality of the consulting relationship because the supervisee is also a consultee. Consider the following situation:

> As a consultant, you agree to supervise John, who is also your consultee. In a meeting, John's immediate superior asks you for some information to be used in his annual evaluation. As both a consultant and supervisor you have noticed some professional skill deficits in John and have been working with him to upgrade his skills.

What kind of information could you share as a supervisor without breaking your obligation to maintain the confidentiality of the consulting relationship? The level of difficulty in answering this question suggests that professional dual relationships involve significant risk in terms of conflicts of interest.

Fourth, consultants need to guard against putting the consultee in interrole conflict in which two roles cause contradictory expectations about a given behavior. For example, consultation focuses on work-related concerns, and counseling focuses on personal concerns. Because it is difficult to differentiate these two foci, it is best to keep the expectations as simple as possible so that the consultee will not confuse the two relationships and bring up personal issues during consultation and work-related ones during counseling.

Fifth, the training of counselors conditions them to move naturally toward affective concerns and personal problems, and it is hard to turn off this tendency in other types of relationships such as consultation. This tendency can be particularly dangerous if the counselor, when consulting, determines that the locus of the work-related concern lies more in the personal issues of the consultee than in the client system itself. Further, it is easy to move toward counseling consultees when they talk about the anxiety they are experiencing in a work-related problem. Counselors might, therefore, have a tendency to want to offer counseling services to a consultee based on the perception that they will benefit both personally and professionally from such an additional relationship. Focusing on the emotional needs and concerns, however, breaks the peer relationship inherent in consultation and should therefore be avoided.

Sixth, the consultee may have an obligation to his or her organization not to use the counselor's services for personal purposes because the organization has provided consultation services for professional, not personal, growth. Further, if the consultant agrees to provide counseling and this is kept private, the consultee might wonder later what other kinds of "cheating" the consultant might do (e.g., breaking confidentiality). Consequently, dual relationships, if not approved by the consultee organization, may well raise some issues regarding the professional behavior of consultant and consultee alike.

Seventh, if the consultant simultaneously engages in consulting and counseling roles with a consultee, word may get out that the consultant is "a great counselor." Many prospective consultees who have work-related concerns may avoid seeking consultation because they are concerned that the consultant will try to counsel them on a personal level.

In summary, professional dual relationships are best avoided whenever possible when consulting. They make these complex processes and relationships even more complex. The additional weight of another relationship makes it more difficult for the parties involved to conduct their business of assisting the client system in being more effective.

Conclusions

In this chapter, we have highlighted the implicit duality that exists in the supervisor–supervisee relationship and have noted the difficulties in determining where the boundary lies between supervision and counseling. Because supervision involves a tripartite relationship among supervisor, supervisee, and clients of the supervisee, supervisors have multiple loyalties. They have obligations not only to the supervisee but also to the clients of the supervisee, the supervisee's employer, and ultimately to the profession. When these loyalties conflict, supervisors are confronted with difficult decisions. Supervisors play a vital role as gatekeepers to the profession.

Although it is not appropriate for supervisors to function as therapists for their supervisees, we contend that good supervision is therapeutic in the sense that the supervisory process involves dealing with the supervisee's personal limitations, blind spots, and impairments so that clients are not harmed. Informed consent is crucial in supervision. Supervisees are owed the same kinds of explanations about the potential problems involved in dual relationships as are clients.

We also explored the conflicts that can occur when a consultant attempts to function in the dual role of consultant and counselor or consultant and supervisor. The dual role of consultant and supervisor should be avoided because supervision involves evaluation and thus violates the peer nature of the consultation relationship. Serving as both consultant and counselor is also to be avoided because consultation is designed to focus on work-related concerns. When a consultant determines that a problem resides more in the personal concerns of a consultee than in the client or client system, the consultant should refer the consultee.

6

Education and Training of Group Counselors

This chapter focuses specifically on the training of group counselors. We have devoted a separate chapter to this topic because there is controversy regarding how group counseling courses should be taught. At the heart of the controversy is the question of how to manage dual relationships that may occur in experiential training. This chapter addresses the challenges involved in learning how to manage multiple roles and responsibilities when combining didactic instruction and participation in an experiential group.

It is common practice to include both didactic and experiential aspects of learning in group work courses, but doing so requires that educators address a number of ethical considerations. Group work educators must manage multiple roles and fulfill many responsibilities to their students. In experiential training, participants engage in self-exploration and deal with interpersonal issues within the training group or class as a way of learning how to facilitate groups effectively. Many group work educators believe the potential risks of experiential methods are offset by the benefits to participants who become personally involved in experiential group work as a supplement to didactic approaches in group courses. These educators see a need for an experiential component to assist students in acquiring the skills necessary to function as effective group leaders. It is essential that instructors be aware of the potential dangers inherent in multiple roles and relationships in teaching group courses, and they must be competent to teach group courses.

Training Standards for Group Trainees

In master's-level counselor education programs, one course typically covers both the didactic and experiential aspects of group process. Some counselor training programs have more than one group course, but many have only one course devoted to teaching knowledge and skills for group counselors (F. R. Wilson, Rapin, & Haley-Banez, 2004). In a survey of group psychotherapy training during predoctoral psychology internship, Markus and King (2003) found that predoctoral clinical psychology internships do not routinely provide adequate group therapy training. The results of Markus and King's survey suggest that there is lack of depth and breadth of group therapy didactic course offerings for psychology interns. For a variety of articles on teaching group work, see the March 2004 special issue of the *Journal for Specialists in Group Work* (Conyne & Bemak, 2004).

Specialized training is essential as a way to obtain proficiency and expertise in group process (Markus & King, 2003). Over the past 20 years, the Association for Specialists in Group Work (ASGW) has developed three foundational documents to guide training and practice in group work (F. R. Wilson et al., 2004). These documents are "Best Practice Guidelines" (ASGW, 1998), which address guidelines in planning, implementation, processing, and evaluation in group work practice; "Principles for Diversity-Competent Group Workers" (ASGW, 1999); and "Professional Standards for the Training of Group Workers" (ASGW, 2000).

The revised "Professional Standards for the Training of Group Workers" (ASGW, 2000) outlines basic aspects in the education and training of group counselors: didactic course work, being involved in experiential group activities, leadership opportunities, and receiving competent supervision. It also specifies two levels of competencies and related training: a set of core *knowledge* competencies and *skill* competencies provide the foundation on which *specialized* training is built. At a minimum, one group course should be included in a training program, and it should be structured to help students acquire the basic knowledge and skills needed to facilitate a group. These group skills are best mastered through supervised practice, which should include observation and participation in a group experience.

The Council for Accreditation of Counseling and Related Educational Programs (CACREP, 2001) standards call for students in an entry-level program to have a theoretical knowledge and understanding of group process. This knowledge includes the purpose of groups, developmental stages of a group, group dynamics, theory applied to practice, methods in group work, styles of group leadership, and ethical and legal issues in group work. The standards also call for skill development necessary to facilitate groups.

Both CACREP and ASGW training guidelines include an experiential component to training group leaders. CACREP (2001) has a 10-hour requirement for direct experience as a participant in a small group. ASGW (2000) requires a minimum of 10 hours of observation and participation in a small group as a member or a leader, with 20 hours being recommended.

The core competencies delineated in the ASGW (2000) training standards are considered the benchmarks for training group workers. The current trend in training group leaders focuses on learning group process by becoming involved in supervised experiences. Both direct participation in planned and supervised small groups and clinical experience in leading various groups under careful supervision are needed to equip leaders with the skills to meet the challenges of group work.

Markus and King (2003) maintained that comprehensive training must include intensive supervision by a competent group therapist. Although

Markus and King endorsed group supervision of group therapy as a powerful cognitive and emotional learning experience, they reported that the majority of internships provided for group trainees use the one-to-one model rather than offering opportunities for group supervision. DeLucia-Waack and Fauth (2004) agreed that group supervision of multiple group leaders has many advantages for learning about group process and receiving supervision.

Combining Experiential and Didactic Approaches

Although combining experiential and didactic methods in training group leaders is quite common, this practice has led to controversy among group work educators. Merta, Wolfgang, and McNeil (1993) found that a large majority of counselor educators continue to use the experiential group in preparing group counselors. Furthermore, there is significant diversity in using alternative training models, and various safeguards are employed. Many group counselor educators consider the experiential component to be essential for group counseling courses. Although there are certain problems in teaching students how groups function by involving them on an experiential level, these difficulties can be resolved. Clear guidelines need to be established so that students know their rights and responsibilities. This arrangement does put a bit more pressure on both the instructor and the students. It calls for honesty, maturity, and professionalism.

Those who teach group counseling courses are faced with many challenges in attempting to meet the professional standards for the training of group workers (Guth & McDonnell, 2004). According to O'Halloran and McCartney (2004), it is a major challenge in teaching group counseling in an entry-level program to effectively cover the standards set forth by ASGW (2000) and CACREP (2001). Akos, Goodnough, and Milsom (2004) recommended a number of strategies in training school counselors, one of which is infusing group concepts throughout the curriculum. They also recommend selecting practicum and internship sites based on opportunities to conduct group work. Killacky and Hulse-Killacky (2004) made a case for teaching generic group competency skills across the counselor education curriculum. Other writers have stressed the importance of incorporating multicultural issues in training group counselors (Bemak & Chung, 2004; DeLucia-Waack & Donigian, 2004). The Association for Specialists in Group Work (1999) publication "Principles for Diversity-Competent Group Workers) helps group workers sensitively address issues of classism, sexism, racism, heterosexism, and ableism. There is increased recognition that all group work is multicultural; thus, effective training of group counselors addresses multicultural dimensions (DeLucia-Waack & Donigian, 2004; Ivey, Pedersen, & Ivey, 2001).

Multiple Roles of Group Work Educators

Faculty who teach group courses often function in multiple roles: facilitator of a group, teacher, evaluator, and supervisor. At various times educators may teach group process concepts, lead a demonstration group in class, set up an exercise to illustrate an intervention in a group situation, and evaluate students' work. Educators may have a monitoring function, especially in intervening when students demonstrate bizarre behavior, are unable to give or receive feedback appropriately, or are unable to relate to others effectively. Group educators have a responsibility to the students, the profession, the community, and the training institution to take action when students in a group course give evidence that they are not suited personally to working as group facilitators.

Faculty members who teach group classes often assume a supervisory role, observing trainees as they facilitate a group. If an instructor also facilitates a process group or an interpersonal process-oriented group, this person will at times carry out therapeutic roles and functions with these same students. Although the instructor may avoid becoming a therapist for a student group, he or she might be called upon to assist participants in identifying personal problems that are likely to interfere with their ability to function effectively in group work. Blending these roles presents some potential ethical problems, and various strategies are being employed to address these issues in the preparation of group counselors. Merta et al. (1993) admitted that no one training model or combination of safeguards is apt to solve the dilemma of protecting students from adverse dual relationships and at the same time provide them with the best possible training.

Educational and therapeutic dimensions are often blended in group courses to enable students to obtain both personal benefits and conceptual knowledge and to acquire leadership skills. One core ethical issue is the level of competence of the person teaching the group course. Faculty who teach group courses need to have experienced a group themselves as a member and be adequately prepared to teach group process. Those who teach group courses must guard against exploiting students by using the group as a way of meeting their own needs. Issues of power and control, the undue use of pressure, and bias can cloud the instructor's objectivity and judgment. It is essential to be aware of the potential pitfalls that grow out of dual relationships and to develop strategies to reduce chances of exploiting or harming students.

It seems clear to us that there is no way to completely eliminate the potential for negative outcomes, especially if the form of learning is intense and meaningful. Students who are informed of their rights and responsibilities are less likely to be exploited. Adequate informed consent prior to admission to the program and prior to taking courses that rely on experiential approaches is a key to successful learning experiences.

The potential dual role conflicts in cases where group work instructors combine didactic and experiential approaches raises a number of controversial ethical issues. Faculty sometimes function in multiple roles and relationships with students and trainees without establishing and clarifying appropriate boundaries. Some students who have been in a group course have talked about the experience as being anything but growth producing or a positive learning experience. For example, in some cases students have not been given any preparation for a group experience, and no attempt has been made to provide for informed consent. In other cases, students are left alone to form their own process group, which is a required part of the group course, with very little guidance and no supervision from the faculty person teaching the course. Undirected group experiences have the potential for being aimless or even damaging. Conflicts may not be properly addressed, and scapegoating of a particular member may take place. There may also be undue group pressure for members to reveal personal secrets, and hidden agendas can result in the group getting stuck.

Some professional educators have expressed concern about the potential pitfalls of experiential training or about the multiple roles and relationships involved in teaching group work. Davenport (2004) observed that the practice of having professors or supervised doctoral students lead experiential groups for students in master's-level group counseling courses is widespread. She suggested an alternative training model in which a prerequisite for students taking the advanced group counseling class is a semester-long growth group experience, which is led by a licensed professional. These groups are usually led by a staff member from her university's student counseling service.

Kottler (2004) observed that dual and multiple relationships are not necessarily problematic and that they can add richness and complexity to life. He added that multiple relationships in training become problematic when they are exploitive and when educators misuse their power by taking advantage of others in a dual role. Kottler suggested safeguarding trainees in an experiential group in the following ways: through informed consent, so that students know what they are getting into; by providing the right to pass; and by not evaluating students on what they say or do not say. Kottler made a very important point in teaching group counseling when he said that the key is not *what* we are doing but *how* we are doing it.

Although some abuses in the attempt to train using experiential approaches have been documented, we do not think this warrants the conclusion that these experiences are necessarily inappropriate or unethical. Furthermore, it is a mistake to conclude that group work educators should be restricted to providing didactic information. Overcorrection of a problem of potential abuse does not seem justified to us. From our perspective, teaching group process by involving students personally is the best way for them to learn how to eventually set up and facilitate groups. We are in agreement with Stockton, Morran, and Krieger (2004), who indicated that there is a fine line between offering experiential activities and safeguarding against gaining information that could be used in evaluating students. Faculty who use experiential approaches are often involved in balancing multiple roles, which requires them to consistently monitor boundaries. Stockton and colleagues emphasized that group work educators need to exert caution so that they offer training that is both ethical and effective.

Kline, Falbaum, Pope, Hargraves, and Hundley (1997) found that students who had a group experience generally had positive reactions to it, even though their group experience entailed some anxiety. The student reactions to their group experience consistently indicated that they valued the opportunity to challenge their interpersonal fears and that they were satisfied with the gains they made from taking risks as a group member.

Kline and his colleagues studied the reactions of participants to the group experience by using both initial and follow-up questionnaires. On the basis of data from their study, they developed a number of hypotheses regarding the benefits of a group experience in counselor education programs, three of which are listed here:

- Concurrent group experiences augment training in counseling skills by increasing awareness and encouraging experimentation with interpersonal behaviors.
- After an initial period of anxiety, the group process can be helpful in teaching students how to give and receive feedback.
- The cognitive and emotional awareness stimulated by the group experience develops a clearer understanding of client experience, acceptance of others who are different, and increased understanding and acceptance of their own emotional experience and that of others.

R. D. Anderson and Price (2001) conducted a survey of students in master's-level courses in group counseling to assess their attitudes toward the use of an experiential group activity as a component of training, as well as the level of instructor involvement in these experiential groups. Approximately 41% of the students in this survey indicated that their instructor did not lead their experiential group and did not observe the group, but did receive feedback about the group's process or members' participation. About 33% of the students indicated that their instructor did not lead their experiential group; however, he or she did observe the group at times. Approximately 22% of the students indicated that the instructor did not lead, observe, or receive feedback about their group. Only 3% of the students indicated that their instructor led the experiential group. On the basis of the students' responses to the survey items, it is apparent that the majority of the students (93%) believe experiential groups are necessary for their development as a group worker. Most of the students (92%) indicate that they benefited from their involvement in the experiential group, even though they felt anxiety and discomfort at times.

R. D. Anderson and Price (2001) maintained that there is research support for the value of experiential groups and that these groups are an effective and necessary part of the training of group counselors. The findings of their survey also suggest that programs need to have safeguards in place such as informed consent, pregroup preparation, and training in appropriate self-disclosure that have been recommended in the literature (Forester-Miller & Duncan, 1990; Merta et al., 1993).

A Contributor's Perspective

Holly Forester-Miller summarizes some perspectives on teaching group counseling and discusses how to implement safeguards. She believes counselor educators have an ethical obligation to require students to participate in group counseling experiences and argues that the benefits of including an experiential aspect outweigh the potential risks to students, especially if safeguards are designed and implemented.

Dual Relationships in Training Group Workers

Holly Forester-Miller

In the past, counselor educators have debated whether it was ethical or appropriate to require students to participate in an experiential group as part of their training in group counseling. The current literature indicates that a group experience is an essential component of training group counselors (M. S. Corey & Corey, 2006; Forester-Miller & Duncan, 1990; Merta et al., 1993; Yalom, 2005). ASGW (2000) concurs, stating that the practice domain should include observations and participation in a group experience, which could occur in a classroom group. Experiential groups are a vital part of training effective group leaders.

In teaching individual counseling skills, we demonstrate and role-play counseling situations for our students. They also practice their skills on each other, for several reasons. First, it gives them a "safe" place to practice. Second, they can give each other valuable feedback based on their counseling knowledge. Third, it gives them the opportunity to experience the counseling process from the client's perspective. These same reasons are relevant to the practice of group counseling skills. In group counseling the process and dynamics are very different from individual counseling, and skills are of no value if the counselor does not understand the process and dynamics that are occurring. Students can read about group process, but until they experience it, I do not believe they can fully understand it. Students have told me time and again that they thought they understood what the book was saying about the stages of a group but that it was so different to actually watch the process occur in our personal growth group. This is especially true of the dynamics that occur during the stage we refer to as the *transition* or *storming* stage. For example, it is extremely helpful for students to see the leadership being challenged, to observe the nondefensive response of an experienced leader, and to be able to discuss that experience with the leader as part of a class discussion.

It seems to me that it is our ethical obligation to require students to participate in a group counseling experience. It is no longer a matter of *whether* it is appropriate; the question now is *how* this group experience can be offered in an ethical and appropriate way.

The *ACA Code of Ethics* (2005) deals with this issue:

> Counselor education programs delineate requirements for self-disclosure or self-growth experiences in their admission and program materials. Counselor educators use professional judgment when designing train-

ing experiences they conduct that require student and supervisee self-growth or self-disclosure. Students and supervisees are made aware of the ramifications their self-disclosure may have when counselors whose primary role as teacher, trainer, or supervisor requires acting on ethical obligations to the profession. Evaluative components of experiential training experiences explicitly delineate predetermined academic standards that are separate and do not depend on the student's level of self-disclosure. Counselor educators may require trainees to seek professional help to address any personal concerns that may be affecting their competency. (F.7.b.)

The personal growth or training group experience built into group counseling courses is very different from a therapy group. The main differences lie in the intensity of the experience and the depth of sharing on the members' parts. Yet the stages of the group and the leadership issues at each stage remain the same, thus offering a wonderful learning opportunity while minimizing the risks to students. As long as counselor educators properly plan for the group experience and, as with any group, design the experience always keeping in mind the purpose and objective of the group and the best interests of the participants, the risk of harm from the dual relationship will be minimal, if any.

Forester-Miller and Duncan (1990) recommended several guidelines and conditions under which the risks to students are minimized. Several that apply here and have not already been mentioned are that the personal growth experience not be related to the process of program screening, whether for admission or for continuing in the program; that students be evaluated only on their level of group skill acquisition; and that students not be allowed to lead a group of their peers without the professional responsible for the group being present. These recommendations are consistent with the standards expressed in the *ACA Code of Ethics* (2005) cited previously as well as in the standards addressing peer relationships.

> Counselor educators make every effort to ensure that the rights of peers are not compromised when students or supervisees lead counseling groups or provide clinical supervision. Counselor educators take steps to ensure that students and supervisees understand they have the same ethical obligations as counselor educators, trainers, and supervisors. (F.6.e.)

In addition to offering guidelines, Forester-Miller and Duncan (1990) provided four alternatives for structuring a group experience for students that meet the conditions suggested:

1. The master's-level group experience is led by postmaster's students under faculty supervision.
2. The instructor leads or coleads the group, using a blind grading system for assessing students' learning and skill acquisition.
3. All students are required to participate in a counseling group that is external to the academic setting.
4. The instructor leads the group with students using the role-play technique.

These are all viable options open to the counselor educator who teaches group counseling.

I prefer to lead the group and use a blind grading system. This approach offers several benefits to students. They are able to experience the "real" thing firsthand: they see the group process at work and at the same time experience it from the perspective of the client. The students have the opportunity to try on the leadership role in an ongoing group with the faculty member present to offer assistance and feedback. The students are provided with an effective leader role model, and the faculty member can feel confident of the skill level being demonstrated and the types of techniques being modeled. This approach also provides a common experience for the students and instructor to use in discussing group process and giving examples. Furthermore, it affords students the unique experience of seeing the faculty member using the skill and applying the strategies that have been discussed, and being able to discuss the effectiveness of the interventions in the various situations.

Davenport (2004) recommended the approach of requiring a personal growth group, prior to taking the advanced group counseling class, that is led by a licensed professional, often staff of the student counseling center. This is consistent with Forester-Miller and Duncan's (1990) alternative number three. The drawbacks to this approach are that some programs do not have access to the resources for providing these groups; the program faculty do not have a means for monitoring the skill levels of the leaders and the skills modeled; the students do not try on the leadership role; and there is no opportunity for the faculty member to discuss the examples from group and use these wonderful teaching moments. But despite these drawbacks, it is clearly better than not requiring a group experience at all.

In 1995, Forester-Miller and Remley surveyed members of ASGW regarding their perceptions of the effectiveness of the group training in their master's-degree counseling programs. At the time ASGW had approximately 3,000 members, and we surveyed 600 of them randomly across the country. The study was based on comparing the perceived effectiveness of the five training methods delineated by Merta et al. (1993). The training methods included no experiential group, no-feedback experiential group, feedback experiential group, instructor-observed experiential group, and instructor-led experiential group. Respondents who were taught using the instructor-led experiential group model indicated that they gained a higher level of competency in processing interactions and in managing groups as the leader than did the other respondents. This supports Merta's (1997) assertion that "the model with the instructor leading the group appears to be most effective in fulfilling training and gatekeeping responsibilities" (p. 91). However, he goes on to say that this model is "least effective in protecting students." These respondents did not indicate any adverse effects. As suggested by Forester-Miller and Duncan (1990) and provided for in the *ACA Code of Ethics* (2005), it is possible to safeguard students in instructor-led experiential groups.

The benefits of such an experience certainly outweigh the risks, especially if the faculty member has planned the experience to minimize these risks. It seems to me that we owe it to our students and to their future clients to provide the best training possible, utilizing the most effective teaching methods available. Therefore, not offering a group counseling experience as part of group counselor training would be neglectful and unethical. Some dual relationships are not only ethical but beneficial.

A Contributor's Perspective

In the following section, Gerald Corey discusses how he teaches a group counseling course using a blend of approaches and how he manages the multiple roles inherent in this work.

Teaching Group Counseling Courses

Gerald Corey

Currently, I teach group courses on both the undergraduate and graduate levels, and I offer training and supervision workshops in group facilitation for both students and mental health professionals. In each of these courses or workshops I blend didactic and experiential approaches, and in doing so I assume multiple roles. In many cases, the courses and workshops that I conduct are composed of voluntary participants, and this brings a different dimension to these experiences than if I were teaching a required course. In addition to teaching group process as a part of the undergraduate program, I also take on the role of supervisor for students in small groups (as part of the group course). I facilitate groups in which students in these classes are exploring their personal concerns, and a variety of interpersonal issues emerge during the unfolding of the group.

The students who sign up for my undergraduate human services program group course are highly motivated and generally willing to engage in significant self-exploration in the context of the group course. In my role as a professor, I am required to grade students, but I am not expected to evaluate students for retention in the major. If I were on a committee charged with making determinations regarding acceptance or dismissal from a training program, and if I was expected to use information about students that I acquired from the group courses, this would prove to be ethically problematic.

The Practicum in Group Leadership Course

One of the undergraduate courses I regularly teach at California State University, Fullerton, is Practicum in Group Leadership. In this course, students get a balanced experience of didactic material on group process and theories of group counseling, opportunities to lead and colead self-directed groups where they can apply what they are learning, supervised experience in group leadership, experiential learning involving working on their own personal issues in a group, and supervision sessions that are therapeutic as well as educational. Thus, in a single course students are exposed to a variety of ways of learning about groups, both cognitive and experiential. I cite this class as an example of the many group leadership courses that typically combine academic learning with opportunities for personal learning.

Students are screened both individually and in a small group before they are allowed to enroll in this course. The course includes supervised experience in coleading a group-oriented class on the campus, and students meet for weekly supervision as a group with the faculty person supervising their work as coleaders. In addition, students meet with me once a week for a 3-hour class session. Each class meeting begins with a didactic focus: a short lecture on group process issues or a consideration of a specific theory of group work and a demonstration group that I lead to illustrate the practice of a particular theoretical orientation. During the second half of the class session, the class is divided into two groups (generally not more than 12 students in each small group) with an experiential focus. The students colead this group for the first 45 minutes of the session, which is followed by 30 minutes of processing time with a supervisor. Another faculty member assists me in supervising these small groups.

The Practicum in Group Leadership course (3 units) is a graded course, but student participation as a group member or as a leader is not a criterion for determining the grade. Weekly reactions papers to assigned readings, a major paper toward the end of the semester, and an objective-type final examination are the criteria for assigning the course grade.

A Weekend Training and Supervision Group

Along with the Practicum in Group Leadership course, students are asked to enroll in a 3-day training and supervision workshop during the first weekend of the semester. In this residential workshop, students have many opportunities to function as group members and as coleaders of their own small groups. Group Process and Membership is a separate course in which students are given one semester unit of credit. The course does not carry a letter grade but is evaluated simply as "Credit" or "No Credit," removing the evaluative component from this kind of experiential group training. To obtain credit, students are required to attend all of the sessions for the weekend (24 contact hours) and also to write a thoughtful reflection paper that conceptualizes their learning based on this group experience.

In addition to my role in this weekend workshop, five other faculty members also function as supervisors during this workshop. Before students enroll in this workshop, they are informed of the nature, purpose, and structure of the class. They indeed do get involved in self-exploration and in dealing with interpersonal issues that grow out of the emergence of the group process. Students each have at least two opportunities to colead a group during the weekend, and each of these sessions is directly supervised. Students colead for the first hour and spend the next 30 minutes discussing group process with the supervisor of that particular session.

Preparing students to colead small groups. When students and supervisors initially meet for the weekend workshop, an orientation meeting is held for the entire group. We offer suggestions aimed at helping students get the maximum benefit from their experience, both as members and as facilitators of their small groups. We urge students not to be overly concerned about making mistakes and encourage participants to share what they are thinking, feeling, perceiving, and experiencing in the here-and-now of the group session. We emphasize that there is no such thing as a "bad group," because everything that occurs in this kind of workshop is an opportunity for learning. We also allow some time for participants to express and explore their concerns and to ask us questions about the workshop. Students often mention a fear of getting stuck and not knowing what to do; concern about being left unfinished; the difficulty they expect to face in switching from member to leader; wondering how far to go with personal issues; and their anxieties about the responsibility of coleading a group. During this time we do our best to create a safe climate in which participants will feel free enough to practice leading and feel trusting enough to share themselves in personal ways so that they can become a working group.

Small-group sessions. During the first small-group session, our main goal is to assist participants in continuing to talk about any fears or expectations they have pertaining to the workshop. We encourage them to identify themselves to one another, which is partly done by defining their personal goals. Through getting acquainted in their small group, participants begin to actively create a trusting environment where they can engage in the self-disclosure necessary for a working group. Another agenda we have for this session is to help the group come up with themes they can use as a focus for their sessions.

Prior to attending the workshop, students are expected to read *Group Techniques* (G. Corey, Corey, Callanan, & Russell, 2004) to familiarize themselves with ways of using and evaluating techniques in facilitating groups. Also, before students attend the workshop, they are told that each of the 90-minute sessions will be structured around themes taken from the book *I Never Knew I Had a Choice* (G. Corey & Corey, 2006), which they have read prior to this workshop. Participants are asked to read this book prior to attending the workshop, but they are not expected to stick rigidly to these themes in a given session; rather, these themes are points of departure and topics for focus. Generally, it is hoped that the student leaders learn that their own personal fears, problems, and unresolved issues will affect the way they lead groups. Other here-and-now issues surface and are dealt with, especially matters such as students' anxiety about not knowing enough to lead groups effectively, fears of being seen as incompetent, discomfort with intense emotions, fear of making mistakes, and concerns about being able to work well with a coleader.

At this preliminary meeting, students are given guidelines regarding how they can actively participate in their small groups. To use the time in their small groups effectively, students are asked to focus on two different aspects in their work. The first level focuses on the here-and-now, which pertains to students' reactions to what is going on in their training group. Students are told that they will be asked to reflect on what they are thinking and feeling as is pertains to being in their small group. Part of this here-and-now emphasis pertains to their fears, concerns, hopes, and goals as they relate to the small group. The expectation is that students will express their reactions to the here-and-now process of the group.

The second level focuses on students' personal goals, or the personal topics they are willing to explore during the workshop. Students hear about the importance of establishing specific and meaningful personal goals. Students are asked to pay special attention to personal topics that have relevance to how an issue is likely to affect their work as a counselor or group leader. The topics or themes in *I Never Knew I Had a Choice* (G. Corey & Corey, 2006) are especially important as material for exploration in the small groups.

In the small groups, we tend to focus on exploring self-defeating cognitions students bring to the workshop. For instance, many students burden themselves with perfectionistic demands that they should already know everything there is to know about a group before they even take the class. Student trainees worry a great deal about their performance and how the supervisors will judge them. Some students are convinced that the supervisors will "discover them" and tell them they cannot continue in the course. They fear being exposed as incompetent. All these concerns make excellent material to work on in the sessions, for it is what is presently on many of their minds. Some of the most useful themes pertain to their concerns about doing well in this workshop and in the group course. We caution participants to avoid discussing such themes in abstract and impersonal ways, and we encourage the leaders to facilitate in a manner that will help members apply these themes to themselves and explore them in personal ways.

During the first hour of group working time, the supervisors take notes that we later share with the students when we process the group. These details can serve as excellent teaching points during the process commentary time that immediately follows. Many aspects of what is going on in the group get our attention: How do the coleaders open the group? How do they introduce techniques? If there is a theme, do the coleaders facilitate group interaction and assist members to deal with the theme in a personal way? Are coleaders able to drop an agenda to pick up on an emerging theme in the group, such as lack of trust? What leadership skills are the coleaders demonstrating? Are they able to orchestrate member interaction, or do they focus on the first person who speaks and ignore others? What are the results of certain interventions? Are the coleaders paying attention to nonverbal language? Are they able to move from one person to another in a natural way? What are the coleaders modeling? How is conflict dealt with in the group? How are the coleaders working together? Do they pick up on each other's interventions? What leadership skills do they need to acquire or refine?

These are a few examples of what the supervisors focus on during the first hour of each session that the students are coleading. We find that participants are most receptive to learning about group process when they have just experienced what we hope to teach.

The process commentary time. The second part of each small-group session (approximately 30 minutes) begins with our request that the coleaders talk to each other about what they were thinking and feeling during the past hour. We then ask the student group members to briefly summarize their experience. Then, as supervisors, we share our observations in such a way that participants are encouraged to interact with us through questions and discussion. During the process commentary, we emphasize that many appropriate clues can be recognized and explored during a group session. What a leader decides to focus on is not a matter of "right" or "wrong"; rather, it is often a function of the leader's interest at the moment. Leaders might make a certain intervention (or avoid doing so) because of their theory, their lack of comfort with certain emotions, their personal blocks, or the mood that seems present in the group. We tend to focus on what the coleaders had in mind with certain interventions and sometimes talk about alternative ways of intervening.

During this process commentary time, we might ask coleaders open-ended questions designed to help them reflect on their own experience as they were leading. Some of these key questions include the following: What was going on with you when . . . ? Were you aware of thinking or feeling something that you did not say? What hunches did you have when . . . ? Where might you go if you were to continue in the next session? Why did you introduce this particular technique at this time? As we discuss the proceedings and provide feedback, we try to be constructive, honest, and sensitive. We encourage students to build on their strengths and try not to discourage them from trying out new ideas and approaches.

Our experience in doing training workshops has shown us that the participants learn best when the material arises from what they actually experience in a session. This ongoing teaching and learning process seems to have an impact on students: What they are conceptualizing has its roots in a problem they have actually faced as either a member or a leader of their training group.

At times we have to give difficult feedback, yet we say what needs to be said in a respectful and sensitive way. We notice that after the first small group and our process commentary, the participants relax greatly and feel much less anxiety. They watch the way we give feedback and see that we treat them with dignity. We respect their level of experience, whatever that may be, and give them room to learn by trial and error. Also, we encourage students to be patient with themselves and not to burden themselves with unrealistic expectations of having to be perfect.

Leading by the supervisors. The other supervisors and I typically colead the small groups during the evening session. During these sessions, participants have no leadership responsibilities. This is their time to bring up any issues that surfaced for them during the day and to go further with them if they choose. Our leading provides a safeguard against members opening up issues without having a means to explore them in greater depth. The participants have an opportunity to work with any personal matters that are unsettled, with anyone in the workshop whom they might have reactions to, or with any of their concerns pertaining to their participation in their small group (either as a member or a facilitator). We realize that going from one session to another, being alternately a member of a group and a leader, working on a feeling level and then a cognitive level, and being in a personal working group and then shifting to a process-oriented discussion group can be unsettling and often demands adjustment.

Our leading during the evening is one way of attending to the feelings that arise from the intense and demanding activities of a typical day in the workshop. It also gives the participants a chance to observe and experience each supervisor's style of leadership. However, we caution students against merely observing what we are doing and studying us. They are reminded that the best way to learn how to lead a group is by getting fully involved as a member, and then later conceptualizing and discussing what they experienced.

In the last small-group session, supervisors lead the groups and help the participants to review and integrate what they have learned during the workshop. During this last review session, our focus can be discerned in the kinds of questions we suggest: What did each of you learn about yourself as a member? as a leader? What stopped you? What facilitated you individually and as a group? What was helpful? not helpful? How would it be if you had a group composed largely of members like yourself? What did you learn about group process that you can apply to groups you lead? We are basically concerned with helping the participants review and consolidate their learning, both about themselves personally and about how groups function.

We conclude the workshop by meeting as an entire group to review and discuss the experiences of the weekend, with particular emphasis on ways participants can apply what they have learned to the groups they will lead. Time is allowed for debriefing and for talking about the meaning this workshop had for each person.

Process paper for weekend workshops. This workshop is a separate one-unit course that is graded on a "Credit/No Credit" basis. We provide the following guidelines to students in structuring their paper.

- What did you learn about yourself through this process?
- Focus on the qualities about yourself that might either enhance or detract from your effectiveness as a group leader.
- Concretely, what did this workshop teach you about being a group member? about group leadership? about *how* groups function or malfunction? about the stages of a group? about techniques?
- Comment on the evolution and development of your supervision group on the weekend. How did your group begin and end? any key transitions? any turning points? any highlights in your group?

- How did the presence of the supervisor affect your group? How did the rotation of student coleaders from session to session affect your group?
- What group norms developed? How were these norms shaped? Were these norms explicit or implicit?
- Comment on the level of cohesion in your group.
- What did you learn about techniques and skills at this weekend supervision and training workshop?
- What factors contribute to a working and productive group?
- How is trust generated within a group?
- When do groups get stuck, and how can they get unstuck?
- How is resistance best dealt with in groups? How is anxiety dealt with?
- How is conflict therapeutically dealt with in groups?
- What have you learned about groups from this workshop that you can apply to groups that you will be leading?

Over the many years of reading student papers that conceptualize their personal learning as well as what they learn about group process and facilitating a group, I continue to find that the majority of students greatly benefit from putting into action what they are learning from reading, lectures, and discussions about group work. Students typically value the opportunities to gain practical experience that results from combining didactic and experiential approaches to learning.

Dual Purpose Cautions

In conducting a didactic and experiential workshop to develop group leadership skills, several cautions must be kept in mind. It is difficult to combine a skills development and cognitive framework of group process with personal involvement for therapeutic purposes. Both the students and the supervisors/instructors need to remind themselves that the workshop has a dual purpose. One aim of the workshop has a *didactic* or teaching focus: learning how groups function, learning about group dynamics, and acquiring specific skills necessary to lead groups effectively. The other aim is *experiential* training. This requires a climate of support and challenge that encourages students to get personally involved sufficiently to acquire some tools to continue taking an honest look at themselves as persons and to assess how their personal characteristics might either facilitate or inhibit their ability to lead groups. Both aims must be kept in mind to provide balance in the overall experience.

You should be on guard against two tendencies that may arise in such a workshop. On one extreme, the focus may be directed toward acquiring cognitive knowledge, skills, and techniques. If the personal investment of dealing with real issues is lacking, this group becomes artificial. If the group is characterized by artificiality, any meaningful learning of leadership skills and techniques becomes difficult. On the other extreme is the tendency to forget matters of group process and learning and practicing those skills and to become simply an "experiential group."

My colleagues and I take care to combine both the experiential and didactic dimensions, based on our conviction that such a balance is essential for learning how to lead groups. However emotionally intense the groups may become, we do not abandon the educational aspects. Participants can be involved in personal self-exploration and still put their learning into a cognitive framework. The focus on exploring their own struggles stems from our belief that leaders cannot inspire others to do what they are not willing to do themselves.

Ethical Considerations and Informed Consent

Prior to the time students enroll in this course, a 3-hour meeting (as a class) is scheduled. This preliminary meeting focuses on what students can expect to learn and what will be expected of them as participants in this form of learning. One of the primary reasons for holding such a meeting for the group courses that I teach is to provide a basis for informed consent. I believe students have a right to be informed of the specific nature of the course and program requirements before they enter a program.

Students are given a detailed course syllabus, which we go over during this preliminary meeting. If students determine that they do not want to participate as a member of a group and learn about group facilitation, they are certainly free not to enroll in the course. By going over all of the components of the course described in the course syllabus, students are prepared for the weekend workshop and all of the academic and personal requirements associated with it. With this information, students are in a position to determine whether this is the kind of learning experience they want for themselves.

At this preliminary orientation session, I discuss with the students some of the potential problems and challenges inherent in a course that combines both academic and personal learning. As a part of the course, students will be cofacilitating (with another student) a process group, or a self-exploration group, that meets each week on the university campus. Students are informed that the experience of leading groups, even under supervision, often touches them in personal ways and brings to the surface their own personal conflicts and struggles. It is essential that they be willing to take their own journey toward self-knowledge if they intend to pursue group work. Generally, students hear that they will not be able to encourage future clients to deal with pain in their lives if the students have not become aware of unresolved personal issues and dealt with their own personal pain. Students are encouraged to consider seeking some form of personal counseling as a way to deal with the personal issues that emerge for them as group trainees. Students will have opportunities for working on their personal issues in a training group. I tell students that this is not a therapy group designed for extensive exploration of their personal problems.

Some Safeguards to Protect Students

It is my belief that the potential risks of experiential methods are offset by the clear benefits to participants who become personally involved in experiential group work as a supplement to didactic approaches to group courses. A number of factors in the design of my group courses reduce the chances of students being harmed by the experience. These measures include the following:

- The screening, selection, orientation, and preparation process results in students who have a clear idea of the nature and requirements of the group leadership course they are considering. The preliminary meeting is particularly useful in helping students become acquainted with one another as well as become oriented to what will be expected of them in a course that is academically rigorous and personally demanding.
- The fact that this course is an elective allows for a more intensive learning experience than if it were required. Students take this kind of group course because they are genuinely interested in learning more about themselves as well as learning skills in facilitating a group.
- The fact that other professionals besides myself serve as supervisors for both the weekend workshop and also the entire semester offers students diverse perspectives on group process and leadership styles.
- Students in the course are informed that they can decide for themselves the nature and extent of their self-disclosures in the group pertaining to their private lives. The focus of such a group is often on here-and-now interactions within the group context rather than an exploration of outside concerns of the participants. Students have plenty to explore in reference to dealing with one another as it pertains to building a cohesive learning group. It is not necessary for students to delve into intimate details of their personal lives.
- In the class and in their supervision group, students frequently explore their anxieties and concerns about being a leader. Because students have opportunities to colead a small group with supervision, they are typically very anxious about performing in front of their peers and the supervisor/instructor. Doing this kind of work can be highly personal and provides genuine material for exploration in the here-and-now context of the group situation. In addition to students' fears and concerns about being a member or cofacilitator of a small group, students have opportunities to express their reactions to resistance they encounter with the members of the groups they are leading outside of the course. They may want to explore ways that assuming total responsibility as a group leader frequently burdens them and hinders their functioning in their group.
- The basic rationale of the course is presented and clarified from the outset. The assumption the course is built upon is that the best way to learn about group process is to participate in the group and learn firsthand about issues such as the creation of trust, dealing with conflicts, and challenging one's resistances. Conceptual learning about groups is integrated with learning that grows out of actually experiencing a group. With this kind of understanding, students are educated about helpful boundaries that will enhance their learning.

I strongly endorse participation in a group as part of a leader's training. Learning from books and lectures is important but has its limitations; certain skills can best be learned experientially. Struggling with trusting a group of strangers, risking vulnerability, receiving genuine support from others, feeling joy and closeness, and being confronted are all vital learning experiences for future group leaders. If for no reason other than because it provides a deep understanding of what clients face in groups, I think that group experience for leaders is indispensable.

- After reading the views of Holly Forester-Miller and Gerald Corey, what are your views regarding the experiential group as a basic component in training group counselors?
- How do you think you might respond in the following situation?

As a part of a master's-degree training program for group counselors, students are engaged in supervised work that involves facilitating an experiential group for the introductory course in counseling taken by all students in the counseling program. Some of these beginning students, who are also required to enroll in a section of a self-exploration group as part of the introductory course, are wondering about the ethics of having other students in the role of facilitator. A few oppose the idea of being expected to self-disclose in a group setting with student leaders, even though these leaders are under the supervision of a faculty member. The complaining students think that this is a dual relationship issue because their student leaders are enrolled in the same program.

- What do you think about the practice of using students to facilitate self-awareness groups for other students, assuming they are given adequate supervision?
- What safeguards can you suggest to protect both the student facilitator and the students who are members of the group?
- If this group were conducted by a faculty member who teaches the group course (and who is likely to have the students in a future class), what issues need to be addressed?
- If you are a counselor educator who teaches group counseling courses, where do you stand on the issues raised in this chapter?
- What safeguards do you think are necessary to protect both your students and the public they eventually will serve?
- If you are a student in a counselor education program, what are your reactions to this controversy?
- What kinds of learning experiences do you think you need in order to become an effective group leader?

Conclusions

The issue of dual relationships in the education and training of group counselors is far from being resolved. As this issue has been framed in some of the literature, conscientious counselor educators may face an ethical dilemma in the way they train group leaders. On the one hand, if we remove ourselves from what many consider to be problematic dual roles (such as combining didactic and experiential learning by performing multiple functions that may include any combination of instructor, supervisor, group leader, and consultant), we are vulnerable to charges that we have abdicated our responsibility to the profession, to the public to assure competent service, and to providing students with the best kind of learning experience to equip them to competently lead groups. On the other hand, if we do teach by combining roles, we may be vulnerable to charges that we have abdicated our responsibilities to respect the privacy of our students.

It seems to us that regardless of the model that instructors use, the key elements are the qualifications of instructors and the way the model is presented. Thus, a given model may not itself present a problem, but how specific instructors implement it may create problems. It is crucial for the instructor to be open, to treat students with respect, and to make the expectations for the course clear from the outset. It is essential to keep in mind the primary purpose of a group counseling course, which is to teach students leadership skills and to provide an understanding of how group process works. Although the main aim of a group course is not to provide personal therapy for students, participating in such a group can and ought to be therapeutic. Students can make choices about what personal concerns they are willing to share, and they can also determine the depth of their personal disclosures. A group course is not designed to be a substitute for an intensive self-exploration experience, but learning how groups function can be enhanced through active and personal participation in the group process.

It seems obvious to us that counselor educators need to continue to work to clarify the question of how group counseling courses can best be taught. If counselor educators choose to keep group experiences free from evaluation, then other procedures need to be implemented within the program to screen out unsuitable candidates. At this point, counselor educators have a wide range of choices in preparing students to be group counselors. We each must choose according to our own stance on the issues, balancing our responsibilities to our students, the profession, and consumers of counseling services.

The Counselor
in the Community

In this part of the book, we turn to multiple relationship issues that confront counseling practitioners in their work, mainly in the community. Chapters 8, 9, and 10 focus on various specialty areas in mental health practice and explore some of the unique boundary issues inherent in these specializations. In this chapter, we address a number of questions that confront all counselors who work in the community, regardless of their particular specialty area of practice:

- Is it ethical to barter with clients for goods or services?
- Under what circumstances, if ever, should a counselor accept a gift from a client?
- Should a counselor ever counsel a friend or social acquaintance?
- What unique issues do rural practitioners face?
- What are the appropriate limits of self-disclosure, and how could overextending these limits create a dual relationship problem?
- Should counselors ever socialize with clients? with former clients?
- What alternative roles do counselors need to assume to serve a culturally and ethnically diverse population effectively?

The choices practitioners make on these issues are likely to either confound or clarify their attempts to practice aspirational ethics within an increasingly diverse world.

A basic theme that runs throughout this chapter is that there is a cultural context to the determination of what are considered to be appropriate therapeutic boundaries. Four guest contributors add their voices to this chapter: Holly Forester-Miller discusses boundary issues that arise for rural practitioners, Derald Wing Sue presents multicultural perspectives on relationship boundaries and multiple roles, and Thomas A. Parham and Leon D. Caldwell examine dual relationship issues from an African worldview.

Bartering for Goods or Services

In the most recent revisions of the ethics codes of mental health profession-als, the standards pertaining to bartering have been refined and expanded. Although bartering practices are not encouraged, the codes of various pro-fessions do recognize that there are circumstances in which bartering may be acceptable and that it is important to take into consideration cultural factors and community standards.

> Counselors may barter only if the relationship is not exploitive or harm-ful and does not place the counselor in an unfair advantage, if the client requests it, and if such arrangements are an accepted practice among professionals in the community. Counselors consider the cultural impli-cations of bartering and discuss relevant concerns with clients and docu-ment such agreements in a clear written contract. (ACA, 2005, A.10.d.)

> Barter is the acceptance of goods, services, or other nonmonetary remu-neration from clients/patients in return for psychological services. Psy-chologists may barter only if (1) it is not clinically contraindicated, and (2) the resulting arrangement is not exploitative. (APA, 2002, 6.05.)

> Marriage and family therapists ordinarily refrain from accepting goods and services from clients in return for services rendered. Bartering for professional services may be conducted only if: (a) the supervisee or client requests it, (b) the relationship is not exploitative, (c) the profes-sional relationship is not distorted, and (d) a clear written contract is established. (AAMFT, 2001, 7.5.)

> Social workers should avoid accepting goods or services from clients as payment for professional services. Bartering arrangements, particularly involving services, create the potential for conflicts of interest, exploita-tion, and inappropriate boundaries in social workers' relationships with clients. Social workers should explore and may participate in bartering only in very limited circumstances when it can be demonstrated that such arrangements are an accepted practice among professionals in the local community, considered to be essential for the provision of services, negotiated without coercion, and entered into at the client's initiative and with the client's informed consent. Social workers who accept goods or services from clients as payment for professional services assume the full burden of demonstrating that this arrangement will not be detri-mental to the client or the professional relationship. (NASW, 1999, 1.13.b.)

Although the ethics codes do not prohibit bartering, there are potential prob-lems even though the practice may be motivated by an altruistic concern for the welfare of clients with limited financial resources. Kitchener and Harding (1990) pointed out that the services a client can offer are usually not as monetarily valuable as counseling. Thus, over time, clients could become trapped in a sort of indentured servitude as they fall further and further behind in the amount owed. Another potential problem concerns what criteria should be used to determine what goods or services are worth an hour of the therapist's professional time.

The practice of bartering could open up more problems than it is worth. As an example, consider a client who pays for therapy by working on the counselor's car. If the mechanical service is less than desirable, the chances are good that the counselor will begin to resent the client on several grounds: for having been taken advantage of, for being the recipient of inferior service, and for not being appreciated. The client, too, can begin to feel exploited and resentful if it takes many hours of work to pay for a 50-minute therapy session, or if the client believes the therapy is of poor quality. Feelings of resentment, whether they build up in the counselor or in the client, are bound to interfere with the therapeutic relationship.

Although bartering is not prohibited by ethics or law, most legal experts frown on the practice. Woody (1998), who is both a psychologist and an attorney, recommended against the use of bartering for psychological services because it could be argued that bartering is below the minimum standard of practice. Woody contended that if therapists enter into a bartering agreement with a client, they will have the burden of proof to demonstrate that the bartering arrangement (a) is in the best interests of the client; (b) is reasonable, equitable, and undertaken without undue influence; and (c) does not get in the way of providing quality psychological services to the client. Because bartering is so fraught with risks for both client and therapist, Woody believed prudence dictates that it should be the alternative of last resort. Even if bartering is monitored carefully to lessen the chance of exploitation, there is a high risk of allegations of misconduct.

Although we can see potential problems in bartering, we think it is a mistake to condemn this practice too quickly. In some cultures or in some communities, bartering is a standard practice, and the problems just mentioned may not be as evident. For instance, rural environments may lend themselves more to barter arrangements. We know a practitioner who worked with farmers in rural Alabama who paid with a bushel of corn or apples. Within their cultural group, this was a normal way (and in some cases, the only possible way) of doing business. Many different kinds of barter arrangements could be agreed upon between counselor and client, as Holly Forester-Miller illustrates in her contribution later in this chapter. There are also alternatives to bartering, such as using a sliding scale or doing pro bono work.

Before bartering is entered into, it is important that both the client and the counselor talk about the arrangement, gain a clear understanding of the exchange, and come to an agreement in writing. Furthermore, problems that might develop should be discussed and alternatives to bartering can be examined. Using a sliding scale to determine fees or making a referral are two possible alternatives that might have merit. Bartering is an example of a dual relationship that allows some room for practitioners, in collaboration with their clients, to use good judgment and consider the cultural context in the situation.

J. Lawrence Thomas (2002), a clinical psychologist and a neuropsychologist, claimed that he has never felt completely comfortable in situations where he has entered into a bartering arrangement, but each time he did so he believed bartering was the best alternative. Although bartering is a troublesome topic, it can be a legitimate means of helping out a person with financial difficulties.

Thomas wrote: "It can serve as a relatively dignified way for the patient to compensate the therapist for professional work" (p. 394). In his view, bartering should not be ruled out simply because of the slight chance that a client might initiate a lawsuit against the therapist. Thomas cautioned that venturing into any dual relationship requires careful thought and judgment. He contended that the vast majority of professional work should be paid by the usual monetary means, yet when this is not possible due to a client's economic situation, allowances should be made so that psychological services might be available. In short, bartering can be a way for the poor but needy client to obtain psychological services.

Thomas recommended a written contract, which should be reviewed regularly, that specifies the details of the agreement between therapist and client. Documenting the arrangement can clarify agreements and can also help professionals defend themselves if this becomes necessary.

- What is your own stance toward bartering?
- Do you see it as unacceptable in your own practice, or can you foresee instances when you might work out a barter arrangement that meets your professional code's criteria for ethical practice?
- What cultural factors would you consider in deciding whether or not to barter?
- What standards within the community would you consider?
- What alternatives to bartering might you consider with your clients who are unable to pay your fee?

Accepting Gifts From Clients

The *ACA Ethics Code* (2005), recognizing the cultural implications of gift-giving, has a new standard on receiving gifts.

> Counselors understand the challenges of accepting gifts from clients and recognize that in some cultures, small gifts are a token of respect and showing gratitude. When determining whether or not to accept a gift from clients, counselors take into account the therapeutic relationship, the monetary value of the gift, a client's motivation for giving the gift, and the counselor's motivation for wanting or declining the gift. (A.10.e.)

The AAMFT (2001) also has a guideline regarding gifts: "Marriage and family therapists do not give to or receive from clients (a) gifts of substantial value or (b) gifts that impair the integrity or efficacy of the therapeutic relationship" (3.10.).

Borys (1988) surveyed counselors about a number of dual relationship questions, including accepting gifts from clients. Only 16% of her respondents believed that it was never or only rarely ethical to accept a gift worth less than $10, but the percentage of those who disapproved rose to 82% when the gift was worth more than $50. Apparently, the monetary value of gifts is a major factor for counselors in determining whether it is ethical to accept them. Although expensive gifts certainly present an ethical problem, it is possible to be overly cautious and, in so doing, damage the therapeutic relationship. Rather than establishing a hard and fast rule, our preference is to evaluate each situation individually.

There are other factors, however, that need to be examined as well. First, counselors need to be sensitive to cultural differences. As Derald Wing Sue points out later in this chapter, gift giving has different meanings in different cultures. The motivation of the client also needs to be considered. If the offering of a gift is an attempt to win the favor of the counselor or is some other form of manipulation, it is best not to accept the gift. In addition to the motivation of the client, the relationship that has developed between the counselor and the client should be considered. Offering a gift might be the client's way of expressing appreciation. An example might be a client who brings a potted plant to a termination session as a way of saying "thank you" for the work that the counselor and client have accomplished together. If the therapist were to simply say "I cannot accept your gift," the client might feel hurt and rejected. However, acceptance of other gifts might be improper. For example, a client who is a corporate executive might offer her counselor a stock tip based on her insider's knowledge. The counselor needs to explain to the client why it is improper to profit financially from information gained through a counseling relationship, and this could lead to a productive discussion about why the client felt a need to make such an offer. As is true of so many ethical dilemmas, one possibility is for the therapist to discuss his or her reactions with the client about accepting a gift.

One way to avoid being put in the awkward position of having to refuse a gift is to include a mention of the policy in your professional disclosure statement. The statement could include the information that although counseling sessions may be intimate and personal, the relationship is a professional one and does not allow you to accept gifts. Although being clear with clients at the outset of the relationship does prevent some later problems, there will be instances when small gifts are offered and might be received in the spirit in which they were offered. Rather than using a price tag or some other arbitrary criterion to determine the ethics of accepting gifts, the counselor might choose to have a full and open discussion with the client about the matter.

- In your own practice, would you ever accept a gift from a client? Why or why not?
- What criteria would you use in making the judgment as to whether to accept or refuse the gift?
- Would you ever be inclined to give a client a gift?

Counseling a Friend or Acquaintance

The *ACA Code of Ethics* (2005) and many writers have cautioned against counseling a friend. Kitchener and Harding (1990) pointed out that counseling relationships and friendships differ in function and purpose. We agree that the roles of counselor and friend are incompatible. Friends do not pay their friends a fee for listening and caring. It will be difficult for a counselor who is also a friend to avoid crossing the line between empathy and sympathy. It hurts to see a friend in pain. Because a dual relationship will be created, there is always the possibility that one of the relationships—professional or personal—will be compromised. It may be difficult for the counselor to confront the client in therapy for fear of damaging the friendship. It will also be problematic for clients, who may hesitate to talk about deeper struggles for fear that their counselor/friend will lose respect for them. Counselors who are tempted to enter into a counseling relationship with a friend might do well to ask themselves whether they are willing to risk losing the friendship.

A question remains, however, as to where to draw the line. Is it ethical to counsel a mere acquaintance? a friend of a friend? a relative of a friend? We think it is going to absurd lengths to insist that counselors should have *no* other relationship, prior or simultaneous, with their clients. Often clients seek us out for the very reason that we are not complete strangers. A client may have been referred by a mutual friend, or might have attended a seminar given by the counselor. A number of factors may enter into the decision as to whether to counsel someone we know only slightly or indirectly.

Borys (1988) found that male therapists, therapists who lived and worked in small towns, and therapists with 30 or more years of experience all rated remote dual professional roles (as in counseling a client's friend, relative, or lover) as significantly more ethical than did their comparison group. Borys speculated that men and women receive different socialization regarding the appropriateness of intruding on or altering boundaries with the opposite sex: Men are given greater permission to take the initiative or otherwise become more socially intimate. In a rural environment or a small town, it is difficult to avoid other relationships with clients, who are likely to be one's banker, beautician, store clerk, or plumber. Perhaps more experienced therapists believe they have the professional maturity to handle dualities, or it could be that they received their training at a time when dual relationships were not the focus of much attention in counselor education programs. At any rate, whatever one's gender, work setting, or experience level, these boundary questions will arise for counselors who conduct their business and social lives in the same community.

A good question to ask ourselves is whether the nonprofessional relationship is likely to interfere, at some point, with the professional relationship. Sound professional judgment is needed to assess whether objectivity can be maintained and role conflicts avoided. Yet we need to be careful not to place too much value on "objectivity." In our view, being objective does not imply a lack of personal caring or of subjective involvement. Although it is true that we do not want to get lost in the client's world, we do need to enter this world to be effective.

A special kind of dual relationship dilemma can arise when a counselor needs counseling. Therapists are people too, with our own problems. Many of us will want to go to our friends, who might be therapists, to hear us out and help us sort out our problems. Our friends can be present for us in times of need and provide compassion and caring, yet not in a formal therapeutic way. We will not expect to obtain long-term therapy with a friend, nor should we put our friends in a difficult position by requesting such therapy.

Issues in Rural Practice

In rural communities, counselors may have to play several roles. In comparison to their colleagues who practice in urban or suburban areas, they often find it more difficult to maintain clear boundaries and are frequently challenged in blending several professional and nonprofessional roles and functions.

Sleek (1994) pointed out that ethical issues plague rural practice and that therapists in sparsely populated areas confront a range of unique ethical dilemmas. For example, a therapist who shops for a new tractor encounters a potential dual relationship issue if the only person in town who sells tractors happens to be a client. However, if the therapist were to buy a tractor elsewhere, this could cause strain in the relationship with the client because of the value that rural communities place on loyalty to local merchants. As another example, consider the matter of clients who want to barter goods or services for counseling. Some communities operate substantially on a swap basis rather than a cash economy. As we have suggested, this does not necessarily have to be problematic, but there is potential for conflicts in the therapeutic relationship if the bartering agreements do not work well.

Campbell and Gordon (2003) offered strategies for evaluating, preventing, and managing multiple relationships in rural practice. They stated that multiple relationships in rural practice are inevitable due to the limited number of rural practitioners, access difficulties, characteristics of rural communities, and characteristics of practitioners in these communities. They suggested that the three criteria offered by the APA (2002) ethics code are helpful in making decisions about multiple relationships: risk of exploitation, loss of therapist objectivity, and harm to the professional relationship.

Younggren and Gottlieb (2004) developed an ethical decision-making model for managing risk when contemplating entering into multiple relationships. Practitioners need to make a careful assessment of potential conflicts of interest, loss of objectivity, and potential consequences for the therapeutic relationship. Counselors are advised to discuss with the client any potential problems involved in a multiple relationship and attempt to involve the client as fully as possible in the process of making decisions. After this assessment and discussion have been done, and if the multiple relationship seems appropriate, then the counselor's task is to document the entire process.

A Contributor's Perspective

Holly Forester-Miller explores how practicing in a rural community might make a difference in the appropriateness of dual relationships and how they can best be managed.

Rural Communities:
Can Dual Relationships Be Avoided?

Holly Forester-Miller

If you were raised in an urban environment and have practiced exclusively in urban or suburban settings, the dual relationship issues experienced in rural communities may never even have occurred to you. Life in rural communities can be quite different from life in cities and can raise some complex issues for mental health providers. I was raised on Long Island, New York, and then lived and worked in several rural communities in various states, so these differences have become all too evident to me. Initially, though, I was caught off guard.

Living in an urban area gives one a sense of anonymity that does not exist in rural communities. As Gainsley (1996) so aptly stated, "Remember, we all shop at the same Wal-Mart." In most rural communities, it is impossible to avoid dual relationships. Everyone lives and works in the community, and paths are bound to cross at some point. In a small town, the issue of counseling acquaintances is a moot point because nearly everyone is an acquaintance. Counselors need to distinguish among levels of acquaintanceship and friendship and set clear demarcations in deciding who will be appropriate to accept as clients. My experience is that familiarity and trust are necessary ingredients to be an effective counselor in rural areas, and this observation has been echoed by other rural practitioners. Moleski and Kiselica (2005) pointed out, "The counselor who is about to begin a dual relationship is not always destined for disaster" (p. 7). They go on to point out that refusing to provide counseling services to an acquaintance in a rural area might prevent that individual from receiving assistance, which certainly raises another dilemma.

Values and beliefs may vary significantly between urban dwellers and their rural counterparts. As counselors we need to work to ensure that we are not imposing values that come from a cultural perspective different from that of our clients. Just because someone may have the same ethnicity as you and have the same socioeconomic status does not mean they share the same cultural perspective and values. Working in rural communities I learned quickly that not all White, middle-class Americans have the same culture. For example, the values and beliefs related to marriage and the role of females in the family are often dramatically different in rural communities than they are in urban areas.

Bartering is a common practice in some regions and offers an opportunity for some individuals to receive counseling services. In the Appalachian culture, for example, it is a matter of pride to be able to provide for yourself and your loved ones. When I practiced in Appalachia, I once counseled a suicidal teenage girl. I had discussed fees with her single-parent mother, who was insistent that she not receive free services. We set a significantly reduced fee. After a short time, it became apparent to me that even this small amount was a drain on the family's resources. So I broached the issue with the mother again, and offered to see her daughter for free. This was not acceptable to her. She stated that she could make it on her own and take care of her family. She then asked if I might like her to make a quilt for me, instead of paying in money. Not wanting to get involved in the details and potential dilemmas of designing and planning a quilt with her, I asked her if she had one already made that she was willing to sell. She said that she did, brought in the quilt, and told me the amount she wanted for it. We arranged for that amount to be on account for her daughter's counseling. I had thought it through in advance and decided that I would accept the quilt no matter what the quality or whether or not I liked the colors. I did not want to put myself in a position to be judging or disapproving of this woman's work. My sole purpose was to help the family, and especially be able to continue to offer services to the daughter. In this case bartering was the best solution because it allowed her daughter to receive needed counseling services and afforded the mother an opportunity to maintain her sense of pride that she could pay her own way and provide for her family.

The *ACA Code of Ethics* (2005) recognizes the realities of bartering as both a helpful payment method and as a potentially exploitive arrangement. The inclusion of the phrases in Section A.10.d. that bartering may be acceptable "if such arrangements are an accepted practice among professionals in the community" and that counselors "consider the cultural implications of bartering" are important acknowledgments of cultural differences and rural traditions.

Group counseling also poses some interesting dilemmas in rural communities. We typically assume group members do not know each other and have no outside relationships. This is an assumption that cannot be made in a rural community. The group members are very likely to know each other and to have relationships with each other, which adds new dimensions to the process of trust building in group work.

Is it possible to avoid dual relationships in rural communities? I seriously doubt it. Counselors in rural communities need to be aware of the issues and challenges of dual relationships so that they are prepared to handle them appropriately and to minimize the risks to their clients.

Limits of Self-Disclosure

In her survey, Borys (1988) found that 65% of her respondents believed it was never or only rarely ethical to disclose details of current personal stressors to a client. The wording of this item may have led to a higher percentage of negative responses than might otherwise have been found: Going into detail about one's own stressors is certainly less appropriate than other forms of self-disclosure. Certainly, it is often relevant for a counselor to disclose his or her reactions to a client in the here-and-now of the therapy session, and this is more likely to have a therapeutic effect than disclosing details of one's personal life to a client. The *purpose* of self-disclosure is what needs to be kept in mind. As with other counseling interventions, self-disclosure must be a thought-out process. We must determine whether our self-disclosures are clinically sound therapeutic interventions or subtle boundary violations. When counselors disclose personal facts or experiences about their lives, the disclosures should be appropriate, timely, and done for the benefit of the client. Yalom (2003) acknowledged that the therapist's practice of revealing aspects of his or her personal life can facilitate the therapeutic process, but he also suggests using caution.

If we find ourselves going into detail about our personal lives with our clients, we need to ask ourselves about our intentions and whose needs we are meeting. Clients are seeking our help for their problems, and they are not there to listen to our stories about our past or present struggles. Self-disclosure is a means to an end, not a goal in itself. If we lose sight of the appropriate professional boundaries with our clients, the focus of therapy might well shift from the therapist attending to the client to the client becoming concerned about taking care of the therapist.

A key ingredient in maintaining appropriate boundaries of self-disclosure is the mental health of the counselor. If we are not being listened to by our significant others, there is a danger that we might use our clients to satisfy our needs for attention. Our clients might become substitute parents, children, or friends, and this kind of reverse relationship is certainly not what our clients need. Instead, when we have conflicts or unresolved personal concerns, we need to address them with a colleague, a supervisor, or a therapist.

Social Relationships With Clients

Caution is recommended when it comes to establishing social relationships with former clients, and increased caution is needed before blending social and professional relationships with current clients. Among Borys's (1988) findings were that 92% of respondents believed that it was never or only rarely ethical to invite clients to a personal party or social event; 81% gave these negative ratings to going out to eat with a client after a session. Respondents felt less strongly about inviting clients to an office or clinic open house (51% viewed this as never or rarely ethical) or accepting a client's invitation to a special occasion (33%).

One important factor in determining how therapists perceive social relationships with clients may be their theoretical orientation. Borys found psychodynamic practitioners to be the most concerned about maintaining professional boundaries. One reason given for these practitioners' opposition to dual role behaviors was that their training promotes greater awareness of the importance of clear, nonexploitive, and therapeutically oriented roles and boundaries. In the psychodynamic view, transference phenomena give additional meaning to alterations in boundaries for both client and therapist. A further explanation is that psychodynamic theory and supervision stress an informed and scrupulous awareness of the role the therapist plays in the psychological life of the client—namely, the importance of "maintaining the frame of therapy."

A counselor's stance toward socializing with clients appears to depend on several factors. One is the nature of the social function. It may be more acceptable to attend a client's special event such as a wedding than to invite a client to a party at the counselor's home. The orientation of the practitioner is also a factor to consider. Some relationship-oriented therapists might be willing to attend a client's graduation party, for instance, but a psychoanalytic practitioner might feel uncomfortable accepting an invitation for any out-of-the-office social function. This illustrates how difficult it is to come up with blanket policies to cover all situations.

- What are your views about socializing with current clients?
- Do you think your theoretical orientation influences your views?
- Under what circumstances might you have contact with a client out of the office?

Social Relationships With Former Clients

Having considered the matter of socializing with current clients, we now look at posttermination social relationships between counselors and clients. Few professional codes specifically mention social relationships with former clients. An exception is the Canadian Counselling Association *Code of Ethics* (1999):

> Counsellors remain accountable for any relationships established with former clients. Those relationships could include, but are not limited to those of a friendship, social, financial, and business nature. Counsellors exercise caution about entering any such relationships and take into account whether or not the issues and relational dynamics present during the counselling have been fully resolved and properly terminated. In any case, counsellors seek consultation on such decisions. (B.11.)

In the first edition of this book, Kitchener (1992) noted that the nature of the relationship once the therapeutic contract has been terminated is one of the most confusing issues for counselors and their clients. Clients may fantasize that their counselors will somehow remain a significant part of their lives as surrogate parents or friends. Counselors are sometimes ambivalent about the possibility of continuing a relationship because they are aware of real attributes of clients that under other circumstances might make them desirable friends, colleagues, or peers.

Nonetheless, there are real risks that need to be considered. Studies have suggested that memories of the therapeutic relationship remain important to clients for extended periods after termination and that many clients consider reentering therapy with their former therapists (Vasquez, 1991). This reentry option is closed if other relationships have ensued. Kitchener (1992) maintained that the welfare of the former client and the gains that have been made in counseling are put at risk when new relationships are added to the former therapeutic one. Kitchener suggested that many of the same dynamics may be operating in nonsexual posttherapy relationships as in sexual ones, although not at the same level of emotional intensity. Her conclusion is that counselors should approach the question of posttherapy relationships with care, and with awareness of their strong ethical responsibility to avoid undoing what they and their clients have worked so hard to accomplish.

Two studies have revealed that there is little consensus among therapists regarding whether nonromantic posttherapy relationships between therapists and former clients are ethical. The majority of the participants in a study by S. K. Anderson and Kitchener (1996) did not hold to the concept of "once a client, always a client" with respect to nonsexual posttherapy relationships. Some participants suggested that posttherapy relationships were ethical if a certain time period had elapsed. Others proposed that such relationships were ethical if the former client decided not to return to therapy with the former therapist and if the posttherapy relationship did not seem to hinder later therapy with different therapists.

Another study by Salisbury and Kinnier (1996) found similar results regarding counselors' behaviors and attitudes regarding friendships with former clients. The major finding was that many counselors are engaged in posttermination friendships and believed that under certain circumstances such relationships are acceptable. Seventy percent of the counselors believed that posttermination friendships were ethical approximately 2 years after termination of the professional relationship. Although most codes of ethics now specify a minimum waiting period for sexual relationships with former clients, the codes do not address the issue of friendships with former clients.

In reviewing the codes of ethics of the various professional organizations, it appears that entering into social relationships with former clients is not unethical, yet the practice could be unwise. The safest policy is probably to avoid developing social relationships with former clients. Even after the termination of a therapeutic relationship, former clients may need or want our professional services at some future time, which would be ruled out if a social relationship has been established. In addition, the imbalance of power may change only slowly or not at all. Counselors should be aware of their own motivations, as well as the motivations of their clients, when allowing a professional relationship to eventually evolve into a personal one, even after termination.

- What are your thoughts about social relationships with former clients?
- Do you think codes of ethics should specifically address nonromantic and nonsexual posttherapy relationships?
- Under what circumstances might such relationships be unethical?
- When might you consider them as ethical?

Alternative Counselor Roles in Working With Diverse Clients in the Community

Counselors who work in the community are likely to encounter challenges in meeting the needs of diverse client populations. Working effectively with culturally and ethnically diverse clients may entail a willingness to assume nontraditional roles and to adopt various roles at different stages in the helping process. Some of this role shifting may look like multiple relating and crossing of boundaries that are traditionally marked, yet some combining of roles may be necessary to counsel effectively in a multicultural community.

Counselors may need to acquire a different perspective and a different set of interventions that go beyond the office. For example, counselors may need to do more outreach work with their clients and provide services outside the office setting. Knapp and Slattery (2004) pointed out that home-based services may be the only way some people can get services because of transportation problems, mobility issues, or cultural barriers to office-based treatment. Providing home-based services can also lead to ethical challenges in managing professional boundaries. When working in the homes of clients, Knapp and Slattery recommended that therapists emphasize informed consent, especially about therapeutic boundaries. They also recommended, as much as possible, considering the impact of boundary crossings on the therapeutic relationship before they occur.

Counselors who work with ethnically diverse clients may need to make a shift in their thinking, for sticking with a singular role may have limitations in reaching certain clients. According to Atkinson, Thompson, and Grant (1993), practitioners are generally best trained to play the role of psychotherapist, yet this is also the role most frequently misapplied in working with racial or ethnic minority clients. Atkinson and his colleagues believe that the conventional role of psychotherapist is appropriate only for clients who are highly acculturated and want relief from an existing problem that has an internal etiology.

D. W. Sue and Sue (2003) have criticized conventional approaches to therapy that focus on a client's intrapsychic conflicts and tend to place undue responsibility on clients for their plight. At the extreme, some interventions can be perceived as blaming client problems on the client rather than as examining real factors in the environment that may be contributing to the client's problem. Many of the writers in the field of multicultural counseling and those with a community orientation have emphasized the necessity of recognizing and dealing with environmental conditions that often create problems for ethnically diverse client groups, rather than merely working to change an individual client's behavior.

In selecting roles and strategies to use with diverse clients, Atkinson et al. (1993) believed it is useful to take into account the client's level of acculturation, the locus of problem etiology, and the goal of counseling. These writers and Atkinson (2004) have suggested that several alternative roles—advocate, change agent, consultant, adviser, and facilitator of indigenous support systems—are appropriate for counselors who work in the community.

Because ethnic minority clients are often oppressed to some degree by the dominant society, counselors can function as *advocates*, speaking on behalf of clients who are low in acculturation and who need help with problems that result from discrimination and oppression. The *ACA Code of Ethics* (2005) acknowledges the importance of advocacy for clients whose problems result from discrimination and oppression (A.6.). In the role of *change agent*, counselors can make use of political power to confront and bring about change within the system that creates or contributes to many of the problems that clients face. In this role, counselors assist clients to recognize oppressive forces in the community as a source of their problems and teach clients strategies for dealing with these environmental problems. By operating as *consultants*, counselors can encourage ethnic minority clients to learn skills they can use to interact successfully with various forces within their community. The client and the counselor work together collegially to address unhealthy forces within the system and to design prevention programs to reduce the negative impact of racism and oppression. The counselor as *adviser* discusses with clients ways to deal with environmental problems that are contributing to their personal problems. For example, recent immigrants may need advice on coping with problems they will face in the job market or that their children may encounter at school.

For many ethnically diverse clients, seeking help in the form of traditional counseling is foreign. Often they are more willing to turn to social support systems within their own community. By acting as *facilitators of indigenous support systems*, counselors can encourage clients to make full use of resources in their communities including community centers, extended families, neighborhood social networks, churches, and ethnic advocacy groups. Counselors need to learn what kinds of healing resources exist within a client's culture. In many cultures, professional counselors have little hope of reaching individuals with problems because these people are likely to put their trust in the healers who are a part of their culture such as folk healers, acupuncturists, and spiritual healers. At times, it may be difficult for counselors to adopt the worldview of their clients, and in such instances it could be helpful to *make a referral to an indigenous healer*. Counselors can then structure their activities to complement or augment healing resources that are available to the client.

For counselors who hope to reach a diverse range of client populations, it is essential to be able to employ therapeutic strategies in flexible ways and to assume various roles in helping clients. Combining roles will be necessary to help many clients effectively. Thus community counseling calls for practitioners who are familiar with community resources, know the cultural backgrounds of their clients, have skills that can be used as needed by clients, and have the ability to balance various roles.

A Contributor's Perspective

Derald Wing Sue expands on some alternative roles in helping that may be implemented in various communities. He eloquently presents an ethical framework for viewing dual or multiple relationships from a multicultural perspective.

 Multicultural Perspectives on Multiple Relationships

Derald Wing Sue

Increasingly, mental health professionals are being confronted with situations that challenge the standards of practice and codes of ethics developed by their professional associations (D. W. Sue & Sue, 2003). Such is the case with dual or multiple relationships. Once counselors have entered into a therapeutic relationship with a client, the role they play becomes relatively prescribed. Traditionally, that role has been defined as working for the "therapeutic good" of clients, avoiding undue influence, allowing clients to make decisions on their own, setting clear boundaries, and maintaining objectivity by preventing personal bias from entering counseling decisions. It is believed that such a therapeutic relationship is sacrosanct, and indeed ethical codes have arisen around it to protect clients from being "taken advantage of" or "harmed."

Codes of ethics have clear guidelines that warn against multiple relationships because such relationships potentially compromise the therapeutic role. There is good reason for the existence of these standards. Yet some mental health professionals have begun to raise questions and issues regarding the universal application of such standards to all situations, problems, and populations (D. W. Sue, Ivey, & Pedersen, 1996). First, concepts of mental health, the therapeutic process, and the roles helping professionals play are grounded in modern European American culture. Some cultural groups may value multiple relationships with the helping professional. Second, some dual relationships may be unavoidable. This is especially true when therapists live in smaller or rural communities where the possibility of other contacts is high. Finally, some mental health professionals believe that multiple relationships based on nontraditional helping roles may be more beneficial than harmful. Let us briefly explore several of these particular arrangements.

The multicultural counseling and therapy movement has sensitized many to the fact that standards of normality and abnormality, the counseling role, and what is considered therapy are culture bound (Parham, 2002; Santiago-Rivera, Arredondo, & Gallardo-Cooper, 2002). In Asian culture, for example, it is believed that intimate matters (self-disclosure) are most appropriately discussed with an intimate acquaintance (relative or friend). Self-disclosing to a stranger (counselor) is considered a taboo and a violation of familial and cultural values. Thus, certain Asian cultures may encourage a "dual" or "multiple" relationship in which the helper is also a relative or close personal friend. An Asian client's desire to have the traditional counseling role evolve into a more personal one is often perceived by a European American–trained counselor as inappropriate and manipulative. In addition, gift giving is a common practice in many Asian communities to show gratitude, respect, and the sealing of a relationship (D. W. Sue & Sue, 2003; S. Sue & Zane, 1987). Such actions are culturally appropriate, yet counselors unfamiliar with such practices may feel that it is inappropriate to accept a gift because it blurs boundaries, changes the relationship, and creates a conflict of interest. They may politely refuse the gift, not realizing the great insult and cultural meaning of their refusal for the giver.

The multicultural counseling movement has also challenged the traditional roles played by counselors. Most counselors are taught that therapy is conducted in an office environment, is directed toward remediation, and is a one-to-one process. They are taught that the counselor is relatively inactive and that clients must make the decisions and take responsibility for their own actions. Yet in many cultural groups, including African Americans, Hispanic/Latino(a) Americans, and Asian Americans, clients prefer to receive advice and suggestions because they perceive the counselor to be an expert, with higher status, possessing special knowledge and expertise. The roles they find helpful may not be the traditional counseling role but other, more active roles. As discussed earlier in this chapter, Atkinson et al. (1993) and Atkinson (2004) have identified different helping roles that the professional needs to develop to become multiculturally competent. These roles are associated with client needs and characteristics: internal versus external locus of the problem, level of acculturation/knowledge of the home culture, and whether the overall goal is one of remediation or prevention. Playing more than one of these roles implies the establishment of a dual or multiple relationship.

In smaller communities and in our historical past, it was not unusual for citizens to play multiple roles such as storekeeper, neighbor, teacher, and friend. With increasing urbanization, such cross-mixing of relationships has become rare in the cities. As Forester-Miller discussed earlier, a counselor or therapist in a smaller community may find it exceedingly difficult not to have other relationships with her or his clients.

Our codes of ethics now recognize that multiple relationships may be unavoidable, that not all such relationships are harmful, and that under certain conditions they may even be therapeutically beneficial. In general, the guidelines discouraging dual relationships are well intentioned and basically sound. However, they must not be rigidly applied to all situations. As we have seen, community characteristics (rural vs. urban, small vs. large, and community acceptance of certain practices such as bartering), multicultural redefinitions of counseling roles, and cultural perceptions of helping practices must be considered. Given the fact that counselors may unavoidably find themselves in a dual relationship or faced with a potential one, what guidelines can be used to minimize potential harm? Here are a few suggestions to consider.

- Personal and professional integrity must be the guiding force behind a decision to enter a dual relationship or maintain one. Such a statement implies that the counselor considers the good of the client first and does not allow personal or professional agendas to interfere with the therapeutic relationship. The decision must be based not solely on "good intentions" but on whether the relationship actually impairs or harms the therapeutic goals or whether the risks for harm are too great.
- Counselors must be thoroughly knowledgeable about their profession's code of ethics and the spirit in which it was developed. Written statements cannot cover all situations. Many, like the examples given earlier, are not covered by clear guidelines, and to stick to "the letter of the law" may actually harm clients.
- Counselors must educate themselves about cultural and community standards of practice. For example, if a counselor decides to accept a

gift from a client or to accept barter as a means of exchange, the actions must be judged according to the client's cultural context and by the community's normative standards.

- If a counselor does not feel comfortable with a dual relationship or if it contains too many potential risks, it is the responsibility of the counselor not only to make this clear to the client but also to offer alternative means by which services can be obtained (other community resources or helpers).
- It is unrealistic to expect any single helping professional to rely solely on self-monitoring as a means for avoiding problematic dual relationships. In all situations when a counselor considers entering into or is unavoidably involved in a dual relationship, it is recommended that consultation with colleagues be sought. Indeed, continual consultation and monitoring of the situation must be the cornerstone of any continuing dual relationship.

A Contributor's Perspective

Derald Wing Sue has made it clear that as counselors working in the community, we need to rethink and revise our traditional definitions of therapeutic boundaries if we are to reach and serve a multicultural clientele effectively. Thomas A. Parham and Leon D. Caldwell agree and further discuss multiple relationship issues from an African-centered worldview.

 ## Dual Relationships Revisited: An African-Centered Perspective

Thomas A. Parham and Leon D. Caldwell

In the previous edition of this book, Parham (1997) called attention to the Eurocentric worldview assumptions that make dual relationships potentially exploitive, and thus part of the enforceable standards that govern counseling behavior. More important, Parham articulated how African-centered worldview assumptions would not only render a different definition of dual relationships but offer another perspective regarding the necessity for dual relationships and multiple roles in the counseling process with African American clients.

In this extensively revised article, the African-centered worldview is explained in more depth to provide guidance to students, practitioners, and supervisors who are challenged to express this worldview against a backdrop of Eurocentric standards regarding relationships. We intend to offer a reprieve to those who themselves are or who provide counseling to culturally conscious African Americans.

Reviewing some of the literature, Parham (1997) contended that framers of ethical standards have anchored their objections to dual relationships in several primary themes. First, dual relationships are discouraged because they potentially compromise the clinician's objectivity and professional judgment. Apparently, it is believed that secondary and tertiary relationships increase the probability that professionals will develop strong emotional ties that potentially compromise their ability to make objective decisions. Second, dual relationships are discouraged to prevent the helpee (either client or student) from projecting inappropriate dependency needs onto the helper. A third rationale centers around the power differential between helper and helpee and the degree to which those dynamics contribute to or invite helpee exploitation by the professional. The latest revision of APA's (2002) ethics code has lessened the imperative to "avoid at all costs" to reflect a more culturally sensitive caveat that dual and multiple relationships must be appropriately managed to avoid exploitation. However, many codes of conduct continue to place blanket prohibitions against dual and multiple relationships. The inherent epistemological and axiological assumptions of these codes should be examined because they may, in fact, prove to be an obstacle or hindrance when African Americans are the subjects in question.

Helms and Cook (1999) extended this notion that ethical standards represent barriers for some ethnic communities by observing that the standards themselves have been influenced by traditional theoretical perspectives. They implied that cultural conflicts potentially emerge when strict adherence to ethics codes bumps against cultural mores values and traditions, because Eurocentrically oriented theories have different foundational values. They further cautioned that cultural conflicts that result from rigid ethical and professional guidelines can lead to negative therapeutic consequences such as cultural conflict, client confusion, and early termination.

To understand the foundation of relationships in an African-centered context, one must first understand the role of a healer, why relationships have power, and why boundaries are permeable rather than rigid. Within the context of an African-centered therapeutic space, professionals are considered to be healers. Healers participate "with their clients" rather than "on their clients" in helping them to confront their intellectual, emotional, behavioral, and spiritual debilitations (Hilliard, 1998; Parham, 2002).

Healers recognize that the resolution of personal challenges occurs through many forms and across many contexts. Therefore, to limit their space is to diminish their opportunity to practice their healing art. Fu-Kiau (1991) helped to articulate this idea by reminding us that therapy in an African context is not confined to a mental health professional's office, nor is it conducted in strict 50-minute hours. Therapy involves multiple activities and can include conversation, but also play, shared meals and cooking, travel, rituals and ceremony, singing or drumming, storytelling, writing, touching, and laughter.

For example, therapy can be conducted while the client and therapist are taking a casual stroll through a neighborhood park or outdoor area near the office. Assignments and suggestions can also be given in which the client may be invited to engage in a playful activity, cooking experience, or journaling exercise. Each of these activities, when performed by the client, has the potential to bring a "healing focus" to the experience. Although the therapist may engage in some of these activities with the client, it is also likely that the client will adopt some of these activities and perform them in the absence of the therapist. In this way, the client begins to understand the healing process.

1. Being "open" to healing experiences is a first step in enhancing a client's self-healing power.
2. Healing can occur anywhere and at any time, including spontaneous experiences with unplanned events, or even people one meets by chance.
3. People and events become "healing" not simply because they exist or occur but because they instigate a thought, feeling, or spiritual insight that helps the client to appreciate some aspect of the self that he or she might have been struggling to understand.

Consequently, a healing aspect of therapy in a traditional office setting might include giving the client a hug to end the session. It may include performing a ritual with the client (e.g., sharing a libation) at the beginning of the session, or processing the particular aspects of a recreational activity the client engages in while the therapist is in attendance and observing the client.

Fundamentally, Africans and people of African descent live in a collective world and see every action in terms of a collective community. Unlike the Eurocentric focus on individuals as independently functioning entities, people of African descent belong to a group and derive their power from the collective energy of the group, tribe, or family. Healers must recognize this and use the community in all of its aspects as potential healing places and spaces.

The nature of relationships for African American practitioners and clients is inherently dualistic. Professional standards of conduct, training environments, and practices that disregard alternative cultural perspectives on relationships place culturally conscious African American students and practitioners at risk for ethnic community alienation or professional misconduct.

In understanding the role of a healer, it is also important to understand why relationships have power. People in many African cultures believe that each person is endowed with a spirit or life force that is divinely inspired. That energy is often referred to as an individual's "self-healing power" (Fu-Kiau, 1991). An individual's power can be diminished by being out of balance with one's rhythm and natural order, or by becoming too distant from the energy of the collective community. Thus, therapeutic practice, irrespective of theoretical orientation, is not simply viewed as an art of healing but as a practice of regenerating an individual's self-healing power. That regeneration occurs through the interaction of therapist and patient, whose relationship creates a synergy that is transformative. Thus, therapeutic practice in an African-centered context has less to do with boundary issues or dual relationships and more to do with what is transformative or healing within a specific therapeutic context.

In remembering that imperative, one can now see why African-centered ethics codes begin and develop in a concern for the quality of human relations. A fundamental African principle states that human beings realize themselves only in moral relations to others. Unlike Eurocentric ethical standards, which appear to be designed to control people's behavior, African-centered ethics invite people to aspire to "right ways of being." The African worldview fundamentally believes in the ontological principle of consubstantiation; that is, elements of the universe are of the same substance. There is an interconnectedness between the helper and the helpee; thus, developing and maintaining emotional and spiritual connections is considered facilitative.

In recognizing that professionals and students alike may have difficulty navigating their way through different culturally congruent and incongruent sets of ethics codes of conduct and professional standards of practice, perhaps there is a need for some suggested methods of approach. We offer the following helpful hints to the African American students and professionals, their supervisors (irrespective of cultural background), training programs, and service delivery agencies and organizations who are invested in applying more culturally sensitive ethics to their practice.

Helpful Hints for African American Trainees

- Be aware of all the professional standards and guidelines that exist within the entire professions of psychology and counseling.
- Be aware of the ethical standards that are adopted in the agency in which you work or train.
- Be cognizant of your position and cultural expertise in the community.
- Be aware of the client's worldview and how it might influence your application of particular ethical principles.

Helpful Hints for Supervisors of African American Trainees

- Develop awareness of your own cultural competence, including your limitations.
- Develop awareness of cultural expectations held by African American and other culturally different trainees, and how those might vary by level of racial identity development.
- Acknowledge that when dealing with African Americans supervisees may be more culturally aware and confident about certain aspects of their work than the supervisor.

Helpful Considerations for Professional Therapists

- Examine your own interpretation of the ethical guidelines and how those inform your practice.
- Engage in some deep thinking about how ethical guidelines may affect your work with particular clients.

- Make appropriate use of the consultation process with colleagues who are more culturally competent and those who can render judgments that broaden the options to consider.
- Support policies that recognize dual relationships are inherent and culturally expected.

Considerations for Training Programs
- Acknowledge multiple perspectives on relationships.
- Train students in ways that highlight relationship management rather than relationship avoidance.
- Teach awareness of exploitation and harm by encouraging peer consultation.
- Help trainees examine what drives the decision-making codes (mandatory ethics versus social constructivism).
- Acknowledge when individual cultural competence may conflict with organizational or institutional competency guidelines. Practitioners can advocate for policy change, education, and general awareness of institutional conflict when this occurs.
- Teach trainees to share with the community what our professional ethical obligations are and how they affect our strengths and limitations.
- Develop a clearly articulated decision-making strategy prior to facing an ethical problem.

Considerations for Agencies and Organizations
- Conduct a cultural audit to examine ways in which the organization's policies and practices might affect the client base served by that agency.
- Examine agency protocol and how power and decision making are used to address cultural competence through ethical practice.
- Recognize that there are multiple perspectives on interpreting ethics codes and professional standards regarding boundaries.
- Conduct retreats and periodic meetings to review ethical standards and dilemmas challenged by developing levels of cultural competence within the agency.

In summary, it is important to consider dual-relationship standards when we provide services to clients or students in our professional roles. However, it is also important to take into account cultural traditions and value systems that differ markedly from those underlying the standards embraced by professional associations as we develop appropriate roles and responsibilities for a profession that is becoming increasingly multicultural. Conducting one's affairs in ways that adhere to established professional codes of conduct can be a challenge. This is particularly true when those standards are congruent with only one cultural perspective to the exclusion of others, and the clients are culturally different as well. Boundary issues are only one element of a list of ethical standards that needs to be examined for cultural sensitivity. In doing so, we enhance our own level of cultural competence and help to ensure that those whom we counsel and teach are treated in ways that best address their needs, and not just our own.

Conclusions

This chapter has underscored the point that managing multiple roles and relationships is not a matter driven by fixed rules. Decisions will depend on the needs of clients, what is customary in a community, the integrity of the counselor, the structure of the counseling relationship, the client population, and many other factors. Counselors who work in the community will be challenged to manage a variety of roles if they are to be effective helpers. As each of our guest contributors has persuasively argued, it is crucial that we focus on what is best for our clients and how we best can reach them.

8
Focus on Specialty Areas

Private Practice
Group Counseling
Couples and Family Counseling

This is the first of three chapters that focus on various specializations practiced by mental health professionals. We begin this chapter with an exploration of boundary issues unique to private practitioners. Because these specialists practice in the community, many of the same themes seen in the previous chapter reemerge. Yet, as Harriet L. Glosoff so aptly demonstrates, they take on their own twists when applied to the specific context of private practice. Later in the chapter, we look at boundary issues that often arise when working with multiple clients in the context of counseling groups, couples, and families. Amy Manfrini addresses boundary issues in couples counseling and family therapy.

Private Practice

For some therapists in private practice, circumstances can make it particularly difficult to maintain boundaries between their professional and personal or social lives. Private practitioners who work and live in small communities may find it impossible to avoid interacting with their clients outside the office. Counselors who share the same political affiliation, sexual orientation, or cultural background as their clients may also experience considerable overlap between the professional and nonprofessional aspects of their lives.

Private practitioners who use their personal residences for their offices may need to exercise particular care in keeping their personal and professional lives separate. Although having a private practice in one's home is not an ethical issue in itself, this practice does open up some potential issues. Both family members and clients need to be considered with this kind of office arrangement. It is not fair to children to banish them from the house, yet it is certainly not fair to clients to subject them to interruptions and household noises. If you do use a home office to see clients, you will need to design a private space for your work with them. Clients should not have to contend with interference during the therapy hour. Another consideration is that therapists, by using their home as an office, are revealing a good deal of information about themselves and their lifestyles. Finally, it is important to assess what clientele are appropriate and inappropriate for a home office practice. For example, clients who are potentially dangerous or who have serious problems recognizing and respecting boundaries should not be seen in such a setting.

A Contributor's Perspective

Harriet L. Glosoff raises additional boundary issues unique to private practitioners, who often face collegial isolation, overlapping community contact with clients, and the struggles inherent in being self-employed.

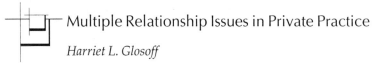 Multiple Relationship Issues in Private Practice

Harriet L. Glosoff

Most counselors, regardless of their work setting, will be faced at some time with the possibility of engaging in either multiple professional or a combination of professional and personal relationships with clients. Although it is clear in the *ACA Code of Ethics* (2005) that it is unethical for counselors to engage in sexual relationships with clients, the issues surrounding nonsexual multiple relationships are not so clear-cut. Some counselors contend that all multiple relationships should be avoided, whereas others argue that some types of multiple relationships may actually be beneficial for clients (Lazarus & Zur, 2002). For private practitioners, the difficulty of dealing with these issues can be compounded by isolation, geographical and cultural factors, and the financial exigencies involved in being self-employed.

Isolation

Work is traditionally one way in which individuals gratify a variety of psychological as well as financial needs. People often look to work settings as one place to meet people with whom they can form friendships or romantic relationships. In many ways, choosing to become a counselor, especially in a private practice setting, limits these opportunities. The relationships formed between counselors and clients are intimate ones, but this intimacy is one way with therapists in the role of "givers" (Hill, 1990; Syme, 2003). Therefore, counselors must look to other personal and work relationships for the chance to be "takers." Private practitioners, even those in group practice, typically cannot rely on work to meet this need. Their days are filled primarily with seeing clients, often individuals they like and admire, and this may leave them feeling more lonely than practitioners in agency or other settings who have greater opportunities to interact with people who are not clients.

One characteristic of most types of harmful multiple relationships with clients is that counselors put their needs above those of their clients (L. Brown, 1994), and their subsequent actions or nonactions are detrimental to clients (Cottone, 2005). This often involves clinicians looking for reciprocity in a relationship that is not, by its nature, reciprocal (Hill, 1990; Syme, 2003). The human needs for intimacy, feeling admired or valued, and for some sense of control or power do not vanish as counselors walk into sessions with their clients. These needs naturally play out in nontherapeutic relationships in which different players get the chance to have their needs take precedence over those of their friends, family members, or partners (Biaggo & Greene, 1995; L. Brown, 1994). However, in counseling relationships, a sense of mutual responsibility for needs cannot occur. L. Brown (1994), referring to "the dance of relationships," noted that "therapy is always a pas de deux in which we [therapists] are the supporting partner" (p. 36).

Private practice affords certain freedoms not found in many other settings: setting one's own hours, determining policies related to payment, and having greater choice over frequency, location, and length of sessions. Yet freedom and choices are accompanied by responsibility and problems not always encountered in more restricted settings. One such problem is that private practitioners often must grapple with their responsibilities and choices without a structure for support and feedback from other colleagues; this can lead to isolation, with an increased potential for emotional stress and burnout (Greenburg, Lewis, & Johnson, 1985). When practitioners feel lonely, experience burnout, or are emotionally stressed, they also may be more likely to engage in behaviors that could be considered violations of appropriate therapist–client boundaries. These behaviors may range from seeking affirmation for being a good counselor to seeking a friendship or a sexual relationship (Hill, 1990).

Counselors need to have a clinical rationale that informs their actions with clients (Syme, 2003) as well as their decisions when faced with an ethical dilemma. Many mental health professionals, however, use their own unique rationalizations when making ethical decisions (Pope & Vasquez, 1998). A sense of loneliness or isolation easily can lead to decisions based on rationalizations instead of on clinical rationales. Depending on one's theoretical orientation, mental health, and client circumstances, it may be relatively easy or difficult to blur this line between rationalization and rationale.

Counselors working from some theoretical approaches, such as traditional psychoanalysis, tend to conceptualize a need for strict boundaries in their relationships with clients. They believe there is a strong clinical need to avoid friendships with clients and see counselor self-disclosure as detrimental to the clinical process (Glosoff et al., 2006). Conversely, counselors who work from other theoretical bases such as humanistic, feminist, existential, or behavioral may view boundaries and self-disclosure in a different way. For example, they see self-disclosure as one way of strengthening therapeutic alliances and equalizing relationships (Freud & Krug, 2002; Glosoff et al., 2006). Regardless of orientation, it is critical that counselors recognize that their self-disclosures may be part of an unconscious agenda to have their own needs met rather than a way to empower clients (Greenspan, 1986). Practitioners in independent private settings may fall prey to unintentionally using self-disclosures in sessions to counter feelings of isolation. Some clients may interpret such counselor self-disclosures as an invitation to develop a friendship or other nonprofessional relationship. Inappropriate self-disclosure may be especially problematic if there are no colleagues with whom to "bounce off' ideas and share reactions to clients. Practitioners in other community settings have more opportunity to receive feedback from their colleagues in both formal and informal ways.

Geographical and Cultural Factors

Professionals who choose to enter private practice do not cease to be members of their communities. They do not become nonsocial, nonpolitical beings. Because of this, it is unlikely that practitioners can totally avoid personal or nonprofessional contacts with their clients. This is especially true for those who live and work in certain cultural and political communities that are close knit.

Clients often seek clinicians who share similar values or characteristics or with whom they can identify (Syme, 2003). Therefore, the political affiliations, sexual orientations, and racial or ethnic backgrounds of counselors may lead to counselors engaging in multiple roles with clients (Smith & Fitzpatrick, 1995; Syme, 2003). This is true for counselors across work settings, but those in private practice must remain vigilant against any temptation to use these factors as a way to solicit business. For example, counselors who serve on a political committee should not use the meetings as a forum for marketing their counseling services.

Counselors who live and work in small communities often find themselves in situations where they see clients outside their sessions. The same is often true for counselors who work for the military; are gay, lesbian, bisexual, or transgendered; are members of ethnic minority, feminist, deaf, or religious communities (Glosoff et al., 2006; Syme, 2003); or are recovering substance abusers (Doyle, 1997). For example, clients may befriend partners or friends of counselors in these communities before knowing about their relationships (L. Brown, 1994; Syme, 2003), leading to an unintentional connection to a therapist's social life. This may be particularly problematic for counselors from such communities whether they live and work in a small town or large city (Biaggo & Greene, 1995; L. Brown, 1994; Glosoff et al., 2006). Regardless of the actual size of their town, counselors may wish to participate in community events and activities that bring them into contact with clients. This creates dilemmas for private practitioners, including how much they can be themselves out in public (such as dancing in the park at a concert or expressing unpopular beliefs at a political meeting). Does this mean that practitioners should not attend community events where clients may be present? Adhering to this as a hard-and-fast rule is overly cautious, in my mind, and can lead to resentment on the part of the counselor. Syme (2003) noted that if counselors "refuse to be active in their community, then they are in danger of being seen as standoffish, of losing credibility, and possibly denying their own membership in the minority group. They also risk becoming isolated from the community to which they belong, which is in itself an emotionally unhealthy position for anybody, whether a therapist or not" (p. 100). In addition, for clients to see their counselors as real people may not be negative (Biaggo & Greene, 1995; Lazarus & Zur, 2002). Furthermore, it is unreasonable to ask counselors in any work setting to never attend a concert simply because a client may have the same taste in music. It is essential, however, for practitioners to discuss with their clients how seeing them outside the office affects them and how these encounters should be handled.

Financial Issues

Finances are another factor that can create ethical quandaries for private practitioners. Berman (1985) raised the point that all therapy involving a fee for services inherently involves a form of multiple relationship—blending a business arrangement with therapy. Clinicians in private practice directly experience the financial impact of clients canceling their sessions or not showing up, insurers not reimbursing for services or limiting the number of sessions, and other fluctuations in income. Obviously, finances may influence how private practitioners conduct business. They may be more tempted to engage in behaviors that keep clients in therapy for longer than necessary. They may unconsciously (or consciously) increase clients' dependence or choose not to challenge clients when it might be therapeutically appropriate to do so for fear that clients may not come back and that they will lose income (Berman, 1985). Further, private practitioners need to recognize that some clients may wish to stay in counseling because it provides a sense of intimacy or closeness that may be lacking in their lives (Moleski & Kiselica, 2005; Syme, 2003). It is essential for private practitioners to assess and monitor client progress, to adjust counseling plans or refer clients who are not making progress, and to learn how to meet their need for income without seeing their clients primarily as objects that produce this income.

Of course, the temptation to increase clients' dependence most likely will be less problematic when working within managed mental health care, due to limitations or caps on the number of sessions allowed. However, at the same time that managed care policies may decrease the problem of prolonging therapy unnecessarily, they create another problem. Regardless of decisions made by third-party payers, practitioners are responsible for making appropriate arrangements for continuation of care as considered clinically necessary. Because of this, counselors may find themselves providing services for little or no fee in order to deliver clinically sound and ethical treatment plans. Obviously, counselors in private practice cannot do this with too many clients and maintain a financially sound practice.

ACA (2005) encourages counselors to engage in pro bono services or activities that yield little or no financial reward (Introduction to Section A). Although private practitioners may build a certain amount of pro bono work into their financial plan, most will be unable to offer this on a regular basis or to many clients. I wonder if managed care will lead to an increased temptation to engage in bartering rather than an increase in the delivery of services pro bono or at a reduced fee. As has been discussed elsewhere, professional codes of ethics do not prohibit bartering, although it is discouraged because it creates a potential to distort therapeutic relationships and exploit clients. At the same time, counselors in private practice are in the position to set their own rules regarding payment and may enter into bartering agreements with clients more easily (with fewer restrictions) than counselors in other settings (Cummings, 2002; Syme, 2003). It is important for counselors in private practice to carefully consider the cultural appropriateness of bartering and the potential for harm to clients. In contemplating possible harm to clients, I suggest that counselors think not only about the individual client who will be part of the bartering agreement but also about their other clients. Because it is unlikely that private practitioners can rely on bartering to maintain their practices, it is helpful to think about what they will do if other clients find out about this practice and also wish to barter for counseling services or request other accommodations in their fees.

Another financial issue that may arise for those in private practice is engaging in different roles with clients over time. For example, Freud and Krug (2002) shared the following scenario:

> A counselor conducted a group for individuals who were recently separated. One of the former group members called the counselors and informed her that she was now on the board of a church and would like to hire the counselor to conduct similar groups for the church and is offering a very good fee arrangement. (p. 489)

Is there any conflict of interest here?

Other common conflicts in private practice may arise when counselors accept clients for counseling services and later are offered the opportunity to be paid to evaluate these clients for court proceedings, or conversely, are asked to change from a forensic evaluative role to a therapeutic one. Similarly, clients may begin seeing counselors for individual work and then want to have the counselor see them for couples or family counseling. It may be tempting to change professional roles with clients when it is financially beneficial to do so and there may or may not be a problem in accepting new and consecutive roles with clients. As previously noted, counselors should be guided in such decisions by their theoretical rationale and the best interests of their client, and not by financial gain. I offer some specific considerations regarding this issue in the next section.

Some Suggestions for Private Practitioners

Hill (1990) noted that she is surprised that boundary violations do not happen more frequently. Given the intimate nature of therapy and the stressors involved with private practice, I share her surprise. However, I wonder how many harmful multiple relationships exist that go unreported because clients are unaware of the harm or potential harm to them. How often have counselors hugged clients to appease their own need to nurture even though such behavior might interfere with clients' growth? Codes of ethics provide guidance in sorting out generally acceptable and unacceptable behaviors. They cannot, however, answer the question of whether it is appropriate to hug a specific client in a specific situation. More important than looking to codes of ethics for strict rules on boundary violations, counselors need to develop for themselves a core set of standards that guide their ethical decisions (Biaggo & Greene, 1995; Lazarus & Zur, 2002). I further believe that counselors should base their actions on theoretically sound principles. Many people believe that common sense can help us see the potential dangers involved with multiple relationships. Alfred Adler once said, "If common sense were so common, everyone would have it" (as quoted in Gottlieb, 1994, p. 287). When we get caught up in our own issues, our common sense often leaves us. I offer the following suggestions as food for thought for counselors in private practice.

- *Recognize the complexity of therapeutic relationships.* First and foremost, I believe therapists must recognize that overlapping relationships do exist. I have seen too many professionals hide their heads in the sand and deny the complexity of balancing the demands of being a therapist and remaining a human being. Refusing to acknowledge the power differential in therapeutic relationships is similar to refusing to acknowledge that we have personal biases that come into our sessions with us. Denial does not make the potential problems disappear, and it precludes developing strategies to prevent them. The *Feminist Therapy Code of Ethics* (Feminist Therapy Institute, 2000, III.A.) states that acknowledging the potential for conflicting interests is essential if therapists are to monitor their actions and prevent potential harm to clients.
- *Attend to self-care.* It is important for counselors to take care of themselves. Both the ACA and Feminist Therapy codes of ethics speak specifically to the responsibility of counselors to engage in self-care activities. For example, counselors recognize their "own needs and vulnerabilities as well as the unique stresses inherent in this work" (Feminist Therapy Institute, 2000, IV.E.), and the introduction to Section C of the *ACA Code of Ethics* (2005) states that "counselors engage in self-care activities to maintain and promote their emotional, physical, mental, and spiritual well-being to best meet their professional responsibilities." Counselors in private practice can attend to self-care by having friends and colleagues who are not clients and by finding ways to meet social and emotional needs other than those that involve a community shared with clients (Berman, 1985; Biaggo & Greene, 1995; Greenburg et al., 1985). Further, practitioners need to examine what possible harm can come to them, as well as their cli-

ents, if they enter into certain types of multiple relationships with clients. For example, counselors may come to resent watching out for their clients who are also friends, or they may actually end up minimizing their own personal needs to a degree that is unhealthy (Biaggo & Greene, 1995; Syme, 2003). This can lead to further erosion of appropriate boundaries with their clients, thus setting a dangerous cycle into motion. Seeking counseling for themselves to prevent or break such cycles is appropriate.

- *Engage in peer consultation.* As noted previously, peer consultation can counter the feelings of isolation experienced by many private practitioners (Greenburg et al., 1985). I strongly recommend that private practitioners formalize some type of regular peer consultation rather than seeking assistance only in emergency situations or when faced with an ethical dilemma.

- *Engage in ongoing self-evaluation.* Peer consultation that focuses on issues of countertransference allows counselors time and support to examine their own reactions, needs, and motivations in their professional work. In addition, critiquing tapes of therapy sessions (with client permission, of course) and keeping a journal of reactions, feelings, and concerns (being careful to protect clients' identity) can be done on one's own. These strategies can help counselors examine whether certain behaviors come up more frequently with some clients than with others and the extent to which interventions are well thought out. Biaggo and Greene (1995) suggested that clinicians check on their tendencies to act impulsively with some clients. They note that this may be a sign that there is tension in the therapeutic relationship that calls for discussion between therapist and client.

- *Take precautions against potential harm to clients when changing roles.* Counselors should consult the *ACA Code of Ethics* (2005) for guidance. They are ethically responsible to obtain informed consent from clients and to let clients know about their right to refuse services related to the change in roles (A.5.e.). In addition, the *ACA Code of Ethics* states that "[c]ounselors do not evaluate individuals for forensic purposes they currently counsel or individuals they have counseled in the past" nor do they "accept as counseling clients individuals they are evaluating or individuals they have evaluated in the past for forensic purposes" (E.13.c.)

- *Acknowledge potential for multiple relationships and possible harm to clients.* Informed consent applies to helping clients understand that their therapists also live in a community. It is important to discuss with clients how meetings outside the office are to be handled along with the potential for the development of multiple relationships and how this may harm clients. It is the therapist's responsibility to educate clients about therapeutic boundaries and how they can identify behaviors that are indicative of inappropriate boundaries. In addition, clients must be informed about avenues for recourse if they believe their therapist has engaged in improper behavior (e.g., reporting them to licensing boards and professional associations).

- *Use sound clinical judgment.* In examining potential for harm to clients, it is essential to examine not only the behavior in question (such as self-disclosure, serving on a committee with a client, or attending religious services in the same setting) but also the individual client(s) involved. For example, therapists will expect clients who are diagnosed as having a personality disorder to interpret counselor behaviors differently from clients who may not have as many boundary issues. Counselors should remember that individuals who are basically healthy may also react in a variety of ways. For example, a therapist's self-disclosure about his or her own experience with adolescent depression may empower one client to think of depression in ways other than as a pathological condition (Greenspan, 1986). Another client, however, may see this same disclosure as intrusive, a shift in focus away from the client's needs, a message minimizing the client's experience, or advice in disguise. Berman (1985) suggested that therapists consider clients' ego strength and ability to self-differentiate before engaging in behaviors that may confuse clients about healthy therapeutic boundaries.
- *Remember the bottom line.* Regardless of theoretical orientation, personal philosophy, or financial situation, counselors are ethically responsible for meeting their clients' therapeutic needs, not the other way around. Clinicians do not have to give up attending social or community events simply because clients may be present. They are not required to ignore the realities of the business aspects of their practice. However, they must think through possible consequences of their behaviors and take responsibility for preventing harm (intentional or unintentional) to their clients.

Group Counseling

Boundary issues can be particularly complex when counselors are dealing not only with multiple roles and relationships but also with multiple clients, as is the case in group counseling. Questions that provide a framework for our discussion here include the following:

- How can group leaders determine what kinds of personal and social relationships with group members are appropriate or inappropriate?
- Are there potential conflicts in admitting a former client into a counseling group? how about a friend or acquaintance?
- What are the limits of group leader self-disclosure? How could overextending the boundaries create a dual relationship?

- In a productive group, when leadership and membership roles may become blurred, what role conflicts might emerge?
- Are role conflicts inherent in serving as both the client's individual counselor and the group counselor?

Personal Relationships in Group Counseling

How can group leaders distinguish between appropriate and inappropriate personal and social relationships with members of their groups? We think it is inappropriate for us to use our professional role to make personal and social contacts, and that it is certainly questionable to develop such relationships with current group members. In fact, we urge group counselors who look to their therapeutic groups as a source of friendships, or as a way to enrich their social lives, to examine their own personal needs and motivations. Group members should not be expected to perform the function of filling gaps in the therapist's personal and social life.

Establishing friendships with current group members can put a strain on the therapeutic relationship and can cause problems for the group leader, the member involved, and other members of the group. The group member might be inhibited from participating fully in the group for fear of jeopardizing the friendship. In addition, singling out an individual member as a friend is bound to affect the dynamics of the group. The members who are not chosen as friends are likely to feel rejected or resentful.

It is more difficult to handle the dual relationship issues that arise when personal and social relationships develop among group members. Pregroup screening can help to identify preexisting relationships among potential members that could be problematic. As Forester-Miller noted in the previous chapter, however, in small towns it may be impossible to form groups composed of people who do not already know each other. Even in urban areas where it is possible to screen for prior relationships, it is probable that as the group progresses, certain members will feel drawn to each other and may want to form personal relationships outside the group. This has its advantages and disadvantages. When members socialize outside group sessions, group cohesion may be increased. Yet such a practice can also destroy the cohesion of a group. If members become a social group that discusses group matters, and if they refuse to bring those matters into the group itself, the progress of the group is inevitably impeded. Other signs that indicate counterproductive socializing include forming cliques and excluding certain members from social gatherings, forming romantic involvements without a willingness to acknowledge these involvements in the group, refusal to challenge one another in the group for fear of jeopardizing friendships, and an exclusive reliance on the group as a source of social life (M. S. Corey & Corey, 2006).

Some group leaders set ground rules at the outset that attempt to prohibit or discourage members from socializing outside of group time, and when the rationale is discussed and understood, this can be a useful approach. It is important that members understand that the primary purpose of a group experience is not for members to acquire friendships within the group but rather to teach participants attitudes and skills that they can use to form friendships in their everyday lives. Yet friendships cannot be prevented from developing, and if this occurs and affects the group's functioning, it is probably best to have an open discussion in the group so that other members can share how they are being affected by these friendships.

Group Counseling for Former Clients

Some counselors form their groups largely from their former clients in individual therapy. They see it as a useful progression to suggest a group experience after a certain number of individual sessions. Such a practice can be useful for a client's growth and, if routinely done in this manner, seems appropriately aimed at maximizing client benefit and minimizing client expenses.

One potential problem that we see, however, is possible jealousy on the part of some clients. When they were seen individually, they had the counselor to themselves for the hour. Now, as group members, they must share their counselor with other group members. This can be therapeutically useful, but it is essential for these clients to discuss their reactions in the group setting. Further, other group members may perceive the person who has had private therapy with the group leader as someone "special," and this reaction needs to be expressed and dealt with in the group.

Admitting a Friend or Acquaintance to a Counseling Group

Admitting a friend or acquaintance is a very different matter than admitting a former client to a group. In the latter case, a professional relationship is already established. In the former case, we have the shifting of roles from a personal relationship to a professional relationship, which we think could create many difficulties for the therapist, the friend or acquaintance who becomes a group member, and possibly for others in the group. Again, the bottom line seems to be the importance of predicting potential problems when dual-role relationships are being considered and discussing them fully. When there is a shifting of roles, and when this is not explored openly, problems can arise in the group. Hidden agendas will block the flow of group process.

Concurrent Individual and Group Counseling

Are role conflicts inherent in serving as both the client's individual counselor and group counselor? When a client participates with the same counselor in both individual counseling and group counseling, the effects can be therapeutic if both modalities are synchronized and are working well together. There are, however, some potential problems that call for careful consideration. Practitioners who see clients on an individual basis and also in a group should have a clinical justification for this practice. As we mentioned earlier, it would not be ethical to engage in this practice primarily to meet one's own financial or psychological needs. Yet it is possible for the same counselor to work beneficially with the same client on an individual basis and in a group setting. For example, we know a clinical social worker in a community agency who works in individual therapy with women with a history of incest and also offers a short-term support group for incest survivors. She screens members carefully and determines which clients could benefit from concurrent private therapy and participation in a support group. Clients in their individual therapy can explore in more depth certain personal issues that they may not have time to explore in the group. Concurrent individual and group counseling can work well if the counselor has a clear rationale for this form of treatment and if the counselor discusses the possible benefits and risks of this approach.

Another clinical social worker who works in a community agency sees many of his clients on an individual basis. He also refers a number of his male clients to a men's group that he and one of his colleagues conduct in the agency. He finds that working with men in individual sessions initially and then progressing to a group to explore common themes is extremely productive. In this case, it is not a situation of simultaneous individual and group counseling but of individual therapy followed by a group. In many instances, clients can benefit from joining a group after their individual therapy is completed. The continuing support they receive can be helpful in maintaining treatment gains and is usually quite affordable.

We think that, generally, counselors are wise to avoid serving as both individual and group counselor for the same client when this situation can be avoided. Of course, in some treatment facilities, these types of dual roles cannot be avoided. Treatment plans in inpatient settings routinely include individual and group counseling, and sometimes both modalities are provided by the same practitioner. Then it is up to the practitioner to take steps to lessen the possible damaging effects of functioning in multiple roles, especially as this applies to any compromising of confidentiality. Clients have a right to know what disclosures will be kept confidential and what information might be shared with other members of a treatment team.

Perhaps the most justifiable approach to meeting the needs of clients who could benefit from both individual and group counseling is for the services to be provided by different counselors. Many private practitioners, for instance, work with individual clients who are also concurrently attending aftercare groups at hospitals or in the community. When concurrent individual and group counseling are provided by different therapists, what is important is for the two clinicians to work cooperatively (with the client's permission to communicate with each other), so that the goals of individual counseling and group counseling are understood by all parties. Decisions regarding concurrent individual counseling and group counseling are multifaceted; they are influenced by the setting in which the counseling takes place, by the client's needs, and by the theoretical orientation and preferences of the practitioner.

Limits of Self-Disclosure

In the previous chapter, we discussed how overextending the boundaries of self-disclosure when counseling an individual client can create dual relationship conflicts or boundary concerns. Such self-disclosure creates special problems in a group setting. As counselors, if we use the groups we lead to obtain our own therapy, we will create confusing relationships. Are we the leaders of the group, or merely another member? As leaders, we need to monitor our self-disclosure so that we are aware of what we are sharing and why we are sharing certain personal information. Group leaders need to think carefully about *what, how much,* and *when* to disclose personal reactions in group counseling and develop guidelines to determine what kinds of disclosure are helpful and what kinds might bog down the group.

This vignette reveals Glen's philosophy and practices regarding self-disclosure:

> Glen makes it a practice to be very self-disclosing in the men's groups that he facilitates in a community agency setting. He believes that one of the best ways to facilitate openness on the part of the other men is for him to model disclosure of his past and current difficulties as a man. He is also willing to take time to explore a present concern if it is getting in the way of his being present as a group leader. Although he is a skilled group leader with considerable training, he firmly believes that his own realness is what helps to create a trusting and cohesive group.

- What are your thoughts about Glen's willingness to be personal in these groups?
- Do you see any potential ethical or clinical problems in Glen's self-disclosures about his past difficulties as a man? about his present concerns or personal issues?
- What dual relationship or boundary concerns, if any, do you have in this case?

It is not the role of group leaders to use group time to work through their personal problems; however, leaders can engage in a wide range of other self-disclosing behaviors. With few words, they can let members know that they are personally affected by the members' sharing of problems. Members can benefit from knowing that the group leader can identify with their struggles. Leaders can also express their persistent reactions to members in a nonjudgmental and timely way and offer feedback to members. They can model appropriate and timely self-disclosure by expressing their here-and-now reactions to what is taking place within the group, including how they are being affected by individual members. Disclosure that is related to what is going on in the group can be very productive. For example, any persistent feelings, thoughts, and reactions leaders are having about what is happening (or not happening) are generally best revealed. If leaders sense a general reluctance in the group, it is best to talk openly about the reluctance. This kind of leader self-disclosure can be quality feedback to the members, and it can facilitate the group process.

In a productive group, leadership and membership roles sometimes become blurred. However, as group leaders we must not forget our primary role and purpose for being in the group. Our main purpose is to facilitate the self-exploration of others, not to work through our own personal problems. If we become aware of problems, we should consider joining a group in which we do not have leadership responsibilities.

Couples and Family Counseling

As is true for group counseling, boundary issues are often complex when counselors have multiple roles in counseling couples or families. Because of the complexity of their work, couples and family counselors are faced with more potential ethical conflicts than are practitioners who specialize in individual therapy. Because most couples and family counselors focus on the family system as the client rather than on the individual's dynamics, ethical dilemmas can arise in the first session. Under the family systems model, counselors avoid becoming agents of any one family member, believing that all family members contribute to the problems of the entire family. Ethical practice demands that counselors be clear at the beginning of the therapeutic relationship about their commitments and responsibilities to each member of the family.

Counselors who work with couples often encounter ethical dilemmas that involve serving one person's best interest at the expense of the partner's interest. This is especially true when the partners do not have a common purpose for seeking counseling. How do counselors carry out their ethical responsibilities when one partner comes for divorce counseling and the other has the expectation of working to improve the marriage? Addressing this conflict can be especially challenging when the motivations of one or both partners for participating in couples counseling are part of a hidden agenda.

Defining boundaries, clarifying the therapeutic goals, and managing multiple roles and relationships are particularly important in couples and family counseling. Questions that provide a framework for our discussion here include the following:

- What unique boundary issues arise in couples and family counseling?
- Are role conflicts inherent in counseling a couple while seeing each of the partners individually?
- Are role conflicts inherent in counseling an individual family member and the entire family?
- Are role conflicts inherent working with a couple while working with the entire family?

Special Considerations for Couples and Family Counseling

As we have mentioned, some boundary issues apply in a special way in couples and family therapy. A counselor's loss of boundaries in couples or family counseling can create inappropriate alliances and render the therapy ineffective.

Consider this example:

> Paul, an intern, was counseling a couple who came to therapy to work out problems in their marriage. Paul increasingly came to view the wife as overbearing and rigid. As the supervisor observed a session, she noted that Paul's responses to the husband were generally supportive, whereas his responses to the wife's verbalizations were often challenging or nonempathic. When the supervisor met with Paul and asked him what he was experiencing in the session, Paul replied, "I don't see how he can stand being married to her!"

In this example, Paul colluded with the husband, in effect lining up with him against the wife.

- If you were Paul's supervisor, how might you work with Paul?
- Might you point out that Paul had created an implicit and unacknowledged dual relationship as the husband's defender and advocate?

Dual relationships can arise for marriage and family therapists in other, more obvious ways. When the therapist has a prior relationship with either a husband or a wife, or with one member of a family, marriage and family therapists recognize the inadvisability of entering into a counseling relationship with the couple or the family. Social relationships with couples or families who are currently in counseling are generally to be avoided. When an individual has been in counseling, and then wishes to change the focus of the counseling to marriage or family therapy, some therapists refer the case to another professional. The prior individual therapeutic relationship might present some difficulties for the newly entering spouse or family members who might not feel on an equal footing.

In marital and family practice, a counselor might see a wife in individual counseling, and then at some point the husband might join the sessions for couples counseling, and at times the entire family might be seen. Some therapists may not be comfortable with this practice, and they may have difficulty in sorting out primary allegiances. In particular, confidentiality questions are likely to arise, and counselors need to be clear about their policies regarding secrets and hidden agendas.

Systems theory is based on a different orientation than individual therapy. In doing individual counseling, we may be sensitive to how an individual's changes affect his or her family, and we may explore ways in which the client's family is now influencing him or her, but the primary focus is on the individual's dynamics. From a systems perspective, one part of the system affects the whole system, and the system affects the individual. Margolin (1982) argued that complex dilemmas can arise when family members are seen together in therapy. Some interventions that serve one person's best interests might burden another family member or even be countertherapeutic. Family counselors need to make intricate judgment calls in attempting to balance their therapeutic responsibilities toward individual family members and toward the family as a whole.

A Contributor's Perspective

In the following article, Amy Manfrini, a marriage and family therapist in private practice, addresses boundary issues of special significance to working with couples and families.

Boundary Considerations in Counseling Couples and Families

Amy Manfrini

Boundaries play a central role in all counseling relationships due in part to the differential power relationship between therapist and client. As a practicing marriage and family therapist for 20 years, I have observed the important and powerful role that boundaries play in a clinical setting.

People often enter treatment in a state of disorganization, feeling vulnerable and fragile. Clients will relinquish some of their own authority, allowing the therapist to be very influential in their lives. As a marital and family therapist, my goal is to establish and maintain a healthy working alliance, rather than one of power or control. This makes it critical that I clearly define the nature and limits for therapy from the outset of a professional relationship.

Couples and families in treatment are often already struggling with boundary concerns and experiencing chaos in their own relationships, making it especially important that I be clear in the description and parameters of the therapy relationship. I don't want to compound their situation, or increase their confusion, by setting poor boundaries myself.

Conversely, being too rigid can cause the therapeutic environment to feel cold and uninviting. Clients need to experience therapy as a safe and secure place where they are supported and encouraged to take risks. I strive for a good balance between being warm, caring, and authentic, yet professional. Boundaries initially are set by clearly conveying my professional role at the initial session. Overall, ethical guidelines regarding boundaries are similar across client groups. When treating couples and families, however, it is important to consider these additional factors regarding boundaries:

- Defining the client: Who will be the focus of treatment? What boundary issues should be considered in couples and family therapy when making this decision? Can this change?
- Avoiding alignment and collusion: How do I prevent crossing or violating boundaries with one particular member of a couple or family? What should I do to avoid this?
- Using self-disclosure: When do I disclose personal information about myself with couples and families, and for what purpose?

Defining the Client

The first decision to make as a marriage and family therapist is who will be the focus of treatment. I begin to consider this as early as the initial phone call. When presenting problems involve couples or family issues, I prefer to see everybody in the relationship for the intake assessment. This allows me to evaluate more accurately whether it will be an individual, couples, or family therapy case. Who my client or clients will be is actually my first boundary consideration. It is important to decide and clearly define who is the focus of treatment from the beginning. Failure to do so can result in a poorly defined professional relationship and, later, confusion for everybody. Consider this scenario:

> In an initial phone call, a distraught wife asking for marriage counseling requests that I meet with her individually for the first session. She wants to share private information regarding her husband and facts about his recent extramarital affair. I let her know that this is actually a fairly common request from new clients, and that although it may be more comfortable for her to share this without him present, I prefer to meet with them together for the initial assessment, as well as for subsequent sessions.

Because I describe my boundaries prior to beginning treatment, this potential client understands where my focus will be and can make an informed decision about selecting me as a therapist.

Sometimes individual treatment, as well as couples or family therapy, is required. Several issues and needs might be identified, leaving the therapist to decide whether to treat only the couple or family or also to provide individual therapy separately. In my own practice, I lean toward treating couples and families as a unit whenever possible rather than seeing any of them individually at the same time. I haven't always practiced this way and have, in fact, treated people in many settings and different configurations throughout the years.

Sometimes a therapist may decide to work with a child individually once family therapy has been completed or to switch to couples therapy following individual treatment with one of the partners. The challenge is to make a clinically sound decision to switch modalities. If the therapist repeatedly switches back and forth between treating the relationship and one or more individuals, it can become confusing, counterproductive to treatment, and even harmful to clients. The focus of treatment should be clear at all times, and a clinically sound rationale should guide the decision to transition. Each case should be considered separately and any risks weighed carefully. The decision should be made collaboratively with the clients, informing them of any ramifications that can be foreseen. It is very important to be proactive and openly address what each client might experience and what concerns he or she may have. This helps redefine clear boundaries around who the client is and reduces the risk of later confusion.

There is no standard rule that dictates how a therapist should make the sometimes difficult decision regarding whom to treat. What informs my decision to see people together primarily is my belief that people's relationships are the most important aspects of their lives. Children want to feel good in their families, and partners want to be fulfilled in their marriages and relationships. I prefer an experiential approach in which people change the way they operate together, or relate to one another, within our sessions. Many therapists do, however, see people both together and separately.

The therapist who is the sole provider of treatment for members of a family or couple together and separately has the advantage of having all the information regarding each member of the couple or family available for evaluation. Thus, treatment goals can be designed to be congruent, compatible, and easily monitored. Another advantage is that clients are generally secure when one therapist provides all of their treatment and often are clearer about what to expect. They may feel less fragmented and less overwhelmed when only one person manages their case. With such an arrangement, there is less chance of having conflicting treatment goals for each case.

Theoretically, this approach can be very valuable as long as clear and healthy boundaries are maintained, but practically speaking I believe this is a challenging task. As a general rule, I work with couples only in conjoint sessions. Remaining clearly focused on a couple or family while treating members separately requires remarkable insight and awareness on my part to avoid becoming overly attached to or aligned with a particular individual. I need to be objective and attentive to the needs of all parties at all times to coordinate treatment effectively.

Other challenges include maintaining equal rapport with each separate client while keeping a solid and equally supportive relationship with the couple or family. Clients may perceive me as more devoted to the needs of their partner or another family member than to the relationship itself. If my focus becomes unclear, I may become more invested in one particular person, which would result in a conflict of interest.

These concerns are very difficult to predict or to control. Although safeguards such as informed consent can help, they may not prevent serious boundary crossings or even violations. This not only risks the integrity of the therapy relationship but can seriously undermine treatment. Therapists should seriously examine the risks to treatment when deciding what method to use. Consider this scenario:

> While working with a couple on communication and intimacy issues, I also agree to treat the wife individually for depression stemming from childhood abuse and explore how this impairs her ability to be close to her husband. I witness her emotional struggle and hard work in individual sessions week after week. Although the husband is aware of her past, he remains frustrated in our couples sessions because things aren't improving more quickly.

Because I witness the wife's struggle, I may tend toward nurturing, supporting, or even defending her in the couples sessions. This would constitute a boundary crossing with serious clinical ramifications. I am blurring my professional role as a therapist with her and assuming a protective position. This is counterproductive to her therapy and undermines her role as an adult. It would undoubtedly damage my rapport with the husband and probably would lead to trust issues, which would undermine the couples sessions. The end results would most likely include confused and frustrated clients, harm to the therapeutic relationship, and poor counseling outcomes.

Another reason I specifically choose to treat couples jointly is based on my view that growth in marriages and partnerships occurs most powerfully within the relationship itself. Productive individual work can occur within the context of joint sessions. One key advantage of seeing people together is that what happens in the session can be directly observed. Rather than simply hearing about how they view themselves as a couple, the therapist can ask them to talk directly to each other. This method fosters increased intimacy and understanding between partners and adds a powerful dimension to the therapy. In cases where couples are not able to work within such an intimate context, for whatever reasons, I might refer them for adjunct treatment with separate therapists. I then would work collaboratively with the other involved therapists to share treatment goals, discuss progress, and avoid conflicting or opposing therapeutic agendas for our clients.

My practice when treating families is to see all members together for at least part of each session. This reinforces the boundary around the whole family as the focus of treatment and keeps the primary emphasis on the family as a whole. Often it is clinically helpful to split families into subgroups, or smaller configurations, for some work, such as parents, siblings, older or younger children, biological or step-family members, brothers, or sisters. Subgroup work can help families establish or redefine unclear or unhealthy boundaries between or among them, as this example shows:

> While treating a recently divorced single father and his two elementary school-age children for adjustment issues, it became apparent to me that both children were very worried about their father. They described him as "sad and lonely." The children reported and appeared to feel responsible for "making him feel better." One of my treatment goals was to assist the father in his adjustment as a single parent, empowering him in this role while also providing him with support. This removed the responsibility from his children, allowing them instead to explore some of their own age-appropriate adjustment issues to their new circumstances. Each week, I met with the three of them for a few minutes, then split them into parent/sibling subgroups. By doing this, I was able to provide the children with time to process feelings and thoughts regarding their experience as children of divorce and assist their father in gaining confidence and adjusting to his new role, while remaining focused on the well-being of their newly configured family unit of three.

When splitting families into subgroups, it is important to explain the process. Children might want opportunities to talk freely without parents present, and parents may need time to discuss parenting or marital issues without children present. My experience is that parents and children usually respond well to the idea of subgroup work, and improvements in the family often emerge as a result of having clear and healthier boundaries reestablished in the therapy setting.

Discussing rules about sharing information outside of counseling is also important. Setting guidelines for communicating once everybody leaves and for continuing discussions at home can be addressed in an effort to keep the therapeutic environment a safe and productive place. This speaks to the importance of clarifying relationships both in and outside of therapy.

Avoiding Alignment and Collusion

Another threat to clear boundaries when working with couples and families is becoming aligned or colluding with a particular individual rather than keeping the relationship the focal point of treatment. Just like individual therapists, relationship therapists can find themselves especially connected or attached to a particular person. It is common to experience strong feelings such as sympathy, frustration, or even anger toward clients. This often occurs unconsciously. We are trained as counselors to be self-aware, regulating and monitoring our countertransference responses. Alignment or collusion is similar and requires the same degree of personal insight on the therapist's part. When regularly working with two or more people in their marriage or family, therapists are likely to have different feelings toward each client. Couples and family therapists need to stay equally focused on the concerns of each client in the relationship and avoid putting their own feelings or needs above those of the couple or family.

Working with a family where both parents are disengaged from a child who presents with depression might elicit strong feelings of sadness from me. I may find myself sympathetic and be tempted to align with and nurture the child. An empathic response here would be normal and therapeutically healthy on my part, but alignment with the child would be clinically inappropriate. If I were to act as the child's rescuer, I would blur the therapeutic boundaries and impair my professional judgment. I should, instead, maintain clear professional limits while addressing the disengagement in this family. I can remain warm and supportive to all family members while providing information and education that will help the parents to assume a more nurturing role with their child.

Using Self-Disclosure

A general guideline regarding therapist self-disclosure is that it should be used to benefit the therapeutic relationship or treatment process. A risk is that self-disclosure can change or distort the boundaries in therapy, complicating treatment. As opposed to being something to avoid, however, I believe that revealing personal information can be very helpful when used appropriately. I am mainly concerned about *when* and *how* to make personal disclosures to clients. It is essential that my disclosures are always done to benefit the client. In the early stages of treatment, developing rapport with new clients can be enhanced through the selective use of disclosure.

When working with children in family therapy, I might compliment a child on her shoes, telling her I have a daughter who likes them as well. This can encourage more conversation and allow us to develop a friendly, easy rapport. Validating a client's experience and conveying empathy can also be an appropriate use of self-disclosure, which can normalize an experience when a client feels isolated or alone.

Families and couples often present similar complaints. Issues of balancing responsibilities, managing finances, parenting styles, communication patterns, and emotional or physical intimacy are common presenting problems in relationships. When two parents work outside the home and struggle with juggling household and child care responsibilities, I often have shared that my husband and I also have faced these demands. In a family where parenting styles differ, I might disclose that most parents, including my husband and myself, bring different strengths and weaknesses to the table, resulting in parenting conflicts.

Disclosure can benefit treatment, but it can also hinder the process and threaten therapeutic boundaries. Timing, frequency, content, and rationale are all aspects to consider, but remain at the discretion of the therapist. When and what to share is a subjective decision. I don't disclose often, nor do I usually disclose deeply personal information. If clients ask for personal information, I consider the length and nature of our working alliance, their ego strength, and the purpose for their interest. Sometimes they simply want to know they aren't alone, or that their situation is not hopeless. Often they need another point of reference. However, at other times clients may simply be curious or want to learn more about me, and this is something that needs to be explored in the therapeutic process.

Questions for Reflection

Some considerations unique to boundaries with couples and families in therapy include identifying the client, keeping the definition of the therapeutic relationship clear, and maintaining a treatment environment that is safe, caring, and productive. My ability to establish and maintain limits in my personal life and interpersonal relationships will affect my ability to do so in my clinical work. Professionals who have boundary issues with interpersonal relationships will likely have difficulties establishing and maintaining appropriate limits with clients. It is useful to explore the following questions when considering your own role in couples or family counseling:

- How were the boundaries in your own family of origin defined? How did this early experience in relationships shape the way you establish and maintain boundaries in your current personal relationships?
- What are your tendencies in your own marriage, or partnership, as they relate to role definitions and boundaries? How might your experience with your significant other influence your expectations regarding roles and boundaries with couples you treat in therapy?
- When working with families in therapy, what potential issues may you need to address pertaining to roles and boundaries, and what areas do you need to further explore to help you set clear and useful boundaries with your clients?

It is of paramount importance that we remain insightful and aware, remembering that clients rely on the therapeutic relationship to be supportive. If we do not recognize the importance of boundaries, or know how to set and maintain them, we invite poor counseling results and in worst case scenarios can do harm.

Clear and clinically sound rules, roles, and limits should be set from the very beginning of treatment and monitored and maintained throughout the course of the professional relationship. Because couples and families often enter therapy confused in their own relationships and face the additional tasks of disclosure and confrontation of loved ones within the therapy context, clarity and safety are particularly important. Keep your clinical position clear, but allow your personal strengths to help create an environment and relationship conducive to growth. Be warm and empathic while also remaining professional and competent. Be cautious about decisions to provide family or marital therapy while also treating the same people in individual therapy, and use personal disclosure wisely.

Through many years of practice, I have come to depend upon these guidelines when working with couples and families. Regardless of what guiding principles you adopt in your own work, considering and respecting their function and importance in the treatment process is imperative.

Conclusions

This chapter is the first of three chapters that focus on specialty areas within counseling. Harriet L. Glosoff discussed boundary issues in private practice, articulating how these issues can be complicated by isolation, geographical and cultural factors, and the financial exigencies involved in self-employment.

Boundary issues are fraught with complexities when counselors work with multiple clients, both in a group format and in couples or family counseling. In group counseling, questions arise regarding personal and social relationships with group members, admitting former individual clients or friends into groups, providing both individual and group counseling to the same client, and group leader self-disclosure. Couples and family counselors must be alert to potential role conflicts as well. Amy Manfrini offered a practitioner's perspective on how to best manage these conflicts.

Focus on Specialty Areas

Substance Abuse Counseling
Counseling Clients Living With HIV
Rehabilitation Counseling
Forensic Psychology and Counseling

In this chapter, we continue our focus on specialty areas, examining boundary questions and concerns that arise in the fields of substance abuse counseling, counseling clients who are living with HIV, rehabilitation counseling, and forensic psychology and counseling. Our own experience with these specializations is limited, so we rely greatly on the expertise of our four guest contributors: Laura J. Veach for substance abuse counseling, Craig D. Kain for counseling clients with HIV, Hal Cain for rehabilitation counseling, and Robert Haynes for forensic psychology.

Substance Abuse Counseling

Substance abuse counselors who are themselves in recovery face some unique boundary issues in their therapeutic relationships with clients. We turn now to Laura J. Veach's thoughts on these issues.

A Contributor's Perspective

Boundary Issues in Addiction and Substance Abuse Counseling

Laura J. Veach

Some of the major challenges for substance abuse/addiction counselors relate to boundary issues. The field of addiction and substance abuse counseling has changed in many ways during the past 20 years. A field once dominated by recovering counselors with a wide range of education and minimal formal training now has a growing prevalence of master's-level counselors. For example, 60% of the National Association for Addiction Professionals (NAADAC, 2003) members surveyed indicated they held a master's degree or doctorate. The addictions counseling field has demonstrated a preference for advanced training and credentials for counselors entering the field. Currently, there are substance abuse/addiction counselor certification or licensure boards throughout the United States and in other countries (International Certification & Reciprocity Consortium/Alcohol and Other Drug Abuse, 2003). In a study reviewing 55 addiction counselor certification boards, including the District of Columbia and the U.S. Navy, representing 32,991 counselors certified in substance abuse or addiction counseling, all participating boards indicated they have formal policies and procedures for filing and investigating any complaint pertaining to ethical issues (St. Germaine, 1997).

Even as ethical guidelines and training are being stressed, some boundary issues unique to substance abuse or addiction counseling settings remain challenging. Toriello and Benshoff (2003) pointed out that "substance abuse counselors operate within an extremely complex environment" (p. 84). On the basis of reviews from a multisite study funded by the National Institute on Alcohol Abuse and Alcoholism (Finney, 2002; Polcin, 2000), there is increasing evidence that the predominant treatment model, with its emphasis on Twelve Step Facilitation (TSF), is effective. Because TSF is a significant part of addiction treatment in the United States, it is important to examine some of the most challenging boundary issues related to counselors working with TSF, which include dual relationships, ethics training, and ethical guidelines.

Dual relationships in addiction counseling can be complicated due to additional contact with clients outside the formal counseling environment; St. Germaine (1996) noted that 47.5% of addiction counselors surveyed inadvertently came across clients outside of their counseling setting. At times, encountering a client outside the formal counseling setting may occur in a mutual-help group, such as a 12 step group. Addiction counselors who are recovering from their own personal addiction often attend local 12 step meetings (Doyle, 1997). In addition, nonrecovering counselors who are working with a TSF treatment model may also attend 12 step groups to learn more about the groups to which they are referring their clients.

Soon after I completed my master's degree in counseling, I accepted a position in a nonprofit agency treating substance abuse and addiction. Both recovering and nonrecovering counselors strongly urged me to attend open 12 step meetings, particularly AlAnon meetings, to learn more about healthy detachment, boundary setting, and enabling. Over 22 years of counseling in the addiction field with the TSF model and other counseling approaches, I am grateful for such astute advice. I learned helpful guidelines to address dual relationships and to minimize inherent problematic issues.

Professional Boundaries and 12 Step Meetings

It is strongly emphasized that counselors who may see current clients in a 12 step meeting keep in mind that "what is heard in meetings, stays in meetings." The 12 step fellowship cites the 12 traditions as important guidelines for its membership, and the 8th tradition clearly indicates there are professional boundaries: "Many of our members are professionals in their own right, but there is no room for professionalism in N.A." (Narcotics Anonymous, 1988, p. 69). Recovering counselors often are faced with deciding which "hat" they are wearing in trying to delineate between their roles as professional counselor and as recovering person (Bissell & Royce, 1994; Doyle, 1997; Polcin, 2000; Powell, 1993). It is important that counselors clearly communicate to clients that they will not act in a professional role as counselor while attending a 12 step meeting. Preferably, this clarification is established in the professional setting *before* a new client faces an awkward encounter with the counselor at a 12 step meeting. The counselor can reiterate the main purpose for attending recovery meetings is for his or her own personal growth. Clear communication with informed consent, clarification about confidentiality guidelines, and caution help clarify this boundary for the counselor and the client.

Another aspect of duality unique to the addiction field relates to counselor self-disclosure in 12 step or alternative meetings with a similar focus on recovery (Polcin, 2000). The potential for harm to a current client can increase if a counselor from the facility where the client is receiving counseling discloses personal issues; for example, current job dissatisfaction at the treatment center. Counselors may limit their personal disclosures in 12 step meetings due to concerns about dual relationship issues and instead are strongly encouraged to share with their sponsor, rather than the entire group, issues that are causing them personal stress. It is often emphasized that significant benefits are experienced by 12 step members who do more listening than talking in a meeting; it can be beneficial to hear how others have handled troubling life issues. It is quite acceptable for a person to bring up a topic around a life struggle without sharing any personal details and request sharing on that topic. A counselor attending a meeting might request sharing on topics such as effective ways to handle work stressors or self-care ideas. The more personal details of struggles (such as job dissatisfaction) are shared with one's sponsor, who is another recovering member with quality recovery who can offer guidance regarding steps toward healthy living. In addition, counselors or supervisors are strongly encouraged to avoid being a sponsor for a client or supervisee (Powell, 1993). Addiction professionals may also find it helpful to attend 12 step meetings or other alternative self-help meetings of their choice that are primarily composed of professionals like themselves. For example, Caduceus groups, primarily composed of recovering physicians, offer support for health care professionals recovering from chemical dependence.

Special Issues of Confidentiality

Facilities that provide counseling for addiction need to provide written guidelines in professional disclosure statements and in their informed consent documents that specifically address the assurance of confidentiality, anonymity, and a distinct separation of the recovering community from the treatment facility (Bissell & Royce, 1994; Dove, 1995; Sayre, 1992).

For example, in some treatment settings, such as a halfway house where recovering addicts often reside after completion of an intensive phase of treatment, clients are expected by clinicians to be employed. Written guidelines need to be developed and clearly communicated to all employees working with clients when potentially exploitive hiring practices are a possibility. Many clients with skills and abilities need to earn money while in early recovery and struggle to do so while experiencing repeated employment rejections. When a client has difficulty securing gainful employment, the addiction professional may be tempted to hire the client on a temporary basis to help the client and benefit the professional with readily available labor for a home project, such as house painting. However, what seems like an innocent means of reaching out has the potential to harm the client. This could be the case if the job is not completed in a satisfactory manner and the counselor is then faced with increasingly negative feelings toward a client. Each agency needs clear and written guidelines discouraging temporary employment and other potentially exploitive practices related to hiring recovering clients (Bissell & Royce, 1994).

Ongoing Supervision and Ethics Training

Ongoing ethics training and supervision are necessary to provide guidelines and direction for addiction counselors faced with dual relationships. It is the responsibility of supervisors and administrators involved in addiction counseling to continue developing policy and training for all addiction staff to provide quality care in the most ethical manner possible. Active supervision using live observation or taping sessions can alert the supervisor to potential boundary issues, and proactive steps can be taken to intervene and thereby reduce possible harm (Powell, 1993).

Encouraging findings in a study by Toriello and Benshoff (2003) noted that those addiction professionals with no more than an associate's degree were found to display more sensitivity to ethical dilemmas than those with a bachelor's degree or beyond and that ethics training was a requirement for certification. Often, addiction counselors with advanced degrees but without knowledge of the recovery community can benefit from ethics training with other addiction professionals who share learning they achieved because of their personal understanding of the 12 step community. Finally, certification requirements often include specific amounts of training in ethics for initial and renewing certification (International Certification & Reciprocity Consortium/Alcohol and Other Drug Abuse, 2003).

Summary

The needs of the substance abuse/addiction counselor involve specific considerations regarding dual relationships, especially related to mutual-help group involvement. Improved understanding of the traditions and functions of 12 step groups can be extremely beneficial. Written agency guidelines, continued supervision, and ongoing ethics training are recommended to provide clear professional boundaries for the counselor working in substance abuse and addiction counseling settings.

Counseling Clients Living With HIV

When a counselor is HIV-positive and works with HIV clients, or when a counselor is in recovery from substance abuse disorder and works with clients who are also recovering, multiple role conflicts are bound to arise. Both the HIV community and the recovery community can be quite tightly knit, and opportunities for boundary blurring are common. HIV-positive clients are another special population whose needs can be met only if we are willing to assume some nontraditional roles, such as advocate, case manager, and change agent.

A Contributor's Perspective

Craig D. Kain points out that the HIV/AIDS community is small, and counselors who work with people living with HIV confront many of the same issues as do rural practitioners. They also face unique issues created by the social, political, legal, and economic context in which HIV-positive clients live.

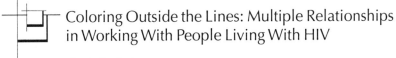

Coloring Outside the Lines: Multiple Relationships in Working With People Living With HIV

Craig D. Kain

It is important that those of us who work with HIV-positive clients demonstrate our humanness in the counseling relationship (Kain, 1996). Because HIV disease is often a dehumanizing illness, at times stripping clients of their physical ability, economic viability, and self-identity, it stands to reason that we must provide them with a genuine, human connection. This may place counselors in a quandary: How do we attend to our clients' needs for genuine human relationship while at the same time maintaining what we believe are good therapeutic practices and boundaries? In my experience, although counselors working with people living with HIV are not required to violate our ethical boundaries, we do need to bend them. We are asked to help our clients draw a picture of their life that, almost by definition, requires coloring outside the lines.

To better understand the quandary, we must first recognize the particular social, political, legal, and economic context in which HIV disease occurs. People living with HIV must contend with social ostracism ranging from mild disapproval to outright prejudice in the form of racism, sexism, and homophobia. They must place their trust for a better future in a political system that influences everything from what types of research on HIV get funded to what types of drugs get approved. People living with HIV must navigate a legal system that regulates crucial aspects of their lives, from the types of disability compensation for which they qualify to the types of visitors they may have in the hospital. Finally, HIV-positive people in this country must work their way through a system that links health care to economic status and thus often provides insufficient health care for those who lack funds. As counselors, we too must work within these contexts. We must keep them in mind because they exert an enormous influence on the decisions we make regarding the types of relationships we will have with our clients.

For these reasons as well as many others, counselors working with HIV-positive clients are often called upon to assume multiple roles (e.g., case manager, client advocate, confidant). It is important for us to remember that these roles define our relationship with our client. To me, it is not so much that we have multiple relationships but rather that our one relationship with our client is determined by these varied roles.

We may be asked to perform tasks often considered within the scope of a case manager, which means we will have relationships with our clients outside the typical counseling session. For example, our clients may need an emergency ride to their primary physician, and we may be the only person they know to ask to arrange for it. Whether we assist the client directly (i.e., physically transport the client) or indirectly (i.e., offer to pay for a taxi), we need to recognize that we have colored outside the lines. Clients may need someone to visit them in the hospital. We may find that they do not want therapy so much as companionship and friendship. Clients may need someone to be their advocate in interactions with a government office. They may assume, often correctly, that our professional status could help them move through bureaucratic delays. In these and other similar situations, our human desire to be of service to others may in our minds overshadow our professional obligations. Still, we always need to be cognizant of the ways in which we are bending our professional boundaries. We will need to discuss these with colleagues and, when appropriate, with our clients.

At times we may find ourselves being asked to counsel others in our clients' lives. We may be called upon to serve as an individual counselor to a significant other, conjoint counselor, or family counselor. Although we may try to refer to others, the crisis nature of HIV counseling often negates our best-made plans. For example, if we are asked to see clients in their homes, others attending to their care may ask to be included (or in our judgment need to be included) in treatment. When these situations occur, we must make certain that all parties are aware of our multiple roles.

Our own personal roles may often come in conflict with more narrowly defined ideas of counselor–client interaction. The HIV/AIDS community is a small one. Thus, if we are actively involved in AIDS education, advocacy, or fund-raising, we are likely to meet clients in social situations. Given the social, economic, and political nature of HIV disease, our involvement in these activities is crucial and thus these situations are not easily avoided.

Another way in which our own personal lives may increase the number of roles we maintain with clients is if we are HIV-positive. Given the limited number of social and support activities for people living with HIV, we may, without anticipating it, find ourselves attending the same functions as our clients. Unlike the situations described previously, in which we maintain our expert status, in these situations we are clients. Similarly, we may unexpectedly run into a client in our physician's waiting area, especially if the physician is a well-known HIV specialist. Although this is not the same as actively seeking out a friendship with a client, it does change the nature of the counseling relationship. Can we in good conscience be in the same support group, attend the same social functions, or wait in the same reception area as our clients? The answer, as is true of many questions about HIV, is not clear-cut. Pursuing other options may be a possibility for counselors in some locales, but in other areas where HIV-related services are more limited, these doctors, groups, and social functions may be the only place where HIV-positive people (clients and counselors) can obtain treatment, support, and camaraderie.

If we are faculty members in counselor education programs and also work within the HIV/AIDS community, our roles may be stretched in different ways. HIV-positive students may see our office as a "safe place" and may disclose their HIV status to us. They may ask us to keep their status confidential, which may place us in an awkward position of balancing our duty to the student with our duty to our educational institution. It is important to remember that our role as faculty member is defined differently from that of counselor or therapist. Students may not always recognize this, and it is our responsibility to inform students of any differences that may exist.

When we work with clients and students living with HIV, we constantly must be alert to how our relationships with them encompass multiple roles. To me, what is important is not whether we enter into these multiple roles (for I am convinced that doing so is an inevitable part of the work we do) but *how* we enter these roles. Do we enter into them with our eyes open or closed? Do we acknowledge these multiple roles with our clients and students, or do we try to minimize them? Do we encourage clients and students to talk with us about the effects on them (both positive and negative) of these multiple roles, or do we avoid such discussions for fear that we will be accused of overstepping our boundaries? Do we actively seek consultation when we become confused (or anticipate becoming confused) about a multiple-role situation, or do we shy away from talking with colleagues for fear of being judged unprofessional or unethical? Are we aware of our own limits when we take on new roles, in terms of our education, experience, and training, to do the new tasks these roles may require? Are we equally aware of our personal limits, of our comfort in taking on new HIV-related roles, and of our emotional capacity to engage in such activities? The clearer we can be about these multiple roles with ourselves, our clients, and those to whom we turn for professional and personal guidance, the more we can rest assured that we are drawing outside the lines in the service of our clients.

Rehabilitation Counseling

Rehabilitation counselors facilitate the personal, social, and economic independence of persons with disabilities and, more specifically, help these persons find or return to employment. Counselors take active measures to eliminate attitudinal barriers toward people with disabilities and strive to increase their own awareness and sensitivity to these individuals. They function in the role of advocate and work toward empowerment of clients by supporting their efforts at self-advocacy both on an individual and an organizational level (CRCC, 2001).

Rehabilitation counselors face some difficult issues involving role conflicts and divided loyalties because they work in both the public and private sectors and serve multiple constituencies. Each of these constituencies has a vested interest in the outcome of counseling, and these interests are often competing and contradictory. For rehabilitation counselors—who may serve as counselor, gatekeeper to services, evaluator, and expert witness—the question is not one of dual roles but rather of multiple roles. Because they have multiple obligations—to the client, to their employer, to the customer (the one who pays the bill), and to society—it is especially important that they be clear about their primary loyalties.

A Contributor's Perspective

In the following contribution, Hal Cain addresses the areas in which multiple relationships and role conflicts are likely to present problems for rehabilitation counselors.

 Roles and Conflicts for Rehabilitation Counselors

Hal Cain

Rehabilitation counseling is a profession within the larger context of counseling professions. Rehabilitation counselors provide services in both the public and private sectors to a diverse group of individuals who have various types of disabilities. The locations and settings for these services include educational settings, medical facilities, industry-based rehabilitation programs, and government agencies. The many roles that an individual rehabilitation counselor must assume, regardless of his or her setting, include advocate, psychotherapist, service broker, job coach, case manager, and educator. It is not uncommon for rehabilitation counselors to be equally involved with employers or school administrators, other professionals, third-party payers, family members, and the client all at the same time.

Because the scope of practice for rehabilitation counseling is broad and the venues in which it takes place vary greatly, rehabilitation counselors, as a group, may have a greater risk potential for role conflict than other counselors. The expanding range of what constitutes rehabilitation counseling makes it impossible to identify all the potential role conflicts for practitioners.

However, there are at least three major areas in which dual relationships and role conflicts are likely to present problems for rehabilitation counselors. These areas are case management, dealing with third-party payer relationships, and advocacy.

Case Management

A role often assumed by rehabilitation counselors is the coordination of clients' rehabilitation service plans. In this role, the rehabilitation counselor becomes the case manager. The dual role of case manager and counselor, which may be seen as inherent in the work of the rehabilitation counselor, carries several potential areas of role conflict.

The nature of case management dictates communication and collaboration with other service providers, intra- or interagency, and often brokering for or purchasing services from these other professionals. Because a case manager is the liaison between a client and other services, he or she is essentially the gatekeeper to other rehabilitation services. This position carries with it the need to be equitable in all professional relationships. A rehabilitation counselor who is also the case manager has to balance the primary client–counselor relationship with these other relationships to avoid conflicts between counseling and management responsibilities.

Having managerial powers over a client's rehabilitation services plan may be seen as advantageous for the rehabilitation counselor in that overseeing beneficial services gives a counselor greater flexibility in assuring comprehensive services geared toward positive outcomes (e.g., competitive employment, independent living). Indeed, many rehabilitation counselors function as case managers, especially in government agencies, and help their clients achieve more independence through acquisition of needed services. Nevertheless, rehabilitation counselors who are case managers may also find themselves torn between the client's wishes and what is deemed by other professionals to be in the client's best interests. For example, a client states during a counseling session that he is unhappy with his occupational therapist (OT) and no longer wants to attend occupational therapy. The rehabilitation counselor has observed that this client tends to avoid difficult situations and suspects that the client's displeasure with the OT is related to the OT's "pushing the limits" (within acceptable practice). As a case manager, the rehabilitation counselor must recognize and respect the client's right to refuse treatment. What "hat" does the rehabilitation counselor wear in this situation? If it is the counseling hat, the counselor is most likely to work with the client on personal issues such as self-efficacy and control. But the counselor wearing a case management hat will want to see the client stay with the rehabilitation plan as written, with a focus on successful case closure. This may involve working with the client on compliance issues or a change of OTs. Either way, the case manager's concern is with program issues and not intrapersonal issues. Although the two hats are not incompatible, one focuses on the treatment plan as priority and the other on individual development.

Another potential conflict resulting from the case manager/counselor dual role has to do with risk to the therapeutic relationship. Clients may lose trust in a rehabilitation counselor if they believe the counselor is more concerned with meeting the needs of others (e.g., service providers, insurance companies) involved with the rehabilitation plan. If case managers/ counselors spend most of their time with clients talking about other team members' reports regarding the client's program, they run the risk of depersonalizing the counselor–client relationship. Discord in the therapeutic relationship can also be created when a client feels pressure to comply with treatment because a rehabilitation counselor, as the case manager, holds the "purse strings" to the client's case.

In addition to role conflicts resulting from a rehabilitation counselor's split focus, caseload size may limit the amount of time spent providing direct counseling services. Many rehabilitation counselors in the public sector, and a growing number in the private sector, have caseloads so large that it is difficult (if not impossible) to meet with clients frequently enough to build good counseling relationships. Some government agency rehabilitation counselors carry a caseload of more than 150 clients. More clients means the case management responsibilities are greater and counseling per se is often forced to take second priority.

Rehabilitation counselors who are having case manager/counselor dual relationships with clients must find some way to differentiate counseling functions from case management activities. One strategy that may help avoid conflicts is to discuss with each client, at the beginning of services, what roles the counselor will have in the rehabilitation process and the limitations and advantages of each role. Involving clients in all aspects of the development of their rehabilitation plan also helps avoid misunderstandings that could lead to conflict. Clear expectations on the part of both the rehabilitation counselor and the client will reduce the risk of role conflict.

Third-Party Payer Relationships

Most rehabilitation counselors, whether working in private or public sector rehabilitation, will deal with third-party payers. Third-party payers can be insurance companies, government agencies, or other funding sources that do not come directly from client fees for service. Whether the counselor is in private practice or works in an agency, role conflict in third-party payer situations stems from confusion as to who is considered the client—the payer or the person who is receiving the rehabilitation services.

The dilemmas that can lead to role conflict for rehabilitation counselors arise from working within the guidelines, limitations, and controls of funding sources. For example, insurance companies usually have limits on the amount of reimbursement for therapy services and adaptive equipment for each rehabilitation case. If a rehabilitation counselor believes a client needs therapy or other expenditures beyond what is provided in the client's insurance policy, this creates problems. Rehabilitation counselors faced with this situation can either revise the rehabilitation plan to accommodate the policy's fiscal constraints or attempt to justify a plan that they believe will best serve the needs of the client.

When funding sources are public or private not-for-profit, limitations on clients' rehabilitation plans are sometimes due to the lack of financial resources. Administrative restrictions that may affect the quality of services provided also will cause role conflict for rehabilitation counselors who, as professionals, have a duty to exercise their best clinical judgment in carrying out their obligations to the person receiving services, that is, the client. Again, the control issue arises.

Rehabilitation counselors may find themselves in a role conflict between being an employee of the funding source and a counselor for the client. The Commission on Rehabilitation Counseling Certification (CRCC, 2001) *Code of Professional Ethics for Rehabilitation Counselors* states that rehabilitation counselors are obligated to make clear to their clients their relationships with third-party payers.

Some realities of the limits imposed due to fiscal resources cannot be avoided. Nevertheless, when artificial boundaries are set on the amount and quality of services deemed necessary by the rehabilitation counselor, ethical decisions need to be made. As an employee of the third-party payer, the rehabilitation counselor will try to contain costs. As a counselor serving the interests of the client, the rehabilitation counselor will try to obtain the optimal service mix regardless of the costs.

Providing rehabilitation counseling within the restrictions of third-party payer relationships can be difficult. Potential role conflicts may be avoided if the rehabilitation counselor is aware of the funding limitations and can legitimately say that the client's rehabilitation plan was developed without undue restrictions from the third-party funding source. In cases where the funding source places restrictions that significantly compromise the chances of the client progressing through rehabilitation, ethically the counselor must find alternative resources or make appropriate referrals.

Advocacy

One of the forces behind rehabilitation counseling is that rehabilitation counselors are advocates for persons with disabilities. Advocating for the rights of persons with disabilities and giving input to policy change at all levels are part of a rehabilitation counselor's professional responsibilities. To reinforce the fundamental role of advocate for rehabilitation counselors, the CRCC (2001) added a section in the *Code of Professional Ethics for Rehabilitation Counselors* specifically dealing with advocacy. Role conflicts associated with being a disability rights advocate occur when rehabilitation counselors lose focus on a client's individual needs.

It is sometimes easy for rehabilitation counselors to get caught up in the disability movement and overgeneralize beyond the needs of the individual who is there for services. Rehabilitation counselors must remember that each person who comes to them for services is unique in his or her own set of issues. In addition, rehabilitation counselors may sometimes be overzealous in their role as advocates and not leave room for clients to share in that activity. In doing so, clients sometimes lose the opportunity to learn to be self-advocates.

Summary

The ultimate goal of rehabilitation counseling is to help individuals with disabilities achieve their full potential in life. To this end, rehabilitation counselors take a holistic approach in serving their clients. Because rehabilitation counselors assume many roles as they carry out their obligations, dual relationships are virtually inevitable. Role conflicts can be minimized if rehabilitation counselors view the client–counselor relationship as the basis of quality service.

Forensic Psychology and Counseling

Psychologists have long been involved in forensic work, and some counselors specialize in working with criminal offenders. With the increasing number of incarcerated criminal offenders and the heightened focus on solving the problems of violent crime, workplace violence, murder and violent behavior among teenagers, and other similar concerns, more psychologists and counselors are entering the criminal justice field than ever before.

A Contributor's Perspective

Robert Haynes draws on his clinical forensic work experience and the 25 years he has invested in guiding clinical and counseling doctoral-level interns through an internship program in a forensic inpatient setting. He describes the challenges of managing multiple relationships in such a setting.

Managing Multiple Relationships in a Forensic Setting

Robert Haynes

In the forensic setting, therapeutic boundaries are often unclear, and the role of the psychologist or counselor is multiple and complex. The mental health professional in a forensic setting serves in a variety of roles and may be called upon to be therapist, evaluator, security enforcer, case manager, expert witness, and predictor of future dangerousness (an imprecise science at best), all for the same client.

A common dilemma for the forensic practitioner is to determine who is the actual client (Lyon & Ogloff, 2000; Monahan, 1980). Is it the individual client, the courts, the state, the victim, or society? For whom, and for whose good, is the practitioner working? Whose goals take priority when conducting therapy? The courts may have mandated therapy to help the client become a law-abiding citizen, but the offender may want to become less guilt ridden about committing a crime. Is it the psychotherapist's role to help the client work for what he or she wants? Or should the therapist challenge or confront the client? It is crucial for the therapist to have a clear picture of the boundaries of the relationship and whose goals take priority before the therapist enters into a professional relationship with the client.

Confidentiality in the true sense is nearly impossible given that the professional is most likely working for the courts, probation, or the state. A trusting relationship is essential in therapy, but it is difficult to achieve in a forensic setting. Therapists can, however, identify with the client those topics that can remain confidential in the therapy relationship and those that cannot. It is then the client's choice whether to delve into areas that cannot be kept confidential. Sometimes a forensic client will venture into the nonconfidential area just to see what the therapist will do and to determine whether the therapist can be manipulated into keeping secrets. Once the therapist keeps confidential any information that should be reported, the therapist has crossed the boundary of the therapeutic relationship and will most likely see an escalation of unusual requests and demands by the client.

When I was working as a psychologist on an inpatient unit, I led group therapy sessions for many clients on the unit. Because I was the only psychologist on that unit, I was often called on to conduct psychological evaluations of clients for the purpose of making recommendations to the court regarding the clients' readiness for release into the community. The dilemmas that I faced involved the ethical issue of being both therapist and evaluator for the same clients and keeping straight the information I had received in the therapeutic setting versus the information I had received in conducting an evaluation. It seems simple to say that one should not function in these multiple roles, yet the workload at the facility and the demands of the courts were substantial. The *Specialty Guidelines for Forensic Psychologists* (American Psychology-Law Society, & Division 41 of APA, 1991) addresses this ethical issue by recommending that

> when it is necessary to provide both evaluation and treatment services to a party in a legal proceeding (as may be the case in small forensic hospital settings or small communities), the forensic psychologist takes reasonable steps to minimize the potential negative effects of these circumstances on the rights of the party, confidentiality, and the process of treatment and evaluation. (Section IV.D.2.)

Although the demands of many forensic settings require the multiple role model of practice, the practitioner can make every effort to minimize conflicts of interest. For example, the practitioner might trade the provision of psychological evaluations with another psychologist to avoid providing both therapy and evaluation with the same client. Therapists must be prepared to identify instances when the ethics of the situation require them to pull back from one or more roles.

Countertransference issues also affect therapeutic boundaries in working with forensic clients. It is important for forensic psychologists and counselors to understand what they can and cannot accomplish with a criminal offender. Much of our training involves learning to support the client and provide a trusting and caring relationship, and we have our own needs to be needed, to be helpful, and to nurture. These needs are often counterproductive with forensic clients and may open the door for the offender to manipulate both the therapist and the system (Meloy, Haroun, & Schiller, 1990; Young, Justice, Erdberg, & Gacono, 2000). Support, trust, and caring may need to be moderated with caution, objectivity, and a watchful eye for manipulation. In particular, working with sociopathic offenders requires a more structured, sometimes confrontive, and always cautious approach.

It is not uncommon for helping professionals in forensic settings to feel dislike, disgust, and even repulsion toward some clients because of the heinous crimes they committed. These feelings can lead professionals to become more comfortable in the role of security enforcer and less comfortable as therapist. The practitioner must be constantly aware of the potential for such feelings and work to keep them in check. According to Mobley (1999), therapists who are most likely to be successful in working with forensic clients are those who can empathize without sympathy, confront without demeaning, care without carrying the client's burdens, direct without controlling, and see manipulation as a poor coping strategy rather than as a personal assault. They find satisfaction in erratic progress toward limited goals, can tolerate the ambiguities and conflicts of the setting, and accept their own limits so that they do not burn out.

Students and supervisees in particular may be faced with judgment calls that require an ability to foresee consequences to their decisions. To give an example, a sociopathic sex offender asked a counseling student to mail a letter to the client's seriously ill sister at the local post office rather than wait for the next day's institutional mail run. The client reported that he was his sister's only family, and that she was depending on him to help her through her life-threatening illness. Although this may appear to be a minor request, if it violates institutional rules, the student who complies has crossed the line and is now assisting the client to violate the rules and work the system. The demands from this client are likely to escalate to more serious violations of institutional policy. In fact, this may be characteristic of the kind of behavior that led to the client's arrest—minor violations that escalated over time.

Not every therapist is suited to work with criminal offenders. Recommendations for psychologists and counselors working in a forensic setting include the following:

- Know your strengths and limitations in working with a forensic population.
- Be aware of how your own values and countertransference issues affect your work.

- Recognize that psychotherapy can be effective with criminal offenders but may require approaches not traditionally taught in graduate school.
- Use colleagues and supervisors as consultants to provide feedback regarding difficult cases and issues.
- Take care of your own mental health. Forensic work can be challenging, exhausting, and demanding.
- Remember that safety and security must be priorities, sometimes at the expense of treatment.
- Become familiar with the standards and principles that apply specifically to forensic psychology, such as the *Specialty Guidelines for Forensic Psychologists* (American Psychology-Law Society, & Division 41 of APA, 1991).

Conclusions

This chapter focused on four distinct specialty areas of practice. They are quite different from each other, yet they share these commonalities: dual and even multiple roles are inherent in the nature of the work, and practitioners need to assume some nontraditional roles if they are to serve their client populations effectively. Certainly, practitioners of many other counseling specialties confront similar issues, and we invite you to consider how the points raised by our chapter contributors might be applied to your own work. For instance, many of the issues raised by Craig D. Kain, regarding work with clients living with HIV/AIDS, and by Hal Cain, with respect to health care delivery in rehabilitation counseling, are equally applicable to counseling clients who are terminally ill in the hospice setting. Many counselors do not consider themselves specialists in forensic work, yet they experience role conflicts when they find themselves involved with the legal system as part of their work with a client. An example of this kind of involvement—when a school counselor has to go to court and testify regarding child abuse or neglect—is discussed in the next chapter.

10

Focus on Specialty Areas

School Counseling
Higher Education

In this chapter, we look at dual or multiple relationship dilemmas that occur in educational settings. We begin with a focus on elementary and secondary schools. Our first guest contributor to this chapter, A. Michael Dougherty, identifies some roles and duties commonly assumed by school counselors that can create dual relationship conflicts. We then move to a discussion of boundary issues in higher education, and Sue Spooner presents her views on this subject.

School Counseling

We believe that school counselors need to be aware of dual relationship issues and that they do encounter multiple role conflicts in their work. These conflicts can arise in subtle and sometimes unexpected ways for school counselors. Two standards in the *Ethical Standards for School Counselors* (ASCA, 2004) address dual relationships.

The professional school counselor:
  a. Avoids dual relationships that might impair his/her objectivity and increase the risk of harm to the student (*e.g.*, counseling one's family members, close friends or associates). If a dual relationship is unavoidable, the counselor is responsible for taking action to eliminate or reduce the potential for harm. Such safeguards might include informed consent, consultation, supervision and documentation.
  b. Avoids dual relationships with school personnel that might infringe on the integrity of the counselor/student relationship. (A.4.a, b.)

Consider these two scenarios involving Wayne and Angelica, both school counselors:

- After school a teacher drops by Wayne's office. Wayne and the teacher are friends. Wayne casually asks, "How's it going?" The teacher's response comes out in a rush. She is feeling tremendously stressed by the demands of raising a child with a handicapping condition, caring for an aging parent, and going to graduate school. When Wayne suggests that she might want to consider seeking counseling, the teacher says, "Where on earth would I find the time or money for that! I hope you won't mind if I just 'bend your ear.'"

• Angelica is conducting a parenting skills group one evening per week. During the fourth session, one of the parents relates an anecdote about the discipline methods he uses. It seems clear to Angelica that these methods are physically abusive.

These two situations seem quite dissimilar, but they both raise potential dual relationship conflicts. In Wayne's case, the teacher hopes to receive—and clearly needs—some free counseling. It might be relatively easy for Wayne to convince himself that it is okay just to listen occasionally in his office after school, and that it is his job to serve the teachers as well as the students. Yet Wayne's friendship with the teacher prohibits him from entering into a counseling relationship.

Angelica, too, might be torn by conflicting wishes. Although she knows she is legally and ethically required to report the child abuse, she foresees the difficulty in attempting to serve both as the parent's ongoing group leader and as reporter of the abuse. She does not want to destroy the parent's trust and perhaps to disrupt the group. She is tempted to avoid or postpone reporting in the hope that the parent will learn nonabusive discipline methods by continuing in the group.

• If you were in Wayne's place, what might you do?
• How might you respond to your friend's request, in a way that both preserves the friendship and assists her to get the help she needs?
• What might you do if you were Angelica?
• How could you best balance the requirements of the law, the needs of the child, the needs of the parent, and the needs of the group?

The situation in which Wayne found himself, in the first scenario, is not at all uncommon. Friendships between teachers and school counselors are a natural outgrowth of their similar interests and daily contacts. In addition, many school counselors were teachers before they became counselors, and sometimes they counsel in the same school where they taught. When the transition first occurs from teacher to counselor, difficulties can arise. Teachers who are accustomed to the open sharing that takes place among colleagues may resent that the counselor, in his or her new role, has a different perspective on student concerns and is less forthcoming with certain kinds of information due to the need to protect student confidentiality. These transitional difficulties can probably best be resolved through open communication in which the counselor clearly defines and explains the rationale that guides decisions in her or his new role.

Another problem relates to school counselors who are also still teachers. Can they balance both roles? Being a teacher might help the counselor to better understand students, yet the teacher role could get in the way of forming the counseling relationship. When a professional must serve simultaneously as a teacher and a counselor, every effort should be made to have a caseload of counselees who are not taking classes taught by the teacher/counselor.

Inevitably, school counselors will have friends who are also parents. When a friend's child attends the counselor's school and is assigned as a counselee, an uncomfortable dual role conflict may develop. The counselor must maintain clear boundaries around the professional relationship with the child and the personal relationship with the child's parents, which can be a difficult task.

Particularly in small towns and rural communities, it is difficult for school counselors to avoid some overlap between their personal and professional lives. When the counselor's friends are also the parents or teachers of their student clients, some role conflicts may be inevitable. For example, Gerald and Marianne Schneider Corey once consulted with school counselors in Alaska who are assigned to several schools in remote villages often accessible only by plane. Thus, the counselor serves many schools, often performs many functions, and is sometimes even a relative of some of the schoolchildren. This example reminds us that the dual relationship issues pertaining to school counseling need to be considered within the context of the community.

School counselors serve multiple constituencies. ASCA's *Ethical Standards for School Counselors* (2004) spell out the counselor's responsibilities to students, parents, colleagues and professional associates, school and community, self, and the profession. According to Glosoff and Pate (2002), school counselors need to balance their ethical and legal responsibilities to the students they serve, to the parents/guardians, and to the school system. Because school counselors are part of an educational community, they often consult with parents, teachers, and administrators. During these consultations, school counselors need to make clear that their primary client is the student (Glosoff & Pate, 2002). When school counselors try to balance their responsibilities to students with their responsibilities to parents, conflicts can arise, particularly around confidentiality issues. Counselors are legally responsible to the parents but ethically more responsible to the students. Minor clients have a right to know what information they reveal to their counselors will be kept secret and what might be shared with parents (or teachers or administrators). The meaning and the limits of confidentiality need to be explained to students in a way they can understand. One way to lessen the impact of some role conflicts is to conduct sessions with the student and parents in those situations when the parent wants information about the child.

School counselors are often faced with ethical dilemmas if their roles are not clearly defined, or if school policies exist that impinge on their effectiveness. To whom does the school counselor owe primary allegiance—the student, the student's parents, the school, or the community? ASCA (2004) provides guidance on this question:

The school counselor] recognizes his/her primary obligation for confidentiality is to the student but balances that obligation with an understanding of the legal and inherent rights of parents/guardians to be the
guiding voice in their children's lives. (A.2.g.)

If counselors are expected to carry out disciplinary functions, their
capacity to serve as effective personal counselors is severely restricted. If
they are expected to report student drug use to parents or administrators,
this will affect their ability to form counseling relationships with many
students. If counselors are required to inform parents about details in
cases concerning birth control or abortion, some students may avoid their
counselors. Sometimes school counselors are asked to monitor tardiness
or truancy, police the restrooms or cafeteria, enforce school policies, or
supervise school events. Carrying out duties associated with any of these
roles can make it more difficult for counselors to establish personal counseling relationships with students.

The School Counselor as Consultant

School counselors are increasingly being expected to serve as consultants to
teachers, administrators, and parents. This can create role conflicts. The
counselor role assumes that the counselor's primary function is to establish a
therapeutic relationship with the student's welfare as the primary consideration. The consultant role, in contrast, emphasizes the process of working with
other professionals when this is in the interest of the client. Ferris and Linville
(1985) raised some important questions about these conflicting goals: How can
counselors uphold their responsibility for the student's best interest if they are
working only indirectly with the student in a consultant role? What are the
ethical implications of giving a measure of responsibility for intervention and
treatment to consultees (parents, teachers) who are not trained as counselors?

Consulting is not the same as counseling, and the two roles should be
kept separate. In their role as consultants, school counselors are most likely
to encounter ethical issues pertaining to dual relationships when they are
involved in situations in which boundaries are not clearly drawn. Being
aware of the issues involved in the consultant/consultee/client relationship, and the rights of consultees, can enable counselors to identify and
deal with ethical problems that arise. School counselors who function as
consultants need to develop a well-defined set of mutually agreed-upon
expectations regarding the nature of consultation. As A. Michael Dougherty
noted in Chapter 5, the consultant's focus must be on work-related concerns.
Thus, school counselors should avoid discussing the personal concerns of a
teacher or an administrator during consultation with that person. They
need to avoid their tendency to move toward exploring the personal problems of their consultees and monitor their interventions so that they avoid
creating dependency, using manipulation, or misusing power. They should
strive to maintain a collaborative relationship.

Dealing With Child Abuse

Perhaps no arena has more potential for dual role conflicts than child abuse. When counselors become aware of situations involving suspected child abuse or neglect, they are required to report it. The school counselor's role, however, is rarely limited to making a report. Remley and Fry (1993) noted that school counselors are often asked to perform a multitude of functions—including informant, counselor to the victim or perpetrator, school system employee, court witness, liaison with social services, and counselor to the family—that involve distinct and conflicting roles. These authors pointed out several conflicts that can arise.

First, the counseling relationship with the child may be endangered when a counselor files a report. A child may have conflicting reactions when the counselor reports the abuse. The counselor may be seen as an ally in putting a stop to the abuse, or the child may feel betrayed and angry, particularly if retribution occurs in the home or if the child is removed from the home and perhaps from the school as a result of the counselor's action. Most abused children are left in their parents' custody, and the counselor then has the task of providing ongoing counseling to the child. Treatment of abuse victims can be a lengthy process that severely strains the counselor's resources. A problem can also develop if the counselor does not maintain appropriate boundaries. For instance, some counselors may be tempted to befriend such children or even attempt to "adopt" them. Counselors need to recognize their limits and not allow themselves to become overly involved to the extent that they lose their capacity for objectivity.

Counselors also need to follow procedures that have been established in their school systems. Some systems require that the principal be notified before a report is made, and some systems require that teachers be informed. It is difficult to maintain confidentiality in these instances.

Once a counselor has made a report, he or she may be involved with the court system until an adjudication is made. The counselor will need to work with Child Protective Services caseworkers, the police, and perhaps with attorneys. If the case goes to trial, the counselor may be required to testify as a witness. The multiple roles played by school counselors involved in child abuse cases can severely test the counselor's ability to handle conflicting demands and keep the client's welfare foremost.

A Contributor's Perspective

A. Michael Dougherty believes school counselors should avoid roles that conflict with their primary role as counselor. He offers counselors some strategies for taking a proactive stance in defining their roles.

 Managing Role Conflicts in School Counseling

A. Michael Dougherty

School counselors often are asked as part of their everyday duties to take on roles that might conflict with their primary role as counselors. I believe school counselors should avoid roles such as disciplinarian, substitute teacher, or lunchroom/bathroom/bus monitor that conflict with their primary role as counselors to students. The unique role of the counselor in the school makes the assumption of such roles highly questionable, and doing so is likely to violate some of the basic tenets of the counseling relationship (such as confidentiality). As a consequence, new counseling relationships with students may be inhibited and existing ones may be compromised.

School counselors often engage in both preventive and remedial efforts as part of their overall counseling program. Preventive aspects of the program include group guidance, consultation with teachers and administrators, advocacy, and membership on student support teams. The primary elements of the remedial role of the counselor include individual and group counseling.

Emphasis on the preventive aspects of the school counselor's role has increased during the past two decades. Preventive interventions frequently assume an acceptance of the school counselor by other staff persons as "one of us." One important way to be accepted in such a manner is to engage in the same day-to-day activities in which other staff members engage. Unfortunately, many of these activities jeopardize the counseling role of the school counselor. A critical issue for school counselors, then, is how to gain acceptance by staff and at the same time avoid engaging in roles that may have a negative impact on their counseling relationships with students. It may be tempting for school counselors to give in and take on roles such as bus duty, lunchroom duty, or bathroom monitoring, particularly when there is strong pressure from administrators and teachers for them to do so. However, when they assume these roles, they increase the probability of placing themselves in the position of disciplinarian or informant. These dual roles, even when entered into only briefly, certainly put a counselor in a conflict-of-interest situation. Consider the following scenario as an illustration:

> Maria Sanchez, a middle school counselor, is currently conducting a counseling group for children of divorce. Vanessa is one of the students in the group. Ms. Sanchez, as a member of the school staff, has accepted bathroom monitoring as part of her duties. One day, as she is monitoring the girls' bathroom, she encounters Vanessa smoking a cigarette. Ms. Sanchez must now report Vanessa to the school administration for misconduct.

Even this very simple example points out the necessity for caution on the part of school counselors in taking potentially conflicting roles with the students they counsel. By reporting Vanessa to the administration, Ms. Sanchez could seriously damage the counseling relationship. Other students may hear of this counselor who "asks you to trust her at one time and turns you in at another time," and this could keep prospective clients from seeking out Ms. Sanchez as a counselor.

School counselors often think of their roles in terms of the "three Cs": counseling, consultation, and coordination. There are, however, many other potential roles that the counselor might assume. Smaller roles like taking on bus duty may seem inconsequential. However, when counselors engage in roles that are incompatible with the primary role of counselor, the resulting dual relationships with students can have an adverse impact and therefore should be avoided.

At the outset of each school year, school counselors need to clearly and publicly state their roles to school personnel as well as to students. When staff and students understand the counselor's unique role in the school, potentially harmful dual relationships with students can be avoided. At the same time, school counselors can be accepted as "family" by staff if they take on additional duties that do not create the potential for inappropriate dual relationships, such as working in the concession stand, running after-school parent groups, or conducting professional development activities.

In recent years there has been an increased emphasis on licensure for counselors, and it is now quite common in many states for school counselors to be licensed to conduct private practice. This trend has created the potential for a problematic dual relationship unique to school counselors. Consider the following scenario:

> Leon, a practicing school counselor, is also a licensed professional counselor. One of Leon's specialty areas is family counseling. He maintains a small private practice and counsels with families during the evenings and on weekends. One of Leon's clients at school is Gilbert, a student with ADHD. Leon counsels with Gilbert at school on a regular basis. Gilbert's parents approach Leon about the possibility of him providing family counseling services.

What are some potential problems if Leon agrees to counsel the family? First, it is ethically questionable for a school counselor to use his position to acquire monetary gain outside the school setting. In addition, relationship boundary issues could arise. Both Leon and Gilbert will be placed in dual roles: Leon, as school counselor to Gilbert as an individual and as family counselor to Gilbert's family, and Gilbert, as a student being counseled and as a family member in counseling. What if the parents, during family counseling sessions, try to obtain specific information from Leon about his sessions at school with Gilbert? What if Gilbert does not want to disclose in the family sessions what he has discussed with Leon at school? Are there any circumstances under which it would be appropriate for Leon to terminate the counseling relationship with Gilbert at school and counsel him as part of the family system? Clearly, school counselors interested in opening a private practice must confront these potential ethical dilemmas and establish clear boundaries between their school counselor role and their private practice.

- If you are a school counselor, are you ever asked to take on noncounseling duties that could conflict with your counselor role?
- How do you handle such requests?
- What are the advantages and disadvantages of taking on extra roles and responsibilities?
- If you are in private practice or are considering opening a practice, what boundaries do you need to establish to keep your two roles from coming into conflict?

To sum up, perhaps the best way to minimize dual relationship conflicts is for school counselors to clearly state their primary role and functions as counselors and to communicate this to teachers, parents, administrators, and, most important of all, to students. Demands made by principals, teachers, parents, and outside agencies can sometimes run counter to student clients' best interests. School counselors may feel as though they are placed in a no-win situation. If they object to taking on inappropriate duties such as monitoring restrooms or hallways, they risk being seen as uncooperative by administrators and as "privileged" by teachers. If they agree to take on such duties, they risk jeopardizing their counseling relationships with students. School counselors serve in multiple roles with multiple constituencies and need to have a repertoire of strategies for dealing with any conflicts that may arise. These include consulting with colleagues, clearly defining and publicizing their role and function, networking with others, and practicing personal stress management.

Higher Education

Many professionals who work in college and university counseling centers perform multiple functions as counselors, supervisors, administrators, course instructors, and colleagues to faculty and staff. There is considerable potential for conflict among these roles. College and university student personnel workers who work in residence halls face yet another set of dual relationship dilemmas. A number of potential conflicts seem to be inherent in the multiple roles played by those who work in higher education counseling centers and residence halls.

College and university counseling centers generally have a broad mission to provide supportive services to students, faculty, and staff. Although counseling services are provided primarily to students, what should college and university counselors do when a faculty or staff member seeks counseling from them? Role conflicts certainly are possible if the counselors accept faculty or staff members as clients when they have another, collegial relationship as well. The potential problems deserve a full and open discussion before establishing a therapeutic relationship.

From our perspective, there are more problems involved in counseling an employee than there are potential benefits. One of the main ethical binds in this situation pertains to the power of the counselor/employer to hire and fire and to make or deny recommendations for promotion. For example, what might you do if you were a counseling center director and counselor, and a department secretary asked you to provide personal counseling? One day your secretary asks you if you might be willing to talk with her about her problems with her husband. She adds that the only reason she is making this request of you is because she knows and trusts you and that it is not like her to talk to anyone about her personal life.

We can think of many risks in acceding to this request. When could the counseling sessions take place? What if the counseling went poorly? What are the implications for the work relationship? What if the secretary discloses an abusive relationship with her husband who is a practicing alcoholic? What if she begins going to a shelter when he threatens to become abusive, as you have suggested, and misses work on these occasions? Although you are sympathetic, you are upset when she falls behind in the work she does for you. How do you deal with her absenteeism when it comes time to evaluate her job performance? These are just some of the questions that might arise and that demonstrate the wisdom of avoiding establishing a therapeutic role with an employee. Although we might be willing to listen to this secretary's personal concerns as we might with a neighbor, we would exercise caution in encouraging her to go into much detail about her problems. Instead, we would encourage her to consider getting professional help from a provider in the community.

Potential role conflicts also exist when higher education counselors serve as course instructors. It is not unusual for a college or university counselor to also teach part time in the counselor education program on campus. We do not think it wise for counselors who are also instructors to accept a current student in one of their classes as a client in their practice at the counseling center. But what if the student is a client first who then enrolls in the instructor's class? Is the instructor/counselor free to prevent the student from enrolling in the class? Perhaps there is only one section of the course and it is required in the student's program. In cases such as this, it is a good policy to seek consultation. One way to avoid some of these problems is to have clear policies in place. For instance, students who are interning in the counseling center might be prohibited from taking a class with their supervisor who also teaches in the counseling program. Although such policies could not possibly cover every contingency that might arise, their existence, if known to students, could help those students make informed choices.

On a related note, what are the potential role conflicts when the college or university counseling center serves as an internship site for students in the counselor education program? This is a fairly common practice that does not necessarily create problems. However, in the case of an intern, it is helpful to have a clear contract and understanding with the intern and with the faculty from the graduate counseling program about what is expected. The supervisory role includes evaluation, and supervisors have responsibilities not only to the interns they supervise but also to the interns' clients.

As we discussed in Chapter 5, supervisors serve as gatekeepers to the profession. The supervisor in the counseling center, the intern, and the faculty members of the counseling program who also provide supervision must all understand their responsibilities in this complex relationship.

Are there problems in hiring an intern after he or she graduates? If the intern proves to be an exceptionally competent counselor and could fit well into a vacant position, we do not see an ethical problem in hiring this person. However, once the former intern is hired, he or she is no longer a supervisee but a colleague. This shift in roles can involve a difficult transition for both the former supervisor and the former intern and might necessitate some special sensitivity, awareness, and open discussion.

We know several counselors who work in university counseling centers who also have part-time independent private practices. Is it ever acceptable for these counselors to refer counseling center clients to themselves in their private practice or to their colleagues who may also have independent private practices?

Our immediate reaction is that it is not acceptable for college and university counselors to refer student clients to themselves. It is important for these counselors to follow the policies of the counseling center where they work, as these policies are likely to address the issue. This may not always be a simple matter, however. Consider the situation in which the college or university counseling center has a limitation on the number of times (say, six sessions) that a student can be seen by a counselor. Assume that at the sixth session the student says, "I feel that I am just beginning to make some progress, yet I realize that the college has a policy that ongoing counseling cannot be provided by the counseling center. I know that you have a private practice, and I am willing to see you there. I feel that we have an excellent working relationship, and I really do not want to stop at this point."

- If you were this counselor, how might you respond?
- What might you say to the counselor if he or she were to consult you for advice on this matter?
- What if the counselor suggested a referral and the student resisted, making it clear that he wanted to continue seeing the counselor with whom he began?
- What if no other therapists were within a range of 100 miles?

These questions show how complex this situation is. College and university counselors generally should not accept a student client into their private practice, but an emergency situation could arise. For instance, a suicidal client might be seen by the college counselor for the limited number of sessions allowed and might refuse a referral to another provider. The counselor might assess the risk in continuing to attempt to refer the client as being higher than the risk involved in seeing the client in his or her private practice. In addition, some nonemergency situations call for commonsense judgments. Perhaps a client needs only one or two additional sessions to complete her work in counseling. Referring the client to another counselor does not seem to be the best option, especially because starting over with a new counselor might involve additional expense to the client. In these cases, we recommend that counselors discuss the situation with the center director to see whether an exception can be made.

It is likely that higher education counselors will need to refer some clients whose needs they cannot meet due to constraints of the setting. How do these counselors develop a referral base? A counselor who does not have a private practice may have a colleague in the counseling center who does. We believe it is prudent policy to avoid referring to this colleague. Rather, the referral base should include practitioners in the community for whom no conflict of interest exists. Competent community practitioners should be afforded an opportunity to apply to be included on the referral list. Limiting the list too narrowly to one's friends or associates could raise the issue of restraint of trade.

A Contributor's Perspective

Sue Spooner makes the point that referral sources are not always readily available. She argues for common sense and some flexibility in role definitions, combined with education and awareness, as keys to avoiding many of the serious complications of dual relationships.

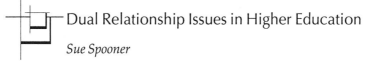

Dual Relationship Issues in Higher Education

Sue Spooner

The potential for dual relationships has been present in higher education for most of this century, if not longer. It exists all across the student affairs realm and beyond, in both the academic and business affairs segments of any campus. Counselor educators and counseling center staff members are obvious targets of approach by staff, students, and colleagues when they consider seeking help for personal or other problems. Other student affairs staff members may or may not be trained as counselors, but if they are viewed as approachable, they also may be sought out by members of the college or university community who want help with personal concerns. This need not always be problematic (indeed, in the case of a student seeking help from the counseling center, it is desirable), but it calls for a special awareness of the issues inherent in offering something as simple as a listening ear to someone who is not a "client." Personal topics arise in the course of casual conversations, in formal supervisory sessions, and in consultations about professional and work-related concerns. Sometimes the lines of demarcation are not entirely clear. In a supervisory session, one might learn that an employee has developed a serious problem with alcohol abuse. Referral is both appropriate and helpful, but so is follow-up. Maintaining the level of trust necessary to accomplish a successful referral calls for good counseling skills, and when these skills exist, we ought to use them.

For those professionals whose skills are fully integrated into their personal styles, it is ridiculous and probably impossible to require that they refrain from responding in a therapeutic way to concerns raised by colleagues, staff, or students. Creating a climate of guilt and anxiety over the use of one's ingrained skills seems counterproductive. It is simplistic to suggest that one should always refer such requests to someone outside the institution. In practice, this is not always feasible. When an institution is situated in a small town, or in a rural environment, the only resources may be those present on the campus itself. In locations where private practitioners are available, the cost may not be covered by insurance and may be too expensive for the help seeker. The colleague who approaches us may have had great difficulty in finding the courage to do so and is indicating a degree of confidence in us that is not only flattering but bodes well for a successful outcome.

The residence hall environment is particularly illustrative of the dual relationship issues that arise in the student affairs domain. Residence life staffs tend to become melded into tightly knit working units. They work closely together 24 hours a day, and their personal lives and their jobs blend into each other almost seamlessly. They know the intimate details of each other's lives, and they share both social and professional concerns with equal freedom. Romantic relationships among staff are common, and they also sometimes occur between students who are staff and residents who are students. Although we may officially frown on such relationships, it is unlikely that they can be eliminated or even limited. Our approach should be to educate staff to the issues surrounding such relationships, with an emphasis on the ethical guidelines to which they should adhere.

Resident life staff typically are aware of problems their students and other staff members have with drugs and alcohol, with school work, with family ties, and with myriad other elements of the lives of the young professionals and the young adult students they serve. They are frequently the best sources of help, at least initially, for both students and colleagues experiencing problems. They also know about referral and tend to use their referral sources wisely and well.

Much the same can be said for other areas of student affairs in which dual relationships may exist. The supervisor–subordinate relationship between boss and employee, the student activities staffer who develops close relationships with student leaders, and the academic adviser who must frequently deal not only with academic planning but also with the personal elements of a student's life all contain the potential for the complications of dual relationships. The key is not to avoid them at all costs but to be aware of the issues and conflicts that can arise and be prepared to deal with them as ethically and professionally as possible.

The climate of higher education has changed noticeably over the last decade. There is less casual sex, both among peers and between students and staff. There is a greater awareness about sexually transmitted diseases, and especially about the issues surrounding sexual harassment. This is not to say that these behaviors do not occur, but generally there is more deliberation before choosing to engage in them. Faculty and staff are more cautious in their relationships with students. Nevertheless, where young staff and the raging hormones of traditional-age students come together, human nature exerts a powerful influence. The office romance is also still with us. When the boss is dating or even living with another staff member, there are endless difficulties, not the least of which ensue when the relationship gets into trouble. Biased employee evaluations, preferential or prejudicial treatment over work assignments, and even fights in the office over problems in the relationship are just some of the complications that arise from such dual relationships. It is wise to discourage them, but it is impossible to prevent them. In most cases, it is agreed that the practice of staff entering into romantic relationships with students is—and should be—prohibited, as specified in our ethics codes. But what of the adult student who has an entire life apart from her or his status as a student? When consenting adults enter into mutually chosen relationships, it is unlikely that we can enforce the prohibition.

Certainly, the professional counselor and the counselor educator have some extra cautions with which to cope. Anyone who has been a sexual partner cannot later become a client. Even after the counseling or teaching relationship has ended, becoming sexually or just personally involved presents risks. Referring a client to oneself, if one has a private practice outside the campus, offers a fertile area for ethical conflicts. As most counseling center directors will tell us, being both an administrator and a counselor is fraught with potential dual roles, most of which cannot be avoided. Counseling center staff frequently teach in the counselor education program and perhaps in the undergraduate program as well. When a student wants to become a client, this is clearly prohibited, but the help seeker needs to be assisted though the referral process. Seeking social outlets with colleagues is a normal and common part of the campus culture but also offers potential problems when friendship and supervision conflict.

In certain cases, the existence of friendships across student service areas can be beneficial. The young professional who works in student activities may be best friends with a staff member in career services. They are apt to discuss situations that arise for either of them around students, other staff, and the general ebb and flow of the institution. Perhaps a student who is deeply involved in activities could use the help of the career services office to weave those experiences into a better resume. A referral is more apt to happen when the staffers have a good relationship. The academic adviser who knows and trusts a colleague on the counseling center staff is more likely to refer to that counselor a student whose personal problems are drawing energy from needed study. We can all help each other as professionals to recognize our limitations and to react appropriately in situations calling for attention to our ethics codes.

Another area in which some change has occurred is in our understanding about boundaries. In the 1960s and 1970s, the term had not been applied to human development. Now, we have a somewhat better understanding of the need to develop a sense of our various roles and to set boundaries between them. If we are clearer about who we are, in the core sense, and how that personhood carries into each segment of our lives, we can better manage to avoid the serious problems of dual relationships, even if we cannot or do not want to avoid them entirely. Consideration of dual relationships needs to become an element of staff training for all areas in student affairs, with presentation of the applicable content from the American College Personnel Association (1995) "Statement of Ethical Principles" and the National Association of Student Personnel Administrators (1996) "Standards of Professional Practice." Even though not all student affairs staff are trained as counselors, there can be a high payoff in exposure to these documents and in an examination of how they apply to the work environment and to our personal lives.

Returning to the case of the colleague or supervisee who presents us with a problem or concern, consciously or unconsciously seeking our help, first there is the question of how long and how deeply to become involved. That decision must be based on knowledge of our own limitations, the seriousness of the situation, and whether other help is available. Some of us feel obligated to offer help when asked but limit the help to a more consultative mode, suggesting alternatives and resources. Faculty members should not enter into long-term psychotherapeutic relationships with colleagues, but neither should they ignore or rebuff any cry for help. Maintaining a list of referral sources is an obvious but easily overlooked necessity. Other commonsense approaches include helping those in supervisory roles understand the conflicts they encounter, encouraging all staff training to include codes of ethics, and taking care that activities that involve intense self-disclosure are led by those who are properly trained to lead them and who do not have supervisory responsibility for the participants.

Education for staff, students, and colleagues should be ongoing. Awareness of the hazards of dual relationships while recognizing their inevitability should go far toward eliminating serious complications from the many roles that student services personnel in higher education play on a day-to-day basis.

Conclusions

Clearly, the potential for multiple role conflicts exists in educational institutions across the entire spectrum from elementary schools through graduate programs. As both of our contributors to this chapter have noted, awareness and training are key elements in our ability to recognize potential problems and to deal with them in an appropriate manner. We think Sue Spooner's point is especially cogent for practitioners of every counseling specialty: The clearer we can be about who we are, in the core sense, and how that personhood carries into every aspect of our professional and personal lives, the better we will be able to manage multiple relationship dilemmas.

This chapter concludes our examination of multiple role and relationship issues in counseling practice. We have touched on many specialty areas, but others might just as easily have been included. We hope that we have raised representative issues and discussed strategies and solutions that all readers can relate to and apply in their work.

Key Themes, Questions, and Decision Making

In this concluding chapter, we highlight some key concepts or themes that have emerged throughout the book and present questions for reflection and integration. We also offer a model of a decision-making process that we find helpful when confronted with potential multiple relationships.

Ten themes (or concepts) have been woven throughout the tapestry of this work.

Key Themes

1. *Multiple relationship issues affect virtually all mental health practitioners, regardless of their work setting or clientele.*

   No helping professional remains untouched by potential multiple role conflicts and dilemmas. We have examined how these relationships affect professionals in many settings and in a number of specialty areas of practice. We explored these issues as they apply to working with individual clients, couples, families, and groups. We also looked at the complex questions that arise when relationships are tripartite, such as those involving supervisor/supervise/client, and consultant/consultee/client system.

   We have attempted to cover a broad range of issues, but we realize that a number of special areas of concern have not been addressed. Despite the fact that we have not been able to discuss multiple relationship concerns in all counseling specializations, we believe that dual and multiple role conflicts are indeed pervasive in the mental health professions.

2. *Most professional codes of ethics caution against forming dual relationships, but the newer codes also acknowledge the complex nature of these relationships.*

   Consulting the codes of ethics can be helpful when we look for guidance regarding multiple relationship dilemmas. However, it seems clear to us that codes of ethics cannot provide most of the answers to the questions we face. A crucial ethical principle that applies to all potential multiple relationships is to do no harm. As professionals, it is our ethical responsibility to devise safeguards to prevent harm to clients, students, or supervisees who may be involved in dual or multiple relationships with us. At the same time, it is imperative that we involve clients, students, and supervisees in open discussion of the possible risks and benefits of any dual relationship we consider entering. For students, seasoned practitioners, and clients alike, learning to deal with role conflicts can help us appreciate the complexity in human relationships.

3. *Not all multiple relationships can be avoided, nor are they necessarily always harmful, and they can be beneficial.*
Multiple relationships are fraught with complexities and ambiguities. They are unavoidable in some situations and settings, and they sometimes contain potential both for risk and for benefit to clients. Dual and multiple relationships are unavoidable in rural and small communities, in counselor education programs, and in the military, to mention just a few settings. Johnson, Ralph, and Johnson (2005) highlighted the ethical dilemmas and challenges in managing multiple roles in active military units. These authors stated that the dual identities of military psychologist (commissioned officer and clinical provider) often create difficulties in identifying the primary client, balancing client best interests, and avoiding potentially harmful multiple relationships with clients.

We have seen that some forms of role blending can be beneficial, such as the mentoring relationships between professor and student or the teaching of group counseling courses by combining didactic and experiential learning experiences.

4. *Multiple role relationships challenge us to monitor ourselves and to examine our motivations for our practices.*
As practitioners, we need to engage in an ongoing process of self-reflection based on these three questions: What is the right thing to do? Am I doing the right thing? Am I doing the right thing for the right reason? It is all too easy to deceive ourselves into thinking that we have the best interests of our clients in mind. One example that we offered was that of a private practitioner who encourages clients who are in individual therapy to join a group that the practitioner is forming. This may not be what clients need, and if we are not honest with ourselves, we run the risk of exploiting our clients. Whenever a multiple role issue arises, it is essential that we ask ourselves whose needs are being met.

5. *Whenever we consider becoming involved in a dual or multiple relationship, it is wise to seek consultation from trusted colleagues or a supervisor.*
A willingness to seek consultation and to document this process is a sign of professionalism. We may also save ourselves a costly and

painful malpractice judgment if we are able to demonstrate that we acted in good faith and sought consultation. Colleagues can help us to gain another perspective on potential problem areas that we may have overlooked. They can also help us maintain our objectivity and can enhance our ability to appraise situations honestly.

6. *There are few absolute answers that can neatly resolve dual or multiple relationship dilemmas.*

   Rather than thinking in terms of "finding the answer," it may be better to consider that there may be more than one acceptable way to respond to ethical dilemmas in multiple relationships. Answers that may be appropriate for us may not be appropriate for you in your situation. Simply because we have differing views about a specific issue does not mean that one of us is right and the other is wrong. The therapeutic styles and preferences of the practitioner and the unique needs of each client must be taken into account. Thus, we need to be able to tolerate ambiguity, and we will not find security in the absolute answers that some others may be quick to offer us.

7. *Decisions whether to enter into dual or multiple relationships should be for the benefit of our clients or others served rather than to protect ourselves from censure.*

   Although it does appear that mental health professionals are increasingly being sued for malpractice, we hope that we will not be so driven by fear of lawsuits, by fear of having an ethics complaint lodged against us, or by fear of censure from a licensing board that we fail to consider what our clients need and the role of our ethical reasoning skills when we are faced with potential multiple roles and relationships. In the final analysis, there is no substitute for our professional judgment, integrity, and goodwill.

8. *In determining whether to proceed with a dual or multiple relationship, consider whether the potential benefit of the relationship outweighs the potential for harm.*

   Generally, dual relationships may be entered into only when the risks of harm are small or when there are strongly offsetting ethical and clinical benefits for the client. It is prudent to consider the risks to the client and the professional involved as well as the possible effects on other consumers, other professionals, the profession itself, and society. Although we may identify benefits to certain multiple roles, we must be cautious in proceeding.

9. *It is the responsibility of counselor education programs to introduce boundary issues and explore multiple relationship questions with students.*

   It is important to teach students ways of thinking about alternative courses of action. When students first enter their graduate program in the helping professions, they may have given little thought to the complexities involved in multiple relationships. Lazarus and Zur (2002) asserted that training programs tend to instill a fear of malpractice and do not give enough attention to educating trainees about personal integrity, personal ethics, and how to navigate the complex issues of dual relationships, boundaries, and intimacy in therapy. We suggest that the issues we have raised in this book be discussed extensively in ethics courses and in courses such as group supervision, practicum, and internship. When students are involved in supervised field placements, they are bound to encounter some dilemmas related to maintaining boundaries with their clients. As counselor educators and supervisors, we do well to encourage students to bring their concerns about these dilemmas to us for discussion. We can also introduce issues through case vignettes and role-playing exercises. Counselor educators should do more than provide students with a list of dos and don'ts. They can challenge students to think through their own positions on issues. Handelsman, Gottlieb, and Knapp (2005) have put this matter well:

> Becoming an ethical professional is more complex than simply following a set of rules or doing what one sees one's mentors do, and helping students become ethical psychologists involves more than teaching certain professional rules to morally upright people who will easily understand and implement them. (p. 59)

10. *Counselor education programs have a responsibility to develop their own guidelines, policies, and procedures for dealing with multiple roles and role conflicts within the program.*
    Faculty should be engaged in continuing discussion about ways to prevent harmful dual relationships within the training program. As educators and supervisors, if we cannot deal with multiple relationships effectively, what chance will we have to teach students how to deal with these issues? If we are not modeling effective ways of thinking about and dealing with boundary issues, how can we expect our students to grapple constructively with them? Faculty groups, with student representation, can develop practical guidelines and procedures in a proactive manner.

Questions for Reflection and Integration

Throughout this book, in each chapter, we have tried to involve you, our readers. We have asked questions intended to encourage you to think about the issues we have raised. Here in the last chapter, we summarize some of the questions that have recurred in various forms. As you review this list, consider your own stance toward the issues and the ways they affect your work as a professional.

- Are *sexual relationships with former clients* (or students or supervisees) ever ethically acceptable? If so, do you think it is a good idea to establish a minimum 5-year time period between terminating the professional relationship and beginning the personal one? What about *social relationships or friendships with former clients* or collegial or peer relationships with former students or supervisees?

- How should the mental health professions deal with the issue of *sexual attraction* between counselors and clients? How can counselor education programs prepare prospective counselors so that they are able to distinguish clearly between feeling a sexual attraction and acting on that attraction? How can sexual attractions best be managed?
- What steps can the profession take to *prevent sexual improprieties* with clients, students, or supervisees? What is your own role in prevention?
- Do the *codes of ethics* that govern your professional identity, work setting, and clientele address boundary issues and multiple relationships in a way that is helpful to you? What guidelines would be useful for you in making decisions?
- If you are a *graduate student*, what kinds of training do you want to receive in order to feel prepared to cope with relationship boundary issues? What kinds of relationships do you want—and not want—to have with your professors?
- What are the appropriate boundaries of a *supervisor's role*? Can supervision address personal concerns of the supervisee without creating a dual role conflict? What kind of boundaries between counseling and supervision are useful?
- Is *bartering* with clients for goods or services or from a client ever acceptable to you in your practice? If so, under what circumstances is it acceptable? If you would not barter, what alternatives might you suggest to clients who are in great financial need?
- What are your thoughts about *accepting a gift* from a client? What factors are you likely to consider in deciding whether to accept a gift?
- What guidelines can you apply to determine the appropriate limits of *counselor self-disclosure*? What boundary issues might be created for you in your work if you were to overextend these limits?
- What special role conflicts do you encounter when you function as a *supervisor or consultant*? To whom do you owe your first obligation—to your supervisee or consultee, or to the client who is ultimately served? What role conflicts do you encounter in attempting to balance these obligations?
- If you function in *multiple roles* in your work—in any combination of such roles as counselor, supervisor, administrator, teacher, client advocate, case manager, colleague, or group leader—what role conflicts do you most frequently encounter? How do you resolve them?

A Decision-Making Model

As a result of examining and pondering these questions, we have developed a model decision-making process that can be useful when confronting dual or multiple relationship dilemmas. (See Figure 11.1) First, we must identify the dual relationship.

Boundary crossings are sometimes confused with dual relationships. Lazarus and Zur (2002) maintained that boundary crossings are not unethical and, in some circumstances, may constitute caring, humane, and effective interventions. A few examples of such boundary crossings might include conducting a home visit with a client who is ill, having lunch with a client with an eating problem, going on a vigorous walk with a depressed client, or attending an event where the client is performing. The 2005 *ACA Code of Ethics* acknowledges these types of interactions with clients as being "potentially beneficial." Counselors need to engage in a decision-making process in determining when boundary crossings or nonprofessional relationships are appropriate and therapeutic.

It seems clear to us that some dual or multiple relationships, built into the counselor's job description or dictated by the unique needs of clients, are indeed unavoidable. Examples include the rehabilitation counselor who must manage the client's case budget; the counselor in a rural community whose clients are also her banker, beautician, and pharmacist; and the school counselor who must report child abuse and then continue to function as the

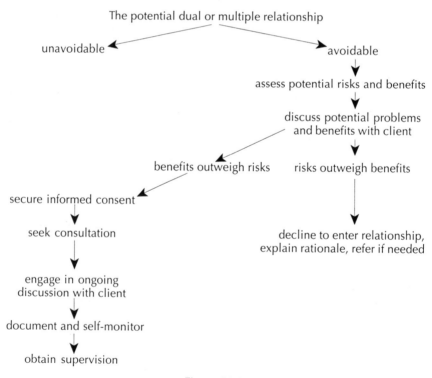

Figure 11.1
The Potential Dual or Multiple Relationship

child's counselor and liaison with Child Protective Services. In these and similar instances, the professional's obligation is to take all possible steps to minimize the risks of harm. The client's informed consent is an ethically important first step that entails a full and open discussion with the client in which the risks are explored. Furthermore, counselors who are engaged in unavoidable dual or multiple relationships are advised to seek consultation both at the time the relationship is entered and periodically throughout its duration. Ongoing self-monitoring and documentation are additional prudent measures. When unavoidable dual or multiple relationships become problematic, it is wise to obtain supervision.

Other types of role blending are avoidable, and in these cases the professional has a choice as to whether to engage in blended or multiple roles. Here it is essential that potential risks and benefits be carefully weighed. A judgment needs to be made regarding factors that create a potential for harm, including differences in expectations, divergent responsibilities, and the power differential. In some instances, when the potential benefits are great and the risks are small, the professional may decide to proceed. Examples include serving as a mentor to a student; teaching a group counseling class in a way that combines didactic and experiential learnings; and working with a client who has AIDS, and the client's family, in a nontraditional, out-of-office environment.

In yet other cases, careful consideration of potential risks will lead the professional to conclude that it is best not to enter into a dual or multiple relationship. Although the temptation to do so might be well motivated, the risk of harm is strong. Examples include entering into a close, personal friendship with a current client, student, or supervisee or entering into a business relationship with a client. When a potential dual or multiple relationship can and should be avoided, professionals need to take steps to ensure that clients understand the rationale for not proceeding with the problematic aspect of the relationship. For instance, in the first example, this might involve acknowledging the attractiveness of the idea of a friendship, discussing the risks to the counseling relationship if a friendship were to develop, and mutually agreeing on what the boundaries of the professional relationship will be.

Although the decision-making model helps to clarify our thinking, each of us will encounter situations in our work that will raise difficult questions for which the answers remain elusive. Our expectation is that we have stimulated thinking and self-examination. In our view, the ability of mental health professionals to reason through ethical issues can be strongly tested by conflicting roles and multiple relationship situations. As is the case with learning to make ethical decisions in other areas of professional practice, many of these situations defy easy answers. To some degree, the personal style of each counselor will dictate the resolution of multiple relationship dilemmas. Some practitioners may be comfortable practicing in the context of multiple roles, but others may need to establish more clear-cut boundaries.

Conclusions

Coauthoring this work about dual or multiple relationships has been a learning experience for both of us. During the revision process, we discovered new slants on issues thought about over the years, rethought many issues in the context of revisions in ethical standards and more recent literature, and learned a great deal from our guest contributors.

Certainties are rare in the helping professions. We make no claim to having discovered answers to the complex and difficult questions about professional relationship boundaries. Rather, our aim has been to raise some important issues, to explore a range of viewpoints, and to discuss our own positions. In writing the various chapters, we hoped to provide material for thoughtful reflection that would act as a springboard for ongoing discussion. We expect that ethically conscientious professionals will continue to struggle with the multiple relationship dilemmas that they face and the multiple roles they will be expected to balance in their work. In the absence of certainties, we must rely on our reasoned professional judgment, openness to discussing issues with clients (or students or supervisees) who are equally affected by the decisions made, and consultation with colleagues. Instead of searching for definitive answers to many of the multiple roles and responsibilities associated with counseling practice, the real challenge is to learn a process of thinking about such dilemmas and clarifying our rationale for the decisions we make in our professional practice.

# References

Akamatsu, T. J. (1988). Intimate relationships with former clients: National survey of attitudes and behavior among practitioners. *Professional Psychology: Research and Practice, 19,* 454–458.

Akos, P., Goodnough, G. E., & Milsom, A. S. (2004). Preparing school counselors for group work. *Journal for Specialists in Group Work, 29,* 127–136.

Allen, V. B. (1986). A historical perspective on the AACD Ethics Committee. *Journal of Counseling & Development, 64,* 293.

American Association for Marriage and Family Therapy. (2001). *AAMFT code of ethics.* Washington, DC: Author.

American College Personnel Association. (1995). Statement of ethical principles. In *ACPA membership directory, 1995–96* (pp. 14–17). Washington, DC: Author.

American Counseling Association. (1995). *Code of ethics and standards of practice.* Alexandria, VA: Author.

American Counseling Association. (2005). *ACA code of ethics.* Alexandria, VA: Author.

American Psychiatric Association. (2001). *The principles of medical ethics with annotations especially applicable to psychiatry.* Washington, DC: Author.

American Psychological Association. (1987). *If sex enters into the psychotherapy relationship.* Washington, DC: Author.

American Psychological Association. (2002). Ethical principles of psychologists and code of conduct. *American Psychologist, 57,* 1060–1073.

American Psychological Association, Ethics Committee. (1987). Report of the Ethics Committee: 1986. *American Psychologist, 42,* 730–734.

American Psychology-Law Society & Division 41 of the American Psychological Association. (1991). *Specialty guidelines for forensic psychologists.* Lincoln: University of Nebraska, Department of Psychology.

American School Counselor Association. (2004). *Ethical standards for school counselors.* Alexandria, VA: Author.

Anderson, R. D., & Price, G. E. (2001). Experiential groups in counselor education: Student attitudes and instructor participation. *Counselor Education and Supervision, 41,* 111–119.

Anderson, S. K., & Kitchener, K. S. (1996). Nonromantic, nonsexual posttherapy relationships between psychologists and former clients: An exploratory study of critical incidents. *Professional Psychology: Research and Practice, 27,* 59–66.

Anonymous. (1991). Sexual harassment: A female counseling student's experience. *Journal of Counseling & Development, 69,* 502–506.

Association for Addiction Professionals (NAADAC). (2003). *Practitioner services network: Survey of NAADAC members.* Alexandria, VA: Author.

Association for Counselor Education and Supervision. (1993, Summer). Ethical guidelines for counseling supervisors. *ACES Spectrum, 53*(4).

Association for Specialists in Group Work. (1998). Best practice guidelines [Electronic version]. *Journal for Specialists in Group Work, 23,* 237–244.

Association for Specialists in Group Work. (1999). Principles for diversity-competent group workers [Electronic version]. *Journal for Specialists in Group Work, 24,* 7–14.

Association for Specialists in Group Work. (2000). Professional standards for the training of group workers [Electronic version]. *Group Worker, 29,* 1–10.

Atkinson, D. R. (2004). *Counseling American minorities* (6th ed.). New York: McGraw-Hill.

Atkinson, D. R., Thompson, C. E., & Grant, S. K. (1993). A three-dimensional model for counseling racial/ethnic minorities. *The Counseling Psychologist, 21,* 257–277.

Austin, K. M., Moline, M. E., & Williams, G. T. (1990). *Confronting malpractice: Legal and ethical dilemmas in psychotherapy.* Newbury Park, CA: Sage.

Bajt, T. R., & Pope, K. S. (1989). Therapist–patient sexual intimacy involving children and adolescents. *American Psychologist, 44,* 55.

Bartell, P. A., & Rubin, L. J. (1990). Dangerous liaisons: Sexual intimacies in supervision. *Professional Psychology: Research and Practice, 21,* 442–450.

Bates, C. M., & Brodsky, A. M. (1989). *Sex in the therapy hour: A case of professional incest.* New York: Guilford Press.

Beauchamp, T. (1982). *Philosophical ethics: An introduction to moral philosophy.* New York: McGraw-Hill.

Bemak, F., & Chung, R. C-Y. (2004). Teaching multicultural group counseling: Perspectives for a new era. *Journal for Specialists in Group Work, 29,* 31–41.

Berman, J. R. (1985). Ethical feminist perspectives on dual relationships with clients. In L. B. Rosewater & L. E. Walker, *Handbook of feminist therapy: Women's issues in psychotherapy* (pp. 287–296). New York: Springer.

Bernard, J. M. (1979). Supervisor training: A discrimination model. *Counselor Education and Supervision, 19,* 60–68.

Bernard, J. M., & Goodyear, R. K. (2004). *Fundamentals of clinical supervision* (3rd ed.). Boston: Allyn & Bacon.

Bersoff, D. N. (2003). *Ethical conflicts in psychology* (3rd ed.). Washington, DC: American Psychological Association.

Biaggio, M., Paget, T. L., & Chenoweth, M. S. (1997). A model for ethical management of faculty–student dual relationships. *Professional Psychology: Research and Practice, 28,* 184–189.

Biaggo, M., & Greene, B. (1995). Overlapping dual relationships. In E. Rave & C. Larsen, *Ethical decision making in therapy: Feminist perspectives* (pp. 88–123). New York: Guilford Press.

Bissell, L. C., & Royce, J. E. (1994). *Ethics for addiction professionals* (2nd ed.). Center City, MN: Hazelden Foundation.

Black, H. C. (1983). *Black's law dictionary.* St. Paul, MN: West.

Bograd, M. (1993, January/February). The duel over dual relationships. *The California Therapist,* 7–16.

Borders, L. D., & Brown, L. L. (2005). *The new handbook of counseling supervision.* Mahwah, NJ: Erlbaum.

Borys, D. S. (1988). *Dual relationships between therapist and client: A national survey of clinicians' attitudes and practices.* Unpublished doctoral dissertation, University of California, Los Angeles.

Borys, D. S., & Pope, K. S. (1989). Dual relationships between therapist and client. A national study of psychologists, psychiatrists, and social workers. *Professional Psychology: Research and Practice, 20,* 283–293.

Bowman, V. E., Hatley, L. D., & Bowman, R. L. (1995). Faculty–student relationships: The dual role controversy. *Counselor Education and Supervision, 34,* 232–242.

Brown, L. (1994). Boundaries in feminist therapy: A conceptual formulation. *Women and Therapy, 15*(1), 29–38.

Brown, R., & Prager, L. (1985). Ethical issues in graduate education, faculty and student responsibilities. *Journal of Higher Education, 56*(4), 403–418.

Burian, B. K., & O'Connor Slimp, A. (2000). Social dual-role relationships during internship: A decision-making model. *Professional Psychology: Research and Practice, 31,* 332–338.

California Department of Consumer Affairs. (2004). *Professional therapy never includes sex.* Sacramento, CA: Author.

Campbell, C. D., & Gordon, M. C. (2003). Acknowledging the inevitable: Understanding multiple relationships in rural practice. *Professional Psychology: Research and Practice, 34,* 430–434.

Canadian Counselling Association. (1999). *Code of ethics.* Ottawa, Ontario, Canada: Author.

Commission on Rehabilitation Counselor Certification. (2001). *Code of professional ethics for rehabilitation counselors.* Rolling Meadows, IL: Author.

Conyne, R. K., & Bemak, F. (Eds.) (2004, March). Special issue on teaching group work. *Journal for Specialists in Group Work, 29*(1).

Corey, G., & Corey, M. (2006). *I never knew I had a choice* (8th ed.). Belmont, CA: Thomson Brooks/Cole.

Corey, G., Corey, M. S., & Callanan, P. (2003). *Issues and ethics in the helping professions* (6th ed.). Pacific Grove, CA: Brooks/Cole.

Corey, G., Corey, M. S., & Callanan, P. (2007). *Issues and ethics in the helping professions* (7th ed.). Belmont, CA: Thomson Brooks/Cole.

Corey, G., Corey, M. S., Callanan, P., & Russell, J. M. (2004). *Group techniques* (3rd ed.). Belmont, CA: Thomson Brooks/Cole.

Corey, M. S., & Corey, G. (2006). *Groups: Process and practice* (7th ed.). Belmont, CA: Thomson Brooks/Cole.

Cottone, R. R. (2001). A social constructivism model of ethical decision making in counseling. *Journal of Counseling & Development, 79,* 39–45.

Cottone, R. R. (2005). Detrimental therapist–client relationships—Beyond thinking of "dual" or "multiple" roles: Reflections on the 2001 *AAMFT Code of Ethics. American Journal of Family Therapy, 33,* 1–17.

Council for Accreditation of Counseling and Related Programs. (2001). *CACREP accreditation manual: 2001 standards.* Alexandria, VA: Author.

Cummings, N. (2002). The last word. In A. A. Lazarus and O. Zur, *Dual relationships and psychotherapy* (pp. 463–468). New York: Springer.

Davenport, D. S. (2004). Ethical issues in the teaching of group counseling. *Journal for Specialists in Group Work, 29,* 43–49.

Davis, A. H. (1997). The ethics of caring: A collaborative approach to resolving ethical dilemmas. *Journal of Applied Rehabilitation Counseling, 28*(1), 36–41.

DeLucia-Waack, J. L., & Donigian, J. (2004). *The practice of multicultural group work: Visions and perspectives from the field.* Belmont, CA: Brooks/Cole-Thomson Learning.

DeLucia-Waack, J. L., & Fauth, J. (2004). Effective supervision of group leaders: Current theory, research, and implications for practice. In J. L. DeLucia-Waack, D. Gerrity, C. R. Kalodner, & M. T. Riva (Eds), *Handbook of group counseling and psychotherapy* (pp. 136–150). Thousand Oaks, CA: Sage.

Dougherty, A. M. (2005). *Psychological consultation and collaboration in school and community settings* (4th ed.). Belmont, CA: Thomson Brooks/Cole.

Douglass, T. K. (1994). Comment: Psychotherapist sexual misconduct: A proposal for legislative change in Missouri. *University of Missouri at Kansas City Law Review, 62,* 777–819.

Dove, W. R. (1995). Ethics training for the alcohol/drug abuse professional. *Alcoholism Treatment Quarterly, 12*(4), 19–30.

Doyle, K. (1997). Substance abuse counselors in recovery: Implications for the ethical issue of dual relationships. *Journal of Counseling & Development, 75,* 428–432.

Egan, G. (2007). *The skilled helper: A problem-management and opportunity-development approach to helping* (8th ed.). Belmont, CA: Thomson Brooks/Cole.

Elman, N. S., & Forrest, L. (2004). Psychotherapy in the remediation of psychology trainees: Exploratory interviews with training directors. *Professional Psychology: Research and Practice, 35,* 123–130.

Emerson, S., & Markos, P. A. (1996). Signs and symptoms of the impaired counselor. *Journal of Humanistic Education and Development, 34,* 108–117.

Feminist Therapy Institute. (2000). *Feminist therapy code of ethics.* Georgetown, ME: Author.

Ferris, P.A., & Linville, M. E. (1985). The child's rights: Whose responsibility? *Elementary School Guidance and Counseling, 19,* 172–180.

Finney, J. W. (2002, November). *High quality community alcohol treatment/ interventions systems: Empirical evidence regarding the efficacy/effectiveness of selected components.* Paper presented to the Join Together Public Policy Panel. Retrieved April 23, 2004, from http://www.jointogether.org/sa/files/word/John_Finney_Paper.doc

Forester-Miller, H., & Davis, T. E. (1995). *A practitioner's guide to ethical decision making.* Alexandria, VA: American Counseling Association.

Forester-Miller, H., & Duncan, J. A. (1990). The ethics of dual relationships in the training of group counselors. *Journal for Specialists in Group Work, 20,* 222–231.

Forester-Miller, H., & Remley, T. P. (1995). *Perceived effectiveness of graduate courses that prepare counselors for group work.* Unpublished manuscript, North Carolina Central University, Durham.

Foster, S. (1996, January). The consequences of violating the "forbidden zone." *Counseling Today,* p. 24.

Freeman, L., & Roy, J. (1976). *Betrayal.* New York: Stein & Day.

Freud, S., & Krug, S. (2002). Beyond the code of ethics: Part II: Dual relationships revisited. *Families in Society: The Journal of Contemporary Human Services, 83,* 483–492.

Fu-Kiau, K. K. K. (1991). *Self healing power and therapy.* New York: Vintage Books.

Gabbard, G. O. (Ed.). (1989). *Sexual exploitation in professional relationships.* Washington, DC: American Psychiatric Association.

Gabbard, G. O. (1994). Teetering on a precipice: A commentary on Lazarus's "How certain boundaries and ethics diminish therapeutic effectiveness." *Ethics and Behavior, 4,* 283–286.

Gabbard, G. O. (1995, April). What are boundaries in psychotherapy? *The Menninger Letter, 3*(4), 12.

Gainsley, J. (1996). In the field: Groups in rural Sumter County. *Together, 24*(3), 9.

Garcia, J. G., Cartwright, B., Winston, S. M., & Borzuchowska, B. (2003). A transcultural integrative model for ethical decision making in counseling. *Journal of Counseling & Development, 81,* 268–277.

Gartrell, N., Herman, J., Olarte, S., Feldstein, M., & Localio, R. (1987). Reporting practices of psychologists who knew of sexual misconduct by colleagues. *American Journal of Orthopsychiatry, 57*(2), 287–295.

Gibson, W. T., & Pope, K. S. (1993). The ethics of counseling: A national survey of certified counselors. *Journal of Counseling & Development, 71,* 330–336.

Gill-Wigal, J., & Heaton, J. A. (1996, Summer). Managing sexual attraction in the therapeutic relationship. *Directions in Mental Health Counseling, 6,* 3–14.

Glaser, R. D., & Thorpe, J. S. (1986). Unethical intimacy: A survey of sexual contact and advances between psychology educators and female graduate students. *American Psychologist, 41*, 43–51.

Glosoff, H. L., Corey, G., & Herlihy, B. (2006). Avoiding detrimental multiple relationships. In B. Herlihy & G. Corey, *ACA ethical standards casebook* (6th ed., pp. 209–222). Alexandria, VA: American Counseling Association.

Glosoff, H. L., & Herlihy, B. (1995, Winter). Teaching, training, and supervision standards in the 1995 ACA code of ethics: What's new, what's different? *ACES Spectrum*, pp. 10–13.

Glosoff, H. L., & Pate, R. H. (2002). Privacy and confidentiality in school counseling. *Professional School Counseling, 6*, 20–27.

Gottlieb, M. C. (1990). Accusations of sexual misconduct: Assisting in the complaint process. *Professional Psychology: Research and Practice, 21*, 455–461.

Gottlieb, M. C. (1994). Ethical decision making, boundaries, and treatment effectiveness: A reprise. *Ethics and Behavior, 4*(3), 287–293.

Gottlieb, M. C., Sell, J. M., & Schoenfeld, L. S. (1988). Social/romantic relationships with present and former clients: State licensing board actions. *Professional Psychology: Research and Practice, 19*, 459–462.

Greenburg, S. L., Lewis, G. J., & Johnson, M. (1985). Peer consultation groups for private practitioners. *Professional Psychology: Research and Practice, 16*, 437–447.

Greenspan, M. (1986). Should therapists be personal? Self-disclosure and therapeutic distance in feminist therapy. *Women and Therapy, 5*, 5–17.

Greenspan, M. (2002). Out of bounds. In A. A. Lazarus & O. Zur (Eds.), *Dual relationships and psychotherapy* (pp. 425–431). New York: Springer.

Guth, L. J., & McDonnell, K. A. (2004). Designing class activities to meet specific core training competencies: A developmental approach. *Journal for Specialists in Group Work, 29*, 97–107.

Gutheil, T. G., & Gabbard, G. O. (1993). The concept of boundaries in clinical practice: Theoretical and risk-management dimensions. *American Journal of Psychiatry, 150*(2), 188–196.

Hammel, G. A., Olkin, R., & Taube, D. O. (1996). Student–educator sex in clinical and counseling psychology doctoral training. *Professional Psychology: Research and Practice, 27*, 93–97.

Handelsman, M. M., Gottlieb, M. C., & Knapp, S. (2005). Training ethical psychologists: An acculturation model. *Professional Psychology: Research and Practice, 36*, 59–65.

Hararr, W. R., VandeCreek, L., & Knapp, S. (1990). Ethical and legal aspects of clinical supervision. *Professional Psychology: Research and Practice, 21*, 37–41.

Haynes, R., Corey, G., & Moulton, P. (2003). *Clinical supervision in the helping professions: A practical guide*. Pacific Grove, CA: Brooks/Cole.

Hedges, L. E. (1993, July/August). In praise of dual relationships. Part II: Essential dual relatedness in developmental psychotherapy. *The California Therapist*, 42–46.

Helms, J. E., & Cook, D. A. (1999). *Issues of race and culture in counseling and psychotherapy.* Boston, MA: Allyn & Bacon.

Herlihy, B. (1996). When a colleague is impaired: The individual counselor's response. *Journal of Humanistic Education and Development, 34,* 118–127.

Herlihy, B. (2001). Managing boundaries. In L. Welfel & E. Ingersoll (Eds.), *The mental health desk reference* (pp. 465–471). New York: Wiley.

Herlihy, B. (2006). Ethical and legal issues in supervision. In J. M. Campbell, *Essentials of supervision* (pp. 18–34). New York: Wiley.

Herlihy, B., & Corey, G. (1992). *Dual relationships in counseling.* Alexandria, VA: American Association for Counseling and Development.

Herlihy, B., & Corey, G. (1994). Codes of ethics as catalysts for improving practice. *Ethical Issues in Professional Counseling, 2*(3), 2–12.

Herlihy, B., & Corey, G. (1996). *ACA ethical standards casebook* (5th ed.). Alexandria, VA: American Counseling Association.

Herlihy, B., & Corey, G. (1997). *Boundary issues in counseling: Multiple roles and responsibilities.* Alexandria, VA: American Counseling Association.

Herlihy, B., & Corey, G. (2006). *ACA ethical standards casebook* (6th ed.). Alexandria, VA: American Counseling Association.

Herlihy, B., & Goldin, L. B. (1990). *Ethical standards casebook* (4th ed.). Alexandria, VA: American Counseling Association.

Herlihy, B., & Watson, Z. E. (2006). Social justice and counseling ethics. In C. C. Lee (Ed.), *Counseling for social justice* (2nd ed.). Alexandria, VA: American Counseling Association.

Hill, M. (1990). On creating a theory of feminist therapy. *Women and Therapy, 9*(1/2), 53–65.

Hill, M., Glaser, K., & Harden, J. (1995). A feminist model for ethical decision making. In E. J. Rave & C. C. Larsen (Eds.), *Ethical decision making in therapy: Feminist perspectives* (pp. 18–37). New York: Guilford Press.

Hillerbrand, E. T., & Stone, G. L. (1986). Ethics and clients: A challenging mixture for counselors. *Journal of Counseling & Development, 64,* 419–420.

Hilliard, A. G., III (1998). *SBA: The reawakening of the African mind.* Gainsville, FL: Makare.

Holroyd, J. C., & Brodsky, A. M. (1977). Psychologists' attitudes and practices regarding erotic and nonerotic physical contact with patients. *American Psychologist, 32,* 843–849.

Hotelling, K. (1988). Ethical, legal, and administrative options to address sexual relationships between counselor and client. *Journal of Counseling & Development, 67,* 233–237.

International Association of Marriage and Family Counselors. (2005). The 2005 Ethical code of the International Association of Marriage and Family Counselors (IAMFC). Retreived February 28, 2006 from http://www.iamfc.com/revised_ethical_code.doc

International Certification & Reciprocity Consortium/Alcohol and Other Drug Abuse. (2003). *Member board lists—Alcohol & Other Drug Abuse Counselor.* Retrieved April 27, 2004, from http://www.icrcaoda.org/boardlist.htm

Ivey, A. E., Pedersen, P. B., & Ivey, M. B. (2001). *Intentional group counseling: A microskills approach.* Pacific Grove, CA: Brooks/Cole.

James, J. (1996, May 11). University to adopt rules that put limits on dating. *Register-Guard*, Eugene, OR, pp. 1, 6A.

Jensen, D. (2005). So, what exactly is a dual relationship? *The Therapist, 17*(4), 16–19.

Johnson, W. B., Ralph, J., & Johnson, S. J. (2005). Managing multiple roles in embedded environments: The case of aircraft carrier psychology. *Professional Psychology: Research and Practice, 36*, 73–81.

Kain, C. D. (1996). *Positive: HIV affirmative counseling.* Alexandria, VA: American Counseling Association.

Kane, A. W. (1995). The effects of criminalization of sexual misconduct by therapists. In J. C. Gonsiorek (Ed.), *Breach of trust: Sexual exploitation by health care professionals and clergy* (pp. 317–332). Thousand Oaks, CA: Sage.

Killacky, J., & Hulse-Killacky, D. (2004). Group work is not just for the group class anymore: Teaching generic group competency skills across the counselor education curriculum. *Journal for Specialists in Group Work, 29*(1), 87–96.

Kitchener, K. S. (1984). Intuition, critical evaluation, and ethical principles: The foundation for ethical decisions in counseling psychology. *The Counseling Psychologist, 12*, 43–56.

Kitchener, K. S. (1988). Dual relationships: What makes them so problematic? *Journal of Counseling & Development, 67*, 217–221.

Kitchener, K. S. (1992). Posttherapy relationships: Ever or never? In B. Herlihy & G. Corey, *Dual relationships in counseling* (pp. 145–148). Alexandria, VA: American Association for Counseling and Development.

Kitchener, K. S., & Harding, S. S. (1990). Dual role relationships. In B. Herlihy & L. Golden, *Ethical standards casebook* (4th ed., pp. 146–154). Alexandria, VA: American Association for Counseling and Development.

Kline, W. B., Falbaum, D. F., Pope, V. T., Hargraves, G. A., & Hundley, S. F. (1997). The significance of the group experience for students in counselor education: A preliminary naturalistic inquiry. *Journal for Specialists in Group Work, 22*(3), 157–166.

Knapp, S., & Slattery, J. M. (2004). Professional boundaries in nontraditional settings. *Professional Psychology: Research and Practice, 35*, 553–558.

Kottler, J. A. (2004). Realities of teaching group counseling. *Journal for Specialists in Group Work, 29*(1), 51–53.

Ladany, N., & Friedlander, M. L. (1995). The relationship between the supervisory working alliance and trainees' experience of role conflict and role ambiguity. *Counselor Education and Supervision, 34*, 220–231.

Lamb, D. H. (1992). Relationships with former clients: Ethical, legal, and clinical considerations. *Register Report, 18,* 13–14.

Lamb, D. H., Catanzaro, S. J., & Moorman, A. S. (2003). Psychologists reflect on their sexual relationships with clients, supervisees, and students: Occurrence, impact, rationales, and collegial intervention. *Professional Psychology: Research and Practice, 34,* 102–107.

Lazarus, A. A., & Zur, O. (Eds.). (2002). *Dual relationships and psychotherapy.* New York: Springer.

Leatherman, C. (1993). In the debate over faculty–student dating, the talk turns to ethics, sex, even love. *Chronicle of Higher Education, 24*(37), A15–A17.

Lloyd, A. P. (1992). Dual relationship problems in counselor education. In B. Herlihy & G. Corey, *Dual relationships in counseling* (pp. 59–64). Alexandria, VA: American Association for Counseling and Development.

Lyon, D., & Ogloff, R. P. (2000). Legal and ethical issues in psychopathy assessment. In C. B. Gacono (Ed.), *Clinical and forensic assessment of psychopathy: A practitioner's guide* (pp. 139–170). Mahwah, NJ: Erlbaum.

Margolin, G. (1982). Ethical and legal considerations in marital and family therapy. *American Psychologist, 37,* 788–801.

Markus, H. E., & King, D. A. (2003). A survey of group psychotherapy training during predoctoral psychology internship. *Professional Psychology: Research and Practice, 34,* 203–209.

McCarthy, P., Sugden, S., Koker, M., Lamendola, F., Maurer, S., & Renninger, S. (1995). A practical guide to informed consent in clinical supervision. *Counselor Education and Supervision, 35,* 130–138.

Meara, N., Schmidt, L., & Day, J. (1996). Principles and virtues: A foundation for ethical decisions, policies, and character. *The Counseling Psychologist, 24,* 4–77.

Meloy, J. R., Haroun, A., & Schiller, E. F. (1990). *Clinical guidelines for involuntary outpatient treatment.* Sarasota, FL: Professional Resource Exchange.

Merta, R. J. (1997). The experiential group: Avoid or manage? In B. Herlihy & G. Corey, *Boundary issues in counseling: Multiple roles and responsibilities* (pp. 90–92). Alexandria, VA: American Counseling Association.

Merta, R. J., Wolfgang, L., & McNeil, K. (1993). Five models for using the experiential group in the preparation of group counselors. *Journal for Specialists in Group Work, 18,* 200–207.

Miller, G. M., & Larrabee, M. J. (1995). Sexual intimacy in counselor education and supervision: A national survey. *Counselor Education and Supervision, 34,* 332–343.

Mobley, M. J. (1999). Psychotherapy with criminal offenders. In I. Weiner & A. Hess (Eds.), *Handbook of forensic psychology* (2nd ed., pp 603–639). New York: Wiley.

Moleski, S. M., & Kiselica, M. S. (2005). Dual relationships: A continuum ranging from the destructive to the therapeutic. *Journal of Counseling & Development, 83,* 3–11.

Monahan, J. (Ed.). (1980). *Who is the client?* Washington, DC: American Psychological Association.

NAADAC. (2003). *Year 2 final report: A survey of early career substance abuse counselors.* Retrieved April 27, 2004, from http://naadac.org/pressroom/files/Year2SurveyReport.pdf

Narcotics Anonymous. (1988). *Narcotics Anonymous* (5th ed.). Chatsworth, CA: Narcotics Anonymous World Services.

National Association of Social Workers. (1999). *Code of ethics.* Washington, DC: Author.

National Association of Student Personnel Administrators. (1996). Standards of professional practice. In *NASPA membership handbook* (pp. 19–20). Washington, DC: Author.

Nerison, R. M. (1992). *Dual client–therapist relationships: Incidence and consequences to clients.* Unpublished doctoral dissertation, University of Iowa.

Neukrug, E. S., Healy, M., & Herlihy, B. (1992). Ethical practices of licensed professional counselors: An updated survey of state licensing boards. *Counselor Education and Supervision, 32,* 130–141.

Neukrug, E. S., Milliken, T., & Walden, S. (2001). Ethical practices of credentialed professional counselors: An updated survey of state licensing boards. *Counselor Education and Supervision, 41,* 57–70.

Noel, B., & Watterson, K. (1992). *You must be dreaming.* New York: Poseidon.

O'Halloran, T. M., & McCartney, T. J. (2004). An evaluation of the use of technology as a tool to meet group training standards. *Journal for Specialists in Group Work, 29,* 65–74.

Oliver, M. N. I., Bernstein, J. H., Anderson, K. G., Blashfield, R. K., & Roberts, M. C. (2004). An exploratory examination of student attitudes toward "impaired" peers in clinical psychology training programs. *Professional Psychology: Research and Practice, 35,* 141–147.

Parham, T. A. (1997). An African-centered view of dual relationships. In B. Herlihy & G. Corey, *Boundary issues in counseling: Multiple roles and responsibilities* (pp. 109–111). Alexandria, VA: American Counseling Association.

Parham, T. A. (Ed.). (2002). *Counseling persons of African descent: Raising the bar of practitioner competence.* Thousand Oaks, CA: Sage.

Pellegrino, E., & Thomasma, D. (1993). *The virtues in medical practice.* New York: Oxford University Press.

Plaisel, E. (1985). *Therapist.* New York: St. Martin's/Marek.

Polanski, P. (2000). Training supervisors at the master's level: Developmental consideration. *ACES Spectrum Newsletter, 61*(2), 3–5.

Polcin, D. L. (2000). Professional counseling versus specialized programs for alcohol and drug abuse treatment. *Journal of Addictions & Offender Counseling, 21,* 2–11.

Pope, K. S. (1988). How clients are harmed by sexual contact with mental health professionals: The syndrome and its prevalence. *Journal of Counseling & Development, 67,* 222–226.

Pope, K. S. (1994). *Sexual involvement with therapists: Patient assessment, subsequent therapy, forensics.* Washington, DC: American Psychological Association.

Pope, K. S., & Bouhoutsos, J. C. (1986). *Sexual intimacy between therapists and patients.* New York: Praeger Press.

Pope, K. S., Keith-Spiegel, P., & Tabachnick, B. G. (1986). Sexual attraction to clients: The human therapist and the (sometimes) inhuman training system. *American Psychologist, 41,* 147–158.

Pope, K. S., Levenson, H., & Schover, L. (1979). Sexual intimacy in psychology training. *American Psychologist, 34,* 682–689.

Pope, K. S., Sonne, J., & Holroyd, J. (1993). *Sexual feelings in psychotherapy: Explorations for therapists and therapists in training.* Washington, DC: American Psychological Association.

Pope, K. S., & Tabachnick, B. G. (1993). Therapists' anger, hate, fear, and sexual feelings: National survey of therapist responses, client characteristics, critical events, formal complaints, and training. *Professional Psychology: Research and Practice, 24,* 142–152.

Pope, K. S., Tabachnick, B. G., & Keith-Spiegel, P. (1987). Ethics of practice: The beliefs and behaviors of psychologists as therapists. *American Psychologist, 42,* 993–1006.

Pope, K. S., & Vasquez, M. J. T. (1998). *Ethics in psychotherapy and counseling* (2nd ed.). San Francisco: Jossey-Bass.

Pope, K. S., & Vetter, V. (1991). Prior therapist–patient sexual involvement among patients seen by psychologists. *Psychotherapy, 28,* 429–438.

Powell, D. J. (with Brodsky, A.). (1993). *Clinical supervision in alcohol and drug abuse counseling: Principles, models, methods.* San Francisco: Jossey-Bass.

Remley, T. P., & Fry, L. J. (1993). Reporting suspected child abuse: Conflicting roles for the counselor. *School Counselor, 40,* 253–259.

Remley, T. P., & Herlihy, B. (2005). *Ethical, legal, and professional issues in counseling* (2nd ed.). Upper Saddle River, NJ: Merrill/Prentice-Hall.

Rest, J. (1982). The major components of morality. In W. Kurtines & J. Gerwitz, *Moral behavior and moral development* (pp. 24–40). New York: Wiley.

Riger, S. (1991). Gender dilemmas in sexual harassment policies and procedures. *American Psychologist, 46,* 497–505.

Robinson, W., & Reid, P. (1985). Sexual intimacies in psychology revisited. *Professional Psychology: Research and Practice, 16,* 512–520.

Roy v. Hartogs, 381 N.Y.S.2d 587 (N.Y. Civ. Ct. 1975).

Rutter, P. (1989). *Sex in the forbidden zone.* Los Angeles: Tarcher.

Salisbury, W. A., & Kinnier, R. T. (1996). Posttermination friendship between counselors and clients. *Journal of Counseling & Development, 74,* 495–500.

Santiago-Rivera, A. L., Arredondo, P., & Gallardo-Cooper, M. (2002). *Counseling Latinos and la familia.* Thousand Oaks, CA: Sage.

Sayre, L. D. (1992). The parallel process in the addiction treatment staff system: An ethical perspective. *Alcoholism Treatment Quarterly, 9*(2), 65–75.

Schafer, C. (1990, March 1). Ethics: Dual relationships come under scrutiny. *Guidepost,* pp. 1, 3, 16.

Schoener, G., & Gonsiorek, J. (1988). Assessment and development of rehabilitation plans for counselors who have sexually exploited their clients. *Journal of Counseling & Development, 67,* 227–232.

Sherry P. (1991). Ethical issues in the conduct of supervision. *The Counseling Psychologist, 19*(4), 566–584.

Shimberg, B. (1986). Preventing sexual exploitation of clients by counselors: A plea for protection. *Journal of Counseling & Development, 65,* 119–120.

Simon, R. I. (1989). Sexual exploitation of patients: How it begins before it happens. *Psychiatry Annals, 19,* 104–112.

Simon, R. I. (1991). Psychological injury caused by boundary violations: Precursors to therapist–patient sex. *Psychiatry Annals, 21,* 614–619.

Simon, R. I. (1992). Treatment of boundary violations: Clinical, ethical, and legal considerations. *Bulletin of the American Academy of Psychiatry and the Law, 20,* 269–288.

Simon, S. (1987). *Clinical psychiatry and the law.* Washington, DC: American Psychiatric Press.

Sleek, S. (1994, December). Ethical dilemmas plague rural practice. *APA Monitor,* pp. 26–27.

Slimp, P. A., & Burian, B. K. (1994). Multiple role relationships during internship: Consequences and recommendations. *Professional Psychology: Research and Practice, 25,* 39–45.

Smith, D., & Fitzpatrick, M. (1995). Patient–therapist boundary issues: An integrative review of theory and research. *Professional Psychology: Research and Practice, 26,* 499–506.

Sonne, J. L. (1994). Multiple relationships: Does the new ethics code answer the right questions? *Professional Psychology: Research and Practice, 25,* 336–343.

Stadler, H. (1986a, September). Making hard choices: Clarifying controversial ethical issues. *Counseling and Human Development, 1,* 1–10.

Stadler, H. (1986b). To counsel or not to counsel: The ethical dilemma of dual relationships. *Journal of Counseling and Human Service Professions, 1*(1), 134–140.

Stadler, H. (1989). Child abuse reporting: A strategy for acting on ethical responsibilities. *The Counseling Psychologist, 17,* 102–110.

Stadler, H. (1992). Counseling relationships between students and educators. In B. Herlihy & G. Corey, *Dual relationships in counseling* (pp. 52–56). Alexandria, VA: American Association for Counseling and Development.

Stockton, R., Morran, D. K., & Krieger, K. M. (2004). An overview of current research and best practices for training beginning group leaders. In J. L. DeLucia-Waack, D. Gerrity, C. R. Kalodner, & M. T. Riva, (Eds.), *Handbook of group counseling and psychotherapy* (pp. 65–75). Thousand Oaks, CA: Sage.

St. Germaine, J. (1993). Dual relationships: What's wrong with them? *American Counselor, 2*(3), 25–30.

St. Germaine, J. (1996). Dual relationships and certified alcohol and drug counselors: A national study of ethical beliefs and behaviors. *Alcoholism Treatment Quarterly, 14*(2), 29–44.

St. Germaine, J. (1997). Ethical practices of certified addiction counselors: A national survey of state certification boards. *Alcoholism Treatment Quarterly, 15*(2), 63–72.

Sue, D. W., Ivey, A. E., & Pedersen, P. B. (1996). *A theory of multicultural counseling and psychotherapy.* Pacific Grove, CA: Brooks/Cole.

Sue, D. W., & Sue, D. (2003). *Counseling the culturally diverse: Theory and practice.* New York: Wiley.

Sue, S., & Zane, N. (1987). The role of culture and cultural techniques in psychotherapy: A critique and reformulation. *American Psychologist, 42,* 37–45.

Sumerel, M. B., & Borders, L. D. (1996). Addressing personal issues in supervision: Impact of counselors' experience level on various aspects of the supervisory relationship. *Counselor Education and Supervision, 35,* 268–285.

Sutter, E., McPherson, R. H., & Geeseman, R. (2002). Contracting for supervision. *Professional Psychology: Research and Practice, 33,* 495–498.

Syme, G. (2003). *Dual relationships in counselling and psychotherapy.* London: Sage.

Tabachnick, B. G., Keith-Spiegel, P., & Pope, K. S. (1991). Ethics of teaching: Beliefs and behaviors of psychologists as educators. *American Psychologist, 46,* 506–515.

Thomas, J. L. (2002). Bartering. In A. A. Lazarus & O. Zur (Eds.), *Dual relationships and psychotherapy* (pp. 394–408). New York: Springer.

Thoreson, R. W., Shaughnessy, P., & Frazier, P. A. (1995). Sexual contact during and after professional relationships: Practices and attitudes of female counselors. *Journal of Counseling & Development, 74,* 84–89.

Thoreson, R. W., Shaughnessy, P., Heppner, P. P., & Cook, S. W. (1993). Sexual contact during and after the professional relationship: Attitudes and practices of male counselors. *Journal of Counseling & Development, 71,* 429–434.

Tomm, K. (1993, January/February). The ethics of dual relationships. *The California Therapist,* pp. 7–19.

Toriello, P. J., & Benshoff, J. J. (2003). Substance abuse counselors and ethical dilemmas: The influence of recovery and education level. *Journal of Addictions & Offender Counseling, 23,* 83–98.

Twemlow, S., & Gabbard, G. O. (1989). The love-sick therapist. In G. O. Gabbard (Ed.), *Sexual exploitation in professional relationships* (pp. 71–87). Washington, DC: American Psychiatric Press.

Tyler, J. M., & Tyler, C. (1994). Ethics in supervision: Managing supervisee rights and supervisor responsibilities. *Directions in Mental Health Counseling, 4*(11), 4–25.

Urofsky, R., & Sowa, C. (2004). Ethics education in CACREP-accredited counselor education programs. *Counseling and Values, 49,* 37–47.

Usher, C. H., & Borders, L. D. (1993). Practicing counselors' preferences for supervisory style and supervisory emphasis. *Counselor Education and Supervision, 33,* 66–79.

Vacha-Haase, T., Davenport, D. S., & Kerewsky, S. D. (2004). Problematic students: Gatekeeping practices of academic professional psychology programs. *Professional Psychology: Research and Practice, 35,* 115–122.

Vasquez, M. J. T. (1988). Counselor–client sexual contact: Implications for ethics training. *Journal of Counseling & Development, 67,* 238–241.

Vasquez, M. J. T. (1991). Sexual intimacies with clients after termination: Should a prohibition be explicit? *Ethics and Behavior, 1*(1), 45–61.

Vinson, J. S. (1987). Use of complaint procedures in cases of therapist–patient sexual contact. *Professional Psychology: Research and Practice, 18,* 159–164.

Walden, S. L. (1996). *Public knowledge of counseling ethics.* Unpublished doctoral dissertation, Kent State University.

Walker, E., & Young, T. D. (1986). *A killing cure.* New York: Holt, Rinehart & Winston.

Welfel, E. R. (2006). *Ethics in counseling and psychotherapy: Standards, research, and emerging issues* (3rd ed.). Belmont, CA: Thomson Brooks/Cole.

Whiston, S. C., & Emerson, S. (1989). Ethical implications for supervisors in counseling of trainees. *Counselor Education and Supervision, 28,* 318–325.

Wilson, F. R., Rapin, L. S., & Haley-Banez, L. (2004). How teaching group work can be guided by foundational documents: Best practice guidelines, diversity principles, training standards. *Journal for Specialists in Group Work, 29,* 19–29.

Wilson, J. (1993). *The moral sense.* New York: Free Press.

Wise, P. S., Lowery, S., & Silverglade, L. (1989). Personal counseling for counselors in training: Guidelines for supervisors. *Counselor Education and Supervision, 28,* 326–336.

Woody, R. H. (1998). Bartering for psychological services. *Professional Psychology: Research and Practice, 29,* 174–178.

Yalom, I. D. (2003). *The gift of therapy.* New York: HarperCollins (Perennial).

Yalom, I. D. (with Leszcz, M.). (2005). *Theory and practice of group psychotherapy* (5th ed.). New York: Basic Books.

Young, M. H., Justice, J. V., Erdberg, P. S., & Gacono, C. B. (2000). The incarcerated psychopath in psychiatric treatment: Management or treatment? In C. B. Gacono (Ed.), *Clinical and forensic assessment of psychopathy: A practitioner's guide* (pp. 313–331). Mahwah, NJ: Erlbaum.

Younggren, J. N., & Gottlieb, M. C. (2004). Managing risk when contemplating multiple relationships. *Professional Psychology: Research and Practice, 35*(3), 255–260.

Zur, O., & Lazarus, A. A. (2002). Six arguments against dual relationships and their rebuttals. In A. A. Lazarus & O. Zur (Eds.), *Dual relationships and psychotherapy* (pp. 3–24). New York: Springer.

Index

A

AAFMT. *See* American Association for Marriage and Family Therapy (AAMFT) Code of Ethics

ACA Code of Ethics
  client dealings
    acceptance of gifts from clients, 118
    advocacy for minority clients, 127
    bartering for goods or services, 116, 123
    culturally appropriate practice and, 48, 132
    friends as clients, 119–120
    sexual relationships with clients, 23, 25
    sexual relationships with former clients, 25, 27
  counselor education
    evaluation of students' competencies, 58
    informed consent of students, 59
    peer roles in, 65
    relationships between student and faculty, 53–54, 63, 64
    relationships between student and student, 53–54, 62, 102
    research credit for students, 60
    self-disclosure of students in, 57, 101–102
      sexual relationships with students, 54, 63
      specifics on, 63
      student responsibilities in, 64
  nonprofessional interactions, 2, 3–4
    avoidance of, 9
    changing role of counselors, 144
    potentially beneficial interactions, 9, 10, 196
    pro bono therapy encouraged by, 141
    self-care of counselors, 143
    supervisory roles, 74–75
      distinguishing between counseling and supervision, 77
      sexual relationships in, 76
ACA Ethics Committee
  guide for ethical decision-making from, 51
  proposed addition of member of general public on, 50
  supervisory role affected by membership on, 83
ACES. *See* Association for Counselor Education and Supervision (ACES) ethical guidelines
Addiction. *See* Substance abuse counseling
Adler, A., 143
Adlerian therapists and collaborative nature of therapy, 44
Administrative relationships and conflict of interest, 64
Advocacy role of therapists
  for minority clients, 127
  in rehabilitation counseling, 166, 169–170

213

African-centered worldview, 131–136
AIDS, counseling clients with, 163–165
Akos, P., 97
Ambivalence of clients and sexual relationships with therapists, 32
American Association for Marriage and Family Therapy (AAMFT) Code of Ethics
    acceptance of gifts from clients, 118
    bartering for goods or services, 116
    nonprofessional interactions, 2, 4
    sexual relationships with clients, 25
    sexual relationships with former clients, 26, 27
    sexual relationships with students, 55, 76
American College Personnel Association "Statement of Ethical Principles," 188
American Counseling Association. See ACA Code of Ethics; ACA Ethics Committee
American Psychological Association (APA)
    code of ethics
        bartering for goods or services, 116
        nonprofessional interactions, 2, 4–5, 9
        nonpsychologist member of general public on Ethics Committee, 50
        sexual relationships with clients, and former clients, 25, 26, 27
        sexual relationships with students or supervisees, 55, 76
    Specialty Guidelines for Forensic Psychologists, 171
American School Counselor Association (ASCA) Ethical Standards for School Counselors, 2, 4, 175, 177–178
Anderson, R. D., 100
Anderson, S. K., 126
APA. See American Psychological Association
ASCA. See American School Counselor Association (ASCA) Ethical Standards for School Counselors
ASGW. See Association for Specialists in Group Work
Asian clients, 129

Association for Counselor Education and Supervision (ACES) ethical guidelines, 74, 75, 76, 77, 88
Association for Specialists in Group Work (ASGW)
    guidance on training and practice in group work, 96, 97, 101
    survey of members on effectiveness of group training courses, 103
Atkinson, D. R., 127, 130
Attitudes and beliefs of clients, 41–42
Austin, K. M., 31

B

Bartell, P. A., 37
Bartering for goods or services, 116–118
    culturally appropriate practice and, 48
    in private practice, 142
    in rural communities, 122–123
Benefits of dual relationships, 6–7, 192
    ACA Code of Ethics on nonprofessional interactions, 10, 196
    client inclusion in ethical decision-making process, 47–49
    in group counselor education, 100
    weighing against potential for harm, 193, 197
Benshoff, J. J., 160, 162
Berman, J. R., 141, 145
Bernard, J. M., 77, 80, 89
Biaggio, M., 61, 144
Blind grading system, 103
Bludworth, Jamie, 84–90
Bograd, M., 8
Borders, L. D., 79, 81–84
Borys, D. S., 42, 118, 120, 123, 124
Boundary crossings
    in couples and family counseling, 152–158
    in decision-making model, 196
    defined, 10–11
    distinguished from boundary violations, 17
    in psychotherapy, 16–19
    role blending, 61, 197
Boundary setting, 15–16
    legal perspective on, 22
    professional assuming control of, 43–44
Boundary violations
    defined, 10–11

distinguished from boundary crossings, 17
sexual. *See* Sexual relationships
Bowman, R. L., 61
Bowman, V. E., 61
Brodsky, A. M., 29
Brown, L., 139
Burian, B. K., 61, 80, 81
Business relationships with supervisees, 80–81

CACREP. *See* Council for Accreditation of Counseling and Related Educational Programs (CACREP) standards on group process
Caduceus groups, 161
Cain, H., 166–170
Caldwell, L. D., 131–136
Callanan, P., 8
Campbell, C. D., 121
Canadian Counselling Association (CCA) *Code of Ethics*
sexual relationships with former clients, 25–26, 27
social relationships with former clients, 125
Case management in rehabilitation counseling, 167–168
Catanzaro, S. J., 56
CCA. *See* Canadian Counselling Association (CCA) *Code of Ethics*
Character disorders of therapists who become sexual offenders, 30
Chenoweth, M. S., 61
Child abuse, school counselor dealing with, 176, 179
Children
See also School counseling
in family therapy, 153, 154, 155–156
therapists' sexual relationships with, 29
Client focus stage of decision-making models during supervision, 87
Client perspective, 41–46
attitudes and beliefs, 41–42
collaborative role in therapeutic process, 44–46, 50
in ethical decision process, 46–52
experiences with dual relationships and, 42–43

implications of, 43–44
Codes of ethics, 2–5, 191–192
See also Ethical standards; *specific associations*
Cognitive behavior therapy and collaborative nature of therapy, 44
Cognitive dysfunction of clients and sexual relationships with therapists, 33
Collaborative role of client in therapeutic process, 44–46, 50
Colleges. *See* Universities and colleges
Collusion in couples and family counseling, 156
Commission on Rehabilitation Counselor Certification (CRCC) *Code of Professional Ethics for Rehabilitation Counselors*
relationships with third-party payers, 169
sexual relationships with former clients, 26, 27
sexual relationships with students or supervisees, 76
Community work of counselors, 115–136
See also Multicultural perspectives; Rural communities
multiple roles of counselors in community, 126–128
Competence
group work training and practice competencies, 96
of students, 58, 69
of supervisees, 89–90
of supervisors, 75–76
Complexity of therapeutic relationships, 143
Confidentiality
See also Informed consent; Self-disclosure
in forensic setting, 171
Consubstantiation, 134
Consultation
defined, 90
dual role conflicts in, 81–84, 90–91
rationale for avoiding, 91–93
with fellow professionals, 15, 192–193
peer consultation, 144
school counselors in consulting role, 178
Contracts between supervisors and supervisees, 88
Cook, D. A., 132

Corey, G., 8, 23, 62, 104–113, 177
Corey, M. S., 8, 177
Cottone, R. R., 45–46
Council for Accreditation of Counseling
  and Related Educational Programs
  (CACREP) standards on group
  process, 96, 97
Counselor education, 53–71
  African-American trainees and,
    134–135
  dual relationships in, 53–54, 62–66
  ethical dilemmas arising in, 63–65
  ethics courses as part of, 65, 66–67,
    193–194
  evaluation of students' competen-
    cies, 58, 69
  group counselors, education of,
    95–114
  informed consent of students, 59
  managing ethical quandaries in,
    65–66, 70
  reflections of recent doctoral
    graduate, 68–71
  relationships between student
    and faculty, 53–54, 60–62
  relationships between student
    and student, 53–54, 62
  reporting of colleagues for
    sexual relationships with
    students, 38–39
  research credit for students, 60
  role conflicts for educators, 56–59
  self-disclosure of students in, 57,
    68
  sexual relationships with
    students, 29, 30, 37–38, 42–43,
    54–56, 63
  teaching group counseling
    courses, 104–113
Countertransference issues
  in counseling, 144
  in forensic setting, 172
  in supervision, 88–89
Couples and family counseling, 150–158
  avoiding alignment and
    collusion in, 156
  boundary considerations in,
    152–158
  defining the client, 153–156
  self-disclosure of therapist in,
    156–157
  special considerations of, 150–152
Criminal offenders, counseling for,
  170–173

Criminal sanctions for sexual relationships with clients, 23–24, 31
Culturally appropriate practice
  See also Multicultural perspectives
  gift giving as, 119, 129
  inclusion of client in ethical
    decision-making process
    and, 48

D

Davenport, D. S., 103
Davis, T. E., 50, 51
Decision-making models, 195–197
  client perspective in, 46–52
  for supervisors, 87
DeLucia-Waack, J. L., 97
Disabilities, counseling of clients with.
  See Rehabilitation counseling
Disclosure by counselors. See Self-
  disclosure
Discrimination
  HIV-positive clients facing, 163
  racial and ethnic. See Multicutural
    perspectives
Divergence of responsibilities for
  counselors, 12–13
Documenting of dual relationships in
  case notes, 16
Dougherty, A. M., 91–93, 178, 179–182
Drug abuse. See Substance abuse
  counseling
Dual relationships
  conflicting views on, 7–9
  decision-making model, 195–197
  defined, 1–2
  difficulty in recognizing, 5–6
  inherent duality, 11
  legal perspectives, 22–24
  potential for harm and, 11–13,
    192, 193
  problems associated with, 5–10,
    193
  risks in, 13–15
  unavoidable conflicts, 9–10, 15,
    191, 192
Duncan, J. A., 102, 103

E

Education
  of consumers, 36
  of counselors. See Counselor
    education

of group counselors. *See* Group
counselors, education of
Egan, G., 87
Emerson, S., 87
Emotional harm in malpractice suit, 23
Emotional lability of clients and sexual
relationships with therapists, 32
Employing of clients, 162
Empowerment of clients, 47–48
Emptiness and isolation of clients and
sexual relationships with therapists,
32
Esalen, 17
Ethical standards, 3–5
*See also specific associations for codes
of ethics*
ability to recognize ethical dilemma
and, 63
aspirational level of, 49
bartering. *See* Bartering for
goods or services
client participation
in creation and adjudication
of ethics codes, 50
in ethical decision-making
process, 42, 46–52
courses in educational programs
on, 65, 66–67, 193–194
culturally appropriate practice
and, 48–49
gifts from clients, 48, 118–119, 129
self-disclosure limits, 123–124. *See*
Self-disclosure
sexual relationships. *See* Sexual
relationships
social relationships. *See* Social
relationships
substance abuse counseling,
training in, 162
supervisory roles. *See* Supervision
Evaluation of student competencies,
58, 69
Experiential approach to couples and
family counseling, 154
Experiential learning in counselor
education, 68–69
in group counselor education,
97, 99, 101–104, 110–111

F

Faculty. *See* Counselor education;
Universities and colleges
sexual relationships with students.
See Sexual relationships

Family therapists. *See* American
Association for Marriage and Family
Therapy (AAMFT); Couples and
family counseling
Fauth, J., 97
Feminine therapists and collaborative
nature of therapy, 45, 50, 51
Feminist Therapy Code of Ethics
(Feminist Therapy Institute), 143
Ferris, P. A., 178
Financial issues in private practice,
141–142
Forensic psychology and counseling,
170–173
contributor's perspective on,
170–173
Forester-Miller, H., 50, 51, 100–104,
121–123, 130, 146
Former clients
group counseling for, 147
sexual relationships with, 25–29
social relationships with, 125–126
Foster, S., 31
Freud, S., 142
Friedlander, M. L., 79, 88
Friends as clients, 119–120
See also Social relationships in
group counseling, 146–147
Fry, L. J., 179
Fu-Kiau, K.K.K., 132

G

Gainsley, J., 122
Garcia, J. G., 48
Gatekeeper role
of educators, 57–58
of supervisors, 89, 93
Gender differences
in sexual relationships between
faculty and students, 55
on counseling of friends, 120
on sexual relationships, 29
Gibson, W. T., 42
Gifts
acceptance of gifts from clients,
118–119
culturally appropriate practice
and, 48, 119, 129
Gill-Wigal, J., 35
Glaser, K., 45
Glaser, R. D., 55
Glosoff, H. L., 138–145, 177

Golden, L., 30
Gonsiorek, J., 30
Goodnough, G. E., 97
Goodyear, R. K., 80, 89
Gordon, M. C., 121
Gottlieb, M. C., 37, 121, 194
Grant, S. K., 127, 130
Greene, B., 144
Group counseling, 145–150
    admitting friends or acquaintances,
        147
    concurrent with individual
        counseling, 147–148
    education of counselors. *See*
        Group counselors, education of
    for former clients, 147
    personal relationships in,
        146–147
    in rural communities, 123
    self-disclosure in, 149–150
Group counselors, education of,
    95–114
    blind grading system in, 103
    combining experiential and
        didactic training methods, 97,
        99, 101–104, 110–111
    informed consent of students in,
        98, 111
    multiple roles of group work
        educators, 97–100
    papers in workshop, 109–110
    Practicum in Group Leadership
        course, 104–105
    process commentary time, 108
    safeguards to protect students
        in, 103, 111–113
    small-group sessions, 106–108
    supervisors, role in, 108–109
    teacher's perspectives on,
        101–113
    training standards for, 95–97
    weekend training and supervision
        group, 105–110
Group Techniques (Corey, G., et al.), 106
Guilt of clients and sexual relationships
    with therapists, 32

Hammel, G. A., 55
Handelsman, M. M., 194
Hararr, W. R., 80

Harden, J., 45
Harding, S. S., 12, 116, 119
Hatley, L. D., 61
Haynes, R., 170–173
Healers in African-centered context,
    132–134
Healy, M., 24
Heaton, J. A., 35
Hedges, L. E., 9
Helms, J. E., 132
Herlihy, B., 8, 24, 62, 77
Hermann, M. A., 22–24
Higher education counseling. *See*
    Universities and colleges
Hill, M., 45, 142
Hillerbrand, E. T., 50
HIV, counseling clients with,
    163–165
Holroyd, J. C., 29
Home-based services, 127
Hotelling, K., 36
Hulse-Killacky, D., 97

I Never Knew I Had a Choice (Corey, G.,
    et al.), 106, 107
IAMFC (International Association of
    Marriage and Family Counselors)
    Code of Ethics, 76
Identity/boundary/role confusion of
    clients and sexual relationships with
    therapists, 32
*If Sex Enters Into the Psychotherapy
    Relationship* (APA), 36
Impaired inability of clients to trust
    and sexual relationships with
    therapists, 32
Impulse control problems of therapists
    who become sexual offenders, 30
Incompatibility of expectations on
    part of client, 12
Incompetence. *See* Competence
Individual counseling concurrent with
    group counseling, 147–148
Informed consent
        of clients, 15, 51–52, 144
            in substance abuse counseling,
                161–162
        of students in counselor
            training, 59
        of students in group counselor
            training, 98, 111

of supervisees, 87–88
Inherent duality, 11
International Association of Marriage
    and Family Counselors (IAMFC)
    Code of Ethics, 76
Interns. *See* Supervision
Interpersonal focus stage of decision-
    making models during supervision,
    87
Isolation
    of clients, 32, 47–49
    of private practitioners, 138–140

Jensen, D., 1, 9
Johnson, S. J., 192
Johnson, W. B., 192
Journal for Specialists in Group Work
    (March 2004 issue) on teaching
    group work, 96

Kain, Craig D., 163–165
Kane, A. W., 23
Keith-Spiegel, P., 38
Killacky, J., 97
King, D. A., 95–96, 96–97
Kinnier, R. T., 28, 42, 126
Kiselica, M. S., 6, 122
Kitchener, K. S., 12, 116, 119, 125, 126
Kline, W. B., 99–100
Knapp, S., 80, 127, 194
Kottler, J. A., 99
Krieger, K. M., 99
Krug, S., 142

Ladany, N., 79, 88
Lamb, D. H., 56
Larrabee, M. J., 55, 56, 76–77
Lazarus, A. A., 3, 7, 9, 11, 16–19, 193,
    196
Leadership, anxiety of students about,
    112
Legal perspectives on dual relationships,
    22–24
Linville, M. E., 178
Lloyd, A. P., 60
Lowery, S., 79, 87

Malpractice, 22–24, 31, 193
Manfrini, Amy, 152–158
Marital counseling. *See* Couples and
    family counseling
Markus, H. E., 95–96, 96–97
Marriage and family therapists. *See*
    American Association for Marriage
    and Family Therapy (AAMFT);
    Couples and family counseling
McCarthy, P., 88
McCartney, T. J., 97
McNeil, K., 97, 98
Meara, N., 66
Mentoring relationships, 60–61
Merta, R. J., 97, 98, 103
Miller, G. M., 55, 56, 76–77
Milliken, T., 24
Milsom, A. S., 97
Minority clients. *See* Multicultural
    community issues
Mobley, M. J., 172
Moleski, S. M., 6, 122
Moline, M. E., 31
Moorman, A. S., 56
Moral virtue, defined, 65
Morran, D. K., 99
Multicultural perspectives
    African-centered perspective,
        131–136
    counselors' work within
        community and, 126–128
    in group work training, 97
    on dual relationships, 128–131
    transcultural integrative
        model for ethical decision-
        making, 50
Multiple relationships. *See* Dual
    relationships
Muratori, Michelle C., 53, 61,
    67–71

Narcotics Anonymous, 160–161
Narrative therapists and collaborative
    nature of therapy, 44
NASW. *See* National Association of Social
    Workers (NASW) *Code of Ethics*

National Association for Addiction Professionals, profile of membership, 159

National Association of Social Workers (NASW) *Code of Ethics*
bartering for goods or services, 116
nonprofessional interactions, 2, 4
sexual relationships with clients, 25
sexual relationships with former clients, 26
sexual relationships with supervisees, 76

National Association of Student Personnel Administrators "Standards of Professional Practice," 188

National Institute on Alcohol Abuse and Alcoholism study on treatment models, 160

Nerison, R. M., 41, 42, 43–44, 46

Neukrug, E. S., 24

Neurotic therapists as sexual offenders, 30

O'Connor Slimp, A., 61

O'Halloran, T. M., 97

Organizational level, promotion of client perspective on ethics, 49–50

Paget, T. L., 61

Parham, T. A., 131–136

Pate, R. H., 177

Paternalism, 43–44

Peer consultation, 144

Peer groups and effects of dual relationships on, 14, 102

Pellegrino, E., 65

Perls, F., 17

Pope, K. S., 7, 31, 34, 35, 38, 42, 46

Power differential between parties involved, 12, 13, 54, 56, 143

A Practitioner's Guide to Ethical Decision Making (Forester-Miller & Davis), 50

Prevention of sexual relationships, 35–39

Price, G. E., 100

Private practice, 137–145
contributor's perspective on, 138–145

financial issues in, 141–142
geographical and cultural factors in, 140–141
isolation of practitioners, 138–140

Pro bono therapy, 117, 141–142

Professional focus stage of decision-making models during supervision, 87

Professional Therapy Never Includes Sex (Calif. Dept. of Consumer Affairs), 36

Prudence, defined, 65–66

Psychologists. *See* American Psychological Association (APA)

Psychotic or borderline personality disordered therapists as sexual offenders, 31

Ralph, J., 192

Referrals to avoid dual relationship, 16

Rehabilitation counseling, 166–170
advocacy role of counselor, 166, 169–170
case management, 167–168
contributor's perspective on, 166–170
third-party payer relationships in, 168–169

Rehabilitation of counselors who engaged in sexual relationships with clients, 39

Remley, T. P., 8, 24, 103, 179

Repeat sexual offenders, 29, 39

Reporting of colleagues for sexual relationships with clients, students, or supervisees, 38–39

Research
faculty issues
credit for students, 60
soliciting research participants, 64
student issues, 65

Rest, J., 63

Rigid boundaries, problems created by, 11

Ripple effect of dual relationships, 14

Risks in dual relationships, 13–15, 193
to consumers, 13
to other consumers, 14
to other professionals, 14
to profession and society, 14–15
to professionals, 13–14
safeguards against, 15–16, 130–131, 144–145

Role blending. *See* Boundary crossings
Roy v. Hartogs (1975), 23
Rubin, L. J., 37
Rural communities
    practitioners in, 9–10, 120–123, 140
    school counselors in, 177

St. Germaine, J., 8, 160
Salisbury, N. A., 28, 42, 126
Schoener, G., 27, 30
School counseling, 175–179
    See also American School
        Counselor Association (ASCA)
    child abuse, dealing with, 176, 179
    consultant role of school
        counselor, 178
    contributor's perspective on,
        179–182
    licensure of school counselors,
        181
    training of school counselors in
        group work, 97
Self-care of counselors, 143–144
Self-disclosure
    to clients, 123–124, 139–140,
        145
        in group setting, 149–150
        in substance abuse
            counseling, 161
    in counselor training, 56–57, 68
        in group counselor
            training, 101–102, 103,
            112, 114
    in couples and family counseling,
        156–157
    not culturally acceptable, 129
Self-focus stage of decision-making
    models during supervision, 87
Self-monitoring for dual relationships,
    192, 197
Self-referrals by college and university
    counselors, 184, 187
Severely neurotic therapists as sexual
    offenders, 30
Sexual Feelings in Psychotherapy (Pope
    et al.), 34, 35
Sexual harassment of students by
    educators, 54–56
Sexual relationships, 2, 21–40
    consumer education on, 36
    consumer views on, 42–43
    counselor education on, 34, 54–56

ethical standards and, 24–25
with former clients, 25–29
gender differences in therapist
    views on, 29
harm to clients, 31–33
incidence, 29–30
legal actions resulting from, 22–
    24, 31
prevention and remediation,
    35–39
professor-student relationships,
    29, 30, 38, 42–43, 54–56, 63,
    186–187
reluctance of female victims to
    report, 37, 42
reporting of colleagues for, 38–39
sexual attraction to clients, 33–35
in supervision, 76–77
support for victims of, 36–37
typical offender profile, 30–31
Silverglade, L., 79, 87
Simon, R. I., 29
Slattery, J. M., 127
Sleek, S., 121
Sliding scale of billing, 117, 142
Slimp, P. A., 80, 81
Social constructionism and collaborative
    nature of therapy, 45, 50
Social relationships
    See also Friends as clients
    with clients, 124–125, 151
    with former clients, 125–126
    with supervisees, 80–81
Sociopathic or narcissistic character
    disordered therapists as sexual
    offenders, 31
Solution-focused brief therapy and
    collaborative nature of therapy, 44–45
Spooner, Sue, 185–188
Stadler, Holly A., 53, 62–66
Standard of care and malpractice, 22–23
State criminal sanctions for sexual
    relationships with clients, 23–24, 31
Stockton, R., 99
Stone, G. L., 50
Students. *See* Counselor education;
    Group counselors, education of
Subgroup work in family counseling,
    155–156
Substance abuse counseling, 159–163
    confidentiality issues, 161–162
    counselor at 12 step meetings,
        160–161
    hiring clients in, 162

Substance abuse counseling
(*Continued*)
    ongoing supervision and ethics
        training for, 162
    Twelve-Step Facilitation (TSF)
        and, 160
Sue, D., 127
Sue, D. W., 119, 127, 128–131
Suicidal risk of clients and sexual
    relationships with therapists, 33
Sumerel, M. B., 79
Supervision, 73–81
    of African-American trainees,
        134
    boundary between counseling
        and supervision, 77–80
        supervisee's perspective
            on, 84–90
        supervisor's perspective
            on, 81–84
    college counseling center as site
        for internships and, 183–184
    competence issues for supervisors,
        75–76
    countertransference issues in,
        88–89
    courses for training in, 75–76
    decision-making models for
        supervisors, 87
    ethical standards, 65–66
    ethics codes and guidelines, 74–75
    incompetence of supervisee,
        89–90
    informed consent in, 87–88
    inherent duality of, 11
    issues related to, 73–94
    liability of supervisor, 89
    reporting of colleagues for
        sexual relationships with
        supervisees, 38–39
    risk requiring supervision of
        practitioner, 15
    sexual relationships in, 76–77
    social and business relationships
        with supervisees, 80–81
    in substance abuse counseling,
        162
Support for victims of sexual relation-
    ships with therapists, 36–37
Suppressed rage of clients and
    sexual relationships with
    therapists, 33

Syme, G., 37, 39, 140
Systems theory, 151

Tabachnick, B. G., 38
Teachers seeking counseling from
    school counselors, 175–176
Third-party payer relationships in
    rehabilitation counseling,
    168–169
Thomas, J. Lawrence, 117–118
Thomasma, D., 65
Thompson, C. E., 127, 130
Thoreson, R. W., 29, 38
Thorpe, J. S., 55
Tomm, K., 8, 9
Toriello, P. J., 160, 162
Transcultural integrative model for
    ethical decision making, 50

Uninformed and naive therapists as
    sexual offenders, 30
Universities and colleges
    counselors at, 182–185
        campus counseling center
            as site for internships,
            183–184
        contributor's perspective,
            185–188
        referrals by, 184–185
        residence hall life and, 186
        in teaching role, 183
    policies forbidding professors and
        administrators from dating
        students, 56
    sexual relationship between
        faculty and student. *See*
        Sexual relationships
Usher, C. H., 79

VandeCreek, L., 80
Vasquez, M.J.T., 7, 31, 35, 37
Veach, Laura J., 159–163

W

Walden, S. L., 24, 42, 46–52
Welfel, E. R., 7, 23, 29
Whiston, S. C., 87
Williams, G. T., 31
Wise, P. S., 79, 87
Wolfgang, L., 97, 98
Woody, R. H., 117

Y

Yalom, I. D., 123
Younggren, J. N., 121

Z

Zur, O., 7, 9, 11, 193, 196